"As Jeff and Sandra glowingl,
coaching approach has become more than just a coaching
technique to many coaches', it's the KEY to scalable levels
of resilience and the demonstration of what a client is truly
capable of - developing a truly 'Fearless' mindset for success at
home or in the boardroom."
— Dr. Cathy Greenberg, best-selling co-author of *What
Happy Working Mother's Know, and Fearless Leaders.*

———————   ———————

"Drs. Auerbach and Foster are outstanding College
of Executive Coaching faculty who thoughtfully and
carefully share a comprehensive body of current
positive psychology and wellbeing research from global
thought leaders and translate it for use in executive
leadership coaching with a variety of straightforward
and relevant applications and tools. I'm grateful for
their contribution, an indispensable resource for anyone
incorporating positivity for coaching leaders, building
teams, and developing healthy organizational cultures."
— Randy Noe, MBA, CFA, and author of *Leading Well: The
Essence of Wholehearted Inspirational Leaders.*

———————   ———————

"*Positive Psychology in Coaching* is a must read! It goes
way outside traditional books on Coaching to broaden
and enlighten us about what is really taking place
inside of human beings when coaching is done well
and with insight and wisdom. Extraordinary coaching
is distinguished by the quality of the connections and

conversations. Every chapter has enlightening takeaways about what coaches can do differently to elevate the coachee's transformation and the coach's capacity for effectiveness and impact."
— Judith E. Glaser, CEO of Benchmark Communications, Inc. and author of best seller *Conversational Intelligence: How Great Leaders Build Trust and Get Extraordinary Results.*

———————————————

"*Positive Psychology and Coaching* masterfully bridges the gap between the theory and its applications that until now have been separated. Jeffrey Auerbach, PhD, and Sandra Foster, PhD, not only talk the talk, but also walk the walk as highly-accomplished instructors and as inspirational mentors. Coaches have been hungry for the practical applications of Positive Psychology, and the wait is now over."
— Andrew Susskind, LCSW, Coach and Author, *From Now On: Seven Keys to Purposeful Recovery*

Positive Psychology in Coaching

Applying Science to Executive and Personal Coaching

❖ ❖ ❖

Sandra L. Foster
Jeffrey E. Auerbach

Executive College Press   •   Pismo Beach, California

Many of the designations used by manufacturers and sellers to distinguish their products are claimed as trademarks. Where those designations appear in this book and Executive College Press was aware of a trademark claim, the designations have been printed in initial capital letters.

Library of Congress Cataloging-in-Publication Data
Foster L. & Auerbach, Jeffrey Ethan.
Positive Psychology in Coaching: Applying Science to Executive and Personal Coaching/ Sandra L. Foster & Jeffrey Ethan Auerbach.—1st ed.
p. cm.
Includes bibliographical references.

ISBN 978-0-9706834-1-0

Library of Congress Control Number: 2015943971

1. Self-actualization (Psychology)
2. Mentoring
3. Executives—Training of.
4. Leadership—study and teaching. I. Auerbach, Jeffrey.

First Edition — First printing 2015

Authors's note: The names and details of the coaching examples provided in this book have been changed when necessary to respect the confidentiality of the coaching relationships. This book is written for educational purposes only and is not intended for use as any type of psychotherapy, diagnostic instrument or legal advice.

PRINTED IN THE UNITED STATES OF AMERICA.

Executive College Press
897 Oak Park Blvd. #271
Pismo Beach, California 93449
(805) 474-4124
http://www.executivecoachcollege.com

DEDICATION

This book is dedicated to the memory of my parents, Margaret and Wayne, and to my life partner, Rolf.

You three continue to teach me about courage, commitment, purpose, contentment, and love that flourishes over time.

And to my 'bro' and colleague, Jonathan Aronoff, PhD. Your wisdom about well-being coaching enriches these pages. Thank you.

— Sandra

This book is dedicated to the College of Executive Coaching faculty and students.

Your commitment to helping the world flourish inspires me.

— Jeff

CONTENTS

CONTENTS

CHAPTER 3

CHAPTER 4

CHAPTER 9

CHAPTER 10

CHAPTER 11

Leveraging Positive Psychology in Culturally Competent Coaching................ 236

CHAPTER 12

CONTRIBUTIONS

The Integration of Positive Psychology and Coaching

N ow that positive psychology is used extensively in coaching, it is hard for us to imagine the one without the other since they complement each other so beautifully. This book applies the science of positive psychology to personal and executive coaching and is a companion to Jeff's well-received first book, *Personal and Executive Coaching: The Complete Guide for Mental Health Professionals*, now in its twentieth printing.[1] Positive psychology theory and techniques are helpful to our clients, whether they are executive coaching clients in organizations or personal coaching clients, yet there have been few practical resources to apply the findings of this rapidly growing field to the practice of coaching. Positive psychology represents the *essence* of excellent coaching in its focus on leveraging strengths and the facilitation of hope, possibility, and goal-directedness in a scientific manner. We believe that coaches can do their best work when they combine their coaching skills with these evidence-based applications from positive psychology.

This book is written for both beginning and experienced coaches. Positive psychology theories and applications will augment the existing skills that long-time coaches have already acquired. This manual will also be an essential guide to new students of coaching interested in integrating positive psychology applications and theories into a science-based process of coaching.

WHAT IS POSITIVE PSYCHOLOGY?

Positive psychology is a domain of psychology which focuses on strengths, optimal functioning, and enhancing well-being for individuals, groups, and communities. While there are historical roots in the human potential movement and in the writings of Abraham Maslow, the therapeutic stance of Carl Rogers, and many other psychologists who advocate the use of strengths, the person most likely to be cited now as the primary figure in positive psychology is Martin E. P. Seligman. His ability to attract talented behavioral scientists and funding for research on a grand scale created a paradigm shift in psychology, a field that has traditionally been oriented toward relieving suffering, following an approach based on the medical model of diagnosing and treating pathology. Positive psychology consists of an accelerating body of scientific research, and there are an increasing number of positive psychology coaching techniques proven to help clients reach key goals.

WHAT IS COACHING?

In the last twenty years several different, yet similar, definitions of coaching have been advanced. I (Jeff) described coaching in 2001 as an ongoing relationship between the professional coach and the client, which focuses on the client's taking action toward the realization of their vision, goals, or desires. Coaching uses a process of inquiry and personal discovery to build the client's level of awareness and responsibility and provides the client with structure, support, and feedback.[2] Tim Gallwey, author of *The Inner Game of Tennis*, describes the essence of coaching as "unlocking a person's potential to maximize their own performance. It is helping them to learn rather than teaching them."[3] Anthony Grant, of the University of Sydney and one of coaching's most prolific researchers, says, "Life coaching can be broadly defined as a collaborative solution-focused, result-oriented and systematic process in which the coach facilitates the enhancement of life experience and goal attainment in the personal and/or professional life of normal, nonclinical clients."[4] At the College of Executive Coaching, where we both teach, we recommend to our aspiring coaches that they use one of these or develop their own conversational definition of coaching.

KEY CONTRIBUTORS TO THE POSITIVE PSYCHOLOGY MOVEMENT

As the strategic thinkers behind a cadre of researchers, theorists, and practitioners, Seligman and his co-investigator Chris Peterson dared to challenge the status quo and created assessment tools that help people zero in on their character strengths and virtues as an alternative to the American Psychiatric Association's *Diagnostic and Statistical Manual of Mental Disorders* (often called the DSM for short), which is used in mental health interventions and in psychotherapy settings. His other well-known colleagues in the positive psychology arena include a number of researchers, such as Mihaly Csikszentmihalyi, and Daniel Kahneman, the first psychologist to receive a Nobel Prize (he received the 2002 Nobel Prize in economics along with now deceased Stanford statistician Amos Tversky for their work in decision theory).

Seligman writes in *Flourish* that his early framework of positive psychology was focused on happiness and life satisfaction in three areas: positive emotions, engagement, and meaning.[5] In the ten years following his first positive psychology book, *Authentic Happiness*,[6] he rigorously examined research findings and questioned his assumptions. His greatest shift was away from the pursuit of happiness to a more thorough construct of well-being. He articulated five domains of well-being using PERMA as an acronym: Positive Emotion, Engagement, Positive Relationships, Meaning, and Accomplishment. He declared that the revised goal of positive psychology was to "increase flourishing" by enhancing functioning in all five elements of well-being.

Another major influencer in positive psychology was the late Donald Clifton of the Gallup organization. As early as 1952, when he was a graduate student, Clifton declared that it was time for psychologists to study what was right with people, rather than remaining solely focused on problems and their solutions. This call to action led to the development of strengths-based assessment tools and recommendations for development of key skills. In 2002, the American Psychological Association honored Clifton with an APA Presidential Commendation, recognizing him as the father of strengths-based psychology.

During construction of this book, we communicated with many key people in positive psychology based on our high regard for their contributions to psychology—and specifically to the practice of coaching—in order to share their work with an audience of coaches. We cite their original studies, their popular books, and the websites they have launched so that you can explore further as your interests lead you. You'll hear about Sonja Lyubomirsky and her research on happiness; Mihalyi Csikszentmihalyi well-known construct of flow and how this relates to engagement at work; Heidi Grant Halvorson, who has brilliantly articulated a large body of research on goals; Robert Emmons's compelling work on the power of gratitude; Roy Baumeister's appealing way of helping us understand what willpower is really about; and Barbara Fredrickson's call to action on the subject of increasing positivity and love.

We'll present the work of Seligman and Chris Peterson and their development of a taxonomy of strengths that has given rise to the VIA (Values in Action) assessments and more recently the VIA Institute on Character. The impressive research on both strengths and well-being by the Gallup organization, and their popular Clifton StrengthsFinder assessment, will be presented. We have included a chapter addressing the sometimes paradoxical nature of strengths and introduce you to thinkers and assessment developers whose work you will find useful in your coaching.

We also look at the topic of coaching through transitions and change, and provide you with the expertise of Randall P. White (a senior faculty member of the College of Executive Coaching and former director of the Executive Coaching Program at the Center for Creative Leadership) on managing the emotion of uncertainty when clients face ambiguity in their places of work and in their lives. Another expert on leadership development, Rob Kaiser, the Editor of the *Consulting Psychology Journal*, will share his thoughts on coaching clients in the workplace to enhance the versatility of their style as they lead others and their enterprises.

The importance of forgiveness is articulated in this volume as a process that our clients can find helpful in making peace and moving forward following the loss of a relationship or a significant setback at work. While some might see forgiveness as a topic better left to pastoral counselors or psychotherapists, we present the work of Fred Luskin and the Stanford Forgiveness Project as a valuable way to coach clients when the context and timing are right.

Before we proceed, we want to look at the language used by those in positive psychology, particularly definitions and what some researchers consider a conundrum in the field: exactly what do we mean by *positive?*

WHAT DO WE MEAN BY POSITIVE?

Positive emotions and positivity are the focus of Barbara Fredrickson's research. Fredrickson is the author of *Positivity*,[7] and we discuss her research in Chapter 2. Positive emotions are often measured by self-reported levels of happiness and life satisfaction. Seligman tied positive emotions to what he termed the "pleasant life," in which a person experiences pleasures like a relaxing holiday or interacting with others in ways that are pleasing and worth repeating. When the word *positive* is used to denote desirable ways of interacting, in referring for example to *positive communication or positive relationships,* the positive aspect is about contributing to the well-being of all the parties involved.

The word *positive* may be taken to mean the opposite or absence of negative emotions or negativity. However, reflecting further, we see that it becomes a bit more complicated. Is positive psychology only about eradicating the experience of negativity in a person's life? Or is it a point of view that all negative emotions are bad and there is no place in our lives for grief, sadness, remorse, self-doubt, or constructive criticism of ourselves and others?

We find compelling the arguments laid out by James O. Pawelski, who directs the Master of Applied Positive Psychology degree program at the University of Pennsylvania. He is also the executive director of the International Positive Psychology Association, which holds a global conference on positive psychology every two years. We invited James to share his analysis of the definition of *positive* as it applies to this domain. He is a philosopher and writes about positive psychology from his unique perspective of "positive humanities." At our request, he provided his thoughts on the debate on the meanings of *positive*. We have summarized his comments here; you can read his full article in the Appendix.

Getting Clear on the Positive in Positive Psychology
—by James O. Pawelski
(condensed version)

Understood as a complement to mainstream psychology, positive psychology seems to be about the best things in life; understood as an approach to the good life … it seems to be about creating the best life we can. These two conceptions are no doubt related … but they are far from identical…. Barbara Fredrickson (1998) … defines positive emotions as those that have a "pleasant subjective feel."[8] Maya Tamir and James Gross (2011), on the other hand, define positive emotions as those that are adaptive for well-being.[9] … Most people would no doubt classify positive emotions as some of the best things in life; if our goal, however, is to create the best life we can, there are at least certain cases where unpleasant emotions may be more useful than pleasant ones.

This debate about how to define the positive in positive psychology is related to a discussion in the second book of Plato's Republic. Glaucon … asks Socrates why we value justice. He makes a distinction between what we would now call intrinsic goods and instrumental goods. Intrinsic goods are things we value for their own sakes, and instrumental goods are things we value for the consequences they bring. Positive psychology defined as a complement to mainstream psychology seems to be a psychology of intrinsic goods ("the best things in life," including things like pleasant emotions); but positive psychology defined as an empirical investigation of the good life seems to be a psychology of instrumental goods (the things that lead to maximal well-being, including, at times, things like unpleasant emotions)....

There is, of course, a third option. This is the option Socrates takes in explaining why we value justice. He argues that justice is both something we value for its own sake and something we value for its consequences.... What is crucial ... is that we be quite clear about whether the work we are doing is a part of intrinsically positive psychology, a part of instrumentally positive psychology, or at the intersection of the two....

It is easy for practitioners to make the tacit assumption that all of positive psychology research is at the intersection of the intrinsically good and the instrumentally good. In this case, any intrinsic goods studied by researchers would be valid means for achieving the instrumental good of human flourishing. The debate about positive emotions ... illustrates how dangerously incorrect this assumption can be. There may well be times where intrinsic goods (like pleasant emotions) are not instrumentally good. In these cases, asking clients to focus on intrinsic goods anyway may diminish their overall well-being and could actually cause them harm....

If the overall goal is human flourishing, the means for achieving it will have to be some optimal balance between the instrumental use and mitigation of the negative and the enhancement of the intrinsically positive.

HOW WE CHOSE TO INTEGRATE POSITIVE PSYCHOLOGY WITH COACHING

Here are our stories of how we came to value a positive psychology approach to coaching. We believe many of you have had similar experiences that led to your interest in this field.

SANDRA'S STORY

As I think back to experiences that led me to my current interest in positive psychology, a key influence was my time studying for my doctorate at Stanford University. On the campus in Palo Alto, I was surrounded by well-known scientists from many fields. It became extremely important to me to practice my craft with my clients from a scholar's point of view. Using theories and techniques that had been put to the test using what behavioral scientists call gold standard research[10] gave me and my recommendations much greater credibility with my clients.

The research base of positive psychology is rich and robust, lending credibility and substance to the applications coaches can use with their clients. In 1993, I came across an article that intrigued me. It described the impact of "optimistic explanatory style" on the productivity of sales professionals. This was Seligman's study of Metropolitan Life Insurance Company sales professionals (who, it should be noted, were also tested as having an aptitude for selling life insurance). A key finding was that optimistic salespeople persisted in contacting their cold calling targets and sold up to 84 percent more policies than their more pessimistic counterparts.[11]

At the 1998 annual convention of the American Psychological Association (APA), Seligman gave the presidential address and laid out two areas which he felt the field of psychology should address. One of these was ethnic conflict around the world; the other was positive psychology. He exhorted the audience to imagine studying the "most positive qualities of an individual: optimism, courage, work ethic, future-mindedness, interpersonal skill, the capacity for pleasure and insight, and social responsibility."[12] He called on those present to imagine a transformational change in the way that psychology focused its research efforts and dollars. Urging psychologists to consider a very different way of thinking, he proposed that the direction of research should fundamentally shift from a singular focus on the amelioration of mental disorders to the study of "what makes life worth living," including research examining how "normal people flourish." [13] Many (including me) who heard

Marty that day sensed that a movement was being born.

I moved to Europe in late 2002 and found that the interest in positive psychology was rapidly growing in Germany and in Italy, where I lived. In 2004, I had the great pleasure of taking part in a positive psychology coaching symposium at the Second European Conference on Positive Psychology, in Verbania, just a few kilometers from my home, north of the city of Milan. In 2006, I was a presenter in Porto, Portugal, at the Third European Positive Psychology Conference. This time, I presented my early efforts to apply positive psychology with executives, as I was now working in a corporate environment in London.

I became a senior faculty member at the College of Executive Coaching in 2002. I later designed a course in positive psychology applications along with my then co-instructor, Todd Kettner. We met in 2004 at the second Positive Psychology Summit in Washington, DC, hosted by the Gallup organization. We both found ourselves invigorated by the research and by the musings of the behavioral scientists there, among them Martin Seligman, Mihalyi Csikszentmihalyi, Roy Baumeister, and Ed Deiner. We were likewise enthused by Connie Rath's description of Gallup's work on deploying strengths in the workplace and the contributions of her colleague, Marcus Buckingham.

We launched the Positive Psychology Applications to Coaching course in 2005 and have since taught the theory and techniques to hundreds of students. I currently co-teach with a very experienced and talented colleague and friend, Jonathan Aronoff, PhD, who has brought to life the research on well-being and how it helps coaches facilitate healthy change for clients. You'll see his contribution on coaching around the topic of well-being in Chapter 4.

As you read through this manual, I think you will find that the emphasis on the science in positive psychology will be of benefit to you when you speak to prospective coaching clients and describe the techniques that have become part of your coaching tool kit. You will have an empirical basis, meaning substantiated by research, for recommending that a client try out a positive psychology application. Particularly when working with business clients, being able to justify and back up an assertion of the likely value of an intervention can give you an edge when selling your coaching services. Now that I have left corporate life and work in my own independent consultancy, I am heartened by what positive psychology theory and applications can offer my coaching clients now and, I believe, for many years into the future.

JEFF'S STORY

As a psychology graduate student, I was fortunate to find a series of mentors who were all characterized by high positivity and high achievement. I remember that when I was a therapist trainee, in our supervision groups, one of my supervisors, Neil Friedman, LCSW, would ask us what our client's strengths were and how those strengths could help them in their situation. This was my first exposure to an intentional strategic use of exploring strengths to help with client success, and since the year was 1983, his approach preceded the current wave of enthusiasm for positive psychology.

During my doctoral studies, my mentors Terrence Olson, a psychobiologist from UCLA, and Dr. George Solomon, known as the grandfather of psychoneuroimmunology, both guided me to explore how optimistic visualization can be a fundamental tool in helping clients. This led to my early research on using positive mental imagery, biofeedback, meditative techniques, and hypnosis to positively impact immune cell function in patients with HIV. In addition to measuring the impact of behavioral intervention on CD4 cells, I also measured its impact on "hardiness." Hardiness had previously been shown to be linked to improved health outcomes in the face of serious illness.[14,15,16] The intervention I used in my research study resulted in an increase in hardiness scores and increased numbers of CD4 cells.[17] Looking back on this research I realize that this fits with what we would now call a positive psychology intervention. I was using psychological approaches to increase elements of hardiness and enhance self-efficacy, which is linked to peak physical health and increased goal accomplishment.

One of my most influential mentors, Ernest Rossi, PhD, was the protégé of the renowned Milton Erickson, MD. Often referred to as a "phenomenon" and a "genius," Milton assisted clients in creative ways, often referring to clients'"resources," which I now view as a precursor to positive psychology's current focus of leveraging strengths. Rossi, the author of over twenty books, taught me in a series of mentoring meetings spanning four years that tuning into one's strengths through reflection, dream journaling, and therapeutic conversation is the secret to unleashing our creative potential. He also taught me a basic principle of well-being: the value of rest for rejuvenation and mental clarity. In a book called *The Twenty Minute Break*, he explains the concept of ultradian rhythms, which are biological cycles of rest and activity that regulate physical and mental health.[18] Approximately every 90 to 120 minutes, we experience shifts in our mental focus which signal the need for rest and change in physical and mental activity. He recommends taking twenty-minute breaks that lead to renewed energy and improved performance. I credit much of my own well-being to the fundamental principles learned from Rossi about the importance of rejuvenation on a regular basis.

In the late 1980s, while working as a licensed therapist and then as a clinical psychologist, I began combining coaching-style approaches with my psychotherapy work. Soon I branched out and began conducting entrepreneurial consulting conversations (although I, and most other people using similar techniques, did not call it "coaching" at the time). Then, in 1998, my colleague Dr. Ana Maria Irueste handed me a book called *Soar with Your Strengths* by psychologist and Gallup founder Dr. Donald O. Clifton. This 1995 book clearly outlined the benefits of focusing on strengths rather than on fixing weaknesses. Clifton's clearly written book preceded the great wave of interest in positive psychology that came with Martin Seligman's official launching of the positive psychology movement when he was APA president in 1998. *Soar with Your Strengths* made a significant impression on my evolving coaching style and contributed to the strengths-based coaching approach that I began teaching in 1999 when I founded the College of Executive Coaching. Clifton's book also influenced the writing of my book *Personal and Executive Coaching* in 2001. One of my proudest moments as a new author was when Clifton approached me at a conference of the Society of Psychologists in Management and told me enthusiastically how much he liked my book.

Fast-forward several years to my position as vice president of the International Coach Federation (the ICF is the largest global nonprofit professional coaching organization, operating in over a hundred countries). As part of our five-year strategic planning effort, I proposed that the top-level goal of the ICF be "to promote humanity's flourishing," and this was unanimously accepted. This is the same goal that Marty Seligman had for the field of positive psychology. I shared this with Marty, and he emailed me back immediately rejoicing in the good news. He also forwarded my message to all the members of the executive board of the International Positive Psychology Association. I received many emails from these board members—the leading researchers around the world in the positive psychology field—expressing their enthusiasm about the natural fit between the science of positive psychology and its practical application to coaching.

POSITIVE PSYCHOLOGY COACHING IS AN OUTGROWTH OF THE RESEARCH

The explosive growth of positive psychology, led by the scholarship and creative influence of Martin Seligman, Mihaly Csikszentmihalyi, and Chris Peterson, created the conditions for an emerging new field of psychology which pulled together the work of many psychologists, helping professionals, and other researchers to fuel a movement that is providing the scientific basis for improved personal and coaching techniques. Since positive psychology is often defined as the scientific study of positive human functioning and flourishing, including the biological, personal, relational, institutional, and cultural dimensions of life, the door is open to a variety of scientifically based psychological interventions to enhance human experiences. Although there are several well-known studies of methods cited as enhancing happiness, such as "gratitude visits" and "counting blessings," coaches are encouraged to develop additional science-based coaching techniques to help with the variety of coaching situations we face. This book is a response to that challenge.

CHAPTER 2

Why Feeling Good Matters: The Science behind Positive Emotions

T his chapter focuses on the research and writings of Barbara Fredrickson and Sonja Lyubomirsky and their findings concerning positive emotions. As coaches, we can benefit from these discoveries by recommending to our clients techniques for generating more positive emotions in their professional and personal lives. The findings show that the experience of greater positivity, specifically happiness, has far-reaching effects, increasing productivity and creativity at work, enhancing physical well-being, fostering resilience in the face of stress and illness, and promoting more satisfying relationships. We're convinced that this research has important implications for personal and business coaching for both individuals and teams. We offer coaching strategies that bring this groundbreaking research to life, having seen encouraging results with our own clients.

We noted in Chapter 1 the shift in psychology from a priority on alleviating the impact of negative emotions to the study of what's right about human functioning, and the historic influence of Martin Seligman and the late Chris Peterson. Fredrickson and Lyubomirsky were among the group of psychology researchers who chose to empirically test the effects of positive emotions.

Fredrickson speculated that one reason positive emotions had received so little attention was that, put simply, it is more difficult to study them.[1] There are fewer of them in the taxonomy of emotions, one positive for every three or four negative. In addition, positive emotions are less differentiated than negative emotions. For example, most of us can readily describe the difference between anger and fear, but explaining just how contentment differs from amusement, or amusement from joy, is much harder.

In contrast, negative emotions have clear-cut signs and effects that can be readily detected and quantified. Think of the facial expressions that alert us that someone is angry, afraid, or repulsed by something. Researchers have found a consistent pattern worldwide of recognizable emotional displays—facial expressions and gestures—of anger, fear, and disgust in primates, including humans. Negative emotions lead to well-defined "specific action tendencies."[2] The emotions of anger and fear trigger a "fight or flight" response. We observe another such response when disgust is triggered and provokes a strong reflex to dispel or avoid the offending object, like spitting out nasty-tasting food or moving away from a noxious smell.

These negative emotions and specific action tendencies are evolutionary adaptations that aided the survival of various species, including our own. Negative emotions temporarily narrow our attention to only that which set off the response—and then prompt us to fight or flee.[3] This survival technique, which ensured that our ancestors identified and avoided harm, helps us stay alive even today; but it has a downside.

Higher cognitive functioning in general, and creative thinking in particular, are not well served by the fight-or-flight response. Negative emotions alone are not helpful when we need to synthesize data, think innovatively, or generate win-win solutions. Even more problematic, the effects of negative emotions can be damaging in the long run, particularly for those who experience prolonged stressful events, especially events over which they have little control. We say more about negative emotions in Chapter 12.

Research by Barbara Fredrickson and others suggests that positive emotions can lead to beneficial effects by "undoing" the harmful consequences of negative emotions and by activating the kind of cognitive activity that is very useful in judgment and reasoning.[4]

BARBARA FREDRICKSON'S RESEARCH ON POSITIVE EMOTIONS

Barbara Fredrickson is the Kenan Distinguished Professor of Psychology and the principal investigator at the Positive Emotions and Psychophysiology Lab at the University of North Carolina, Chapel Hill. She studies the nature and benefits of joy, contentment, gratitude, and love. Her research outcomes have led her to develop her "broaden and build" theory to explain how the effects of feeling good lead to a "broader thought-action repertoire."[5] More recently, she has written about how we can cultivate the powerful positive emotion of love to good effect in our lives. She believes that, if we really want to harness the power of positive psychology to benefit large numbers of people, we have to convince them how and why goodness matters. She has made her work accessible to an audience far beyond academic circles through two popular self-help books, *Positivity*[6] and *Love* 2.0.[7]

About her research hypothesis Fredrickson says, "I call this the broaden-and-build theory of positive emotions. This theory states that certain discrete emotions—including joy, interest, contentment, pride, and love … share the ability to broaden people's momentary thought-action repertoires and build their enduring personal resources, ranging from physical and intellectual resources to social and psychological resources."[8]

Early on, she tested her theory in a study designed to evaluate the effects of positive, neutral, or negative emotion.[9] Subjects were shown one of four brief film clips. These were intended to evoke a mild positive emotion like amusement (footage of penguins playing) or contentment (a happy family gathering); no discernible feeling (neutral emotion—a nature scene); or sadness (a funeral scene).

All four groups were asked to report the emotion they felt after seeing the film clip. Then they were given tasks to complete: a visual matching task and a word puzzle. When subjects reported experiencing positive emotions like amusement or contentment, their thinking was broader and more holistic than that of subjects who reported feeling sadness or no emotion at all.

Fredrickson's colleague, the late Alice Isen, applied this investigative approach in a real-world context.[10] Her research involved asking two groups of physicians to evaluate a case study of a patient with liver disease, provide a diagnosis, and then prescribe a course of treatment. The doctors thought aloud on videotape that was later coded for cognitive style, number and length of replies, and final diagnosis. One group of doctors was first given a small prize, and they subsequently reported experiencing mild positive emotion before they began the task. The other group was given only the task.

The findings were compelling. The physicians who said that they had experienced the mild positive emotion prior to discussing the case synthesized the information more quickly, were less anchored to their initial thoughts during the conversation with their peers, and were less likely to bring their discussion to premature closure than the other doctors.

In her second book, *Love 2.0*, Fredrickson presents her research on love, challenging readers to see this "supreme emotion" in a new light. As she explains her theory, "Love is the momentary upwelling of three tightly interwoven events: first, a sharing of one or more positive emotions between you and another; second, a synchrony between your and the other person's biochemistry and behaviors; and third, a reflected motive to invest in each other's well-being that brings mutual care."[11] She is adamant that love is not just the province of romance or deep feelings between long-time partners. Nor is it only characterized by the care given another, such as a mother's love for her child.

In her book, Fredrickson recommends frequent but small interactions with others that are intended to show positive caring for another person, even a stranger. She also suggests that her readers consider a practice of loving kindness meditation and cites the evidence for its benefits. If you are intrigued by the possible boost to your positivity, you can listen to and download her guided meditation instructions on her website and try them for yourself.[12] You may think of certain coaching clients who might also benefit from practicing loving kindness meditation.

THE GOOD THAT POSITIVE EMOTIONS DO

Let's now consider what we can take away from these findings that will be of benefit to our coaching clients. Experiencing positive emotions, even mild ones (like amusement or contentment), may:

- Encourage what theorists call *approach behavior*, leading to exploration and engagement with one's surroundings.[13]
- Lead to more flexible thought[14] and "broad, flexible cognitive organization and ability to integrate diverse material";[15] this broadening may be linked to increases in dopamine levels in the brain, which are hypothesized to promote enhanced cognitive functioning.[16]
- Lead to more creative thinking[17] or expanded, i.e. broader, attention.[18]
- Help people cope with chronic stress by generating more positive emotions through three strategies: reappraising challenges in positive terms, focusing on solving problems, and interpreting everyday events with positive meaning.[19]
- Result in people's reporting greater life satisfaction in general, as mediated in part by positive emotions, helping build resilience.[19]
- Assist people in demonstrating a more robust immune response when exposed to the virus that causes the common cold.[20]
- Be linked to greater success at work—bosses rate happy people in more favorable terms;[21] and happy people are less likely to resign from their job[22] and may cope more effectively with changes in their organization than employees with low positive affect.[23]

Positive emotions may give rise to specific action tendencies that create a kind of positive chain reaction, even if the tendencies are less specified than for negative emotions.[24] For example, when we feel the positive emotion of interest, we may focus more attention on our surroundings and exploring the environment. When we feel joy, we may want to play, to initiate projects, and to stretch ourselves in creative ways. We may wish to share our pleasure with others, perhaps with affection or kind words. When we feel satisfied and happy about our personal achievements (Fredrickson uses the word *pride*), we may wish to share our accomplishments with others and start imagining our next venture.

There is another benefit to experiencing positive emotions: *it just feels good*. This is the *hedonic* aspect of positivity, experiencing the "pleasant life," as Seligman put it.[25] We will be talking in subsequent chapters about the *eudaimonic* aspect of positivity, or optimal well-being, and the importance to well-being of experiencing the "meaningful and engaged life."

UNDOING THE ADVERSE IMPACTS OF NEGATIVE EMOTION

In one of her earlier investigations, Fredrickson and her colleague Robert Levenson conducted an experiment studying the effects of negative emotions known to have an adverse impact on the cardiovascular system when experienced repeatedly over time.[26] Subjects' heart rate and blood pressure were taken, as markers of vasoconstriction and anxiety.

A mild-to-moderately anxious state was then induced in the subjects by telling them that they had just a short time to prepare and then deliver a speech to others. Subjects' physiological measures were taken again immediately after this experimental induction. A short time later, the subjects were told they did not have to give a speech after all, and were shown one of the four film clips. They were then asked what emotions they felt. These queries were used to measure the time that elapsed from the start of the film clip to the point at which the subject's elevated physiological measures returned to their baseline level. Subjects who viewed a positive-emotion film clip, particularly the amusement clip (penguins), showed the most rapid decrease in the two cardiovascular signs of anxiety. Those who viewed the sad clip (funeral) demonstrated the longest delay in returning to their physiological baseline. Fredrickson and Levenson concluded that experiencing positive emotions appears to help undo the adverse impact of negative emotions like anxiety on physical well-being.[27]

The effects of positive emotions seem to persist. One Fredrickson study found that upward spirals of broadening and building positive thoughts and action seemed to endure for at least five weeks.[28]

APPLICATIONS OF THE RESEARCH TO COACHING

Now, how can we apply these findings to our coaching? We believe we can best assist our clients by helping them increase their experience of positive emotions and general happiness in their daily lives. We often start the discussion by explaining the findings from Fredrickson's research (and that of others like Sonja Lyubomirsky), elaborating on the value of increased positivity to their well-being and performance at work. For some clients, it is crucial to emphasize that the benefits go beyond just feeling good and discuss the importance of *eudaimonia* as well as *hedonia*.

You may also wish to use Fredrickson's brief self-test with your clients using her website.[29] It can offer a client a sense of how positive their mindset is at the present time. We suggest to our clients that they go online and take the test, which is scored immediately. This test asks a person to assess how they have generally felt during the past day. It then poses twenty questions. A typical item is "What is the most amused, fun-loving or silly you felt?" The person rates their emotion on a five-point scale from "not at all" to "extremely."

COACHING QUESTIONS FOR HELPING CLIENTS INCREASE THEIR POSITIVE EMOTIONS

We encourage clients to reflect on activities they liked to do in the past and currently find enjoyable. We coach them in identifying and committing to a variety of ways to experience positive emotions much more frequently, first on a daily basis, then ideally several times during waking hours. You can suggest that such activities fall into categories such as:

- Pleasurable outings—dining out, vacationing to relax, traveling to experience new places and different cultures, seeing a movie or live performance.
- Interpersonal activities—spending time with friends, having lunch or coffee with coworkers or business associates, interacting with one's children, playing with pets, participating in team sports.
- Other pleasant activities—reading, doing puzzles, exercising, cooking, knitting, painting, taking photos, engaging in crafts, gardening, making music, playing individual sports, shopping, visiting museums, being in nature.

The following questions which I (Sandra) developed can be used to guide coaching conversations around increasing the experience of positive emotions:

- Having heard of these possible benefits, what are your thoughts about spending some of our coaching time exploring how you might experience more positive emotions in your daily life?
- What current circumstances have an impact on your experience of both positive and negative emotions?
- Describe your current life circumstances and your sense of the level of positive emotion you experience on a daily basis.
- What current activities seem to have the effect of creating greater positivity in your daily life? These can be related to using your strengths at work or in your personal life;

spending time with friends and family; taking part in sports or other leisure activities you enjoy; and so on.

- What steps could you take in order to spend more time doing activities that you enjoy?
- What are the possible steps you could take that could help you feel more engaged and potentially more positive at work?
- What activities can you engage in that could potentially increase your proportion of positive emotion when you are alone? (If the client does not have many ideas, I sometimes mention a positive success review or thinking about being in a peak performance state to recall and recreate in the present moment the physical, cognitive, and emotional characteristics of that former time. I also mention the beneficial effects of being in nature and exercise on positive mood.)
- What makes you laugh, or at least brings a smile to your face? (If the client does not readily think of a reply, I suggest that looking at cartoons, watching amusing films, attending a comedic play or light-hearted musical, and reading humorous stories are possible ways to invoke smiling and laughter. Other activities might include sharing stories with a particular friend who has a wonderful sense of humor, and looking at pictures of loved ones. I mention that *all* of these activities can also be shared, if the client desires.)
- What activities involving art, movement, or music might be helpful in increasing your experience of positive emotion? (Here I mention listening to and especially *making* music, dancing, visiting a museum, or looking at art books as activities that may increase positive emotion.)
- What social connections might be worth focusing more time on, in order to increase your experience of positive emotion?
- What are some meaningful activities that are important to you? What steps could you take to increase your

involvement in these, which might potentially lead to an increase in positive emotions? (Here I am referring to *eudaimonia*, the meaningful life, and suggest volunteering, becoming active in the community, taking part in spiritual or religious practices, being more conscious about conservation of resources, and helping to clean up and beautify public spaces so that many people might enjoy them.)

I then suggest to the client that, once they have created their list of activities, they add a star next to items that are free or easily accessible. This is a reminder that experiencing positive emotions is not about having substantial discretionary income. Vacations and travel do require money, but many of the experiences that lead to feeling good do not cost much—and plenty of them are free, or nearly so.

I then encourage the client to incorporate their listed activities into their daily life as much as possible. This might mean arranging more time with their friends, enrolling in a dance class, or joining a book club. It might mean surrounding themselves with reminders of things that enrich their life—like photos of loved ones on their smartphone, special laptop screen savers featuring a child's drawing, and so on. I recommend that they keep their list handy, where they will see it often. Finally, I encourage clients to add activities to the list on a regular basis, to help keep their positive emotions practice fresh and invigorating.

RECALLING POSITIVE EXPERIENCES AND SUCCESSES

This next coaching technique is very much like a success review in sport psychology. These are used to deliberately shift an athlete's unsettled state to one more conducive to successful training or competition. While it can indeed create a positive state of mind before going into a challenging sport situation, it also can also help clients who are not competitive athletes increase the time spent experiencing positive emotions in their daily life. Instruct your client, "Allow yourself to engage in positive self- reflection. First, just let your mind wander, to recalling your happiest experiences, your successes, your strengths, and reaching your cherished goals. Next, write down all the positives you can recollect. Consider sharing these reflections with someone you love and trust."

A COACHING TECHNIQUE FOR SHIFTING FROM A NEGATIVE STATE TO ONE MORE POSITIVE

I (Sandra) find the following technique very helpful for a client who feels stymied or distracted by negative emotions at work or in some other venue of importance to them. This process is intended to enable clients to shift from a negative state toward a more positive one and redirect their focus to actions that will further their objectives.

Please note that this technique is *not* appropriate for a person whose history of abuse or unprocessed trauma blocks their access to positive emotions, thoughts, and recollections. In such a situation, psychotherapy, rather than coaching, is indicated.

Instructions

1. Ask the client to identify a negative state currently in effect at work, such as feeling overwhelmed, confused, unfocused, or stressed.
2. Ask the client to imagine (with eyes open or closed) this negative state becoming more positive—not how to achieve this, but just imagining a more positive reality.
3. Ask how this negative state might be changed so it would be more positive six months from now. Have the client notice whether their feelings about the negative situation now feel more positive.
4. Ask the client to think of and say aloud some positive words or statements to strengthen the positive state. Here are some positive words that my clients have found helpful:

Breathe.

Focus.

I'm OK.

What is it I am supposed to be doing right now?

I can get a grip on my thoughts.

I've got this.

Just settle down.

Smile a little. It helps.

I can get on track.

I can manage this.

I can break this enormous task down into pieces and tackle each one, step by step.

What's my task here? I can do what I can see/define/clarify.

We can do it together if we [the team] support each other and work together.

Some of you may be reminded of Donald's Meichenbaum's classic book *Stress Inoculation Training* as you read these.[30]

5. Ask the client whether the words they chose generate entirely positive feelings in the body. If not, encourage them to find other positive words, to create as positive a feeling in the body as possible.

6. Later, taking a page from Fredrickson's research, spend time on coaching the client in developing "broaden and build" action steps to accompany the positive words. Here are a few possible strategies.

    *   *Make a list* that answers an important question, such as "What do I need to do?" or "What else might help in this situation?"

    *   Think of *different ways to solve the problem,* such as new resources or input from different people. Some provocative questions include "If I collaborated with ___ [a coworker], what positive outcomes might occur?" or "What different team interaction might help us better solve this problem?"

- *Get perspective.* Step back and consider how this situation might look a year, three years, or five years from now. "What's the big picture here? Am I 'in the weeds' and too caught up in details? Is my perspective too narrow?"

7. Once the positive words and one or more broadening strategies have been selected, ask the client to again imagine the positive state with the specific actions in mind. See if they can feel even more confident than in the first imagining. Should the client experience any negative physical sensations, try different positive words and broadening tactics to reach a positive state. Make certain that the client truly has the skills needed to execute and achieve the desired goals and has done the preparation crucial for performing well. Assist the client in reducing any performance anxiety that may be present.

8. Once you have created a workable action plan, ask your client to share it with someone they trust ("You know me. How does this sound to you?") and to make any needed refinements based on the feedback. Then ask the client to practice in the real-life situation and to report back to you.

Note. This coaching technique is meant to give your client a temporary means for short-circuiting a negative state to prevent a downward spiral. This is tactical tool and should not take the place of more in-depth reflection about the actual situation at work and whether there are other actions the client should take. Once the client is able to manage the negative state at work, encourage them to explore, in depth, the situation and their options for changing the circumstances as well as their emotional response to it.

Positive emotions are fleeting, yet they have cumulative and lasting benefits. Diener and his colleagues suggested years ago that the *frequency* of positive emotions is more important to one's subjective well-being than the *intensity* of a discrete positive emotional experience.[31]

When we actively cultivate the frequency of our experience of them and encourage clients to do so, positive emotions can help us shift to a more coherent, capable, and competent (strengths-based) state of mind and body. We are then better prepared to take immediate action when caught in a negative state, after which we can ponder and decide what steps are needed for substantive change.

Fredrickson's Ratio Challenged

In 2013, Nicholas Brown, Alan Sokol, and Harris Friedman challenged Fredrickson's assertion in Positivity that her research demonstrated that a 3:1 ratio of positive to negative emotions signaled flourishing while people whose ratios fall below 3:1 would languish.[32] Fredrickson had teamed up in these declarations with Marcial Losada, a Chilean mathematician, who said that his work was based on the mathematical field of nonlinear dynamics, also known as chaos theory. In 2005, they published these assertions in an article in the same journal, the American Psychologist.[33] Losada and his colleague Emily Heapy claimed that his research found a ratio of positive to negative interactions of 3:1 in high-performing teams and 1:1 in the lowest-performing teams at a US corporation, EDS. Performance was measured by business indicators.[34]

The critics laid out a detailed analysis, and Fredrickson's reply appeared in the same issue.[35] Losada did not respond to the critics' arguments then, and still has not done so at the time of this writing.

Essentially, Brown, Sokol, and Friedman questioned Losada's use of "differential equations drawn from fluid dynamics, a subfield of physics, to describe human emotions over time," and concluded: "The lack of relevance of these equations and their incorrect application lead us to conclude that Fredrickson and Losada's claim to have demonstrated the existence of a critical minimum positive ratio of 2.9013 is entirely unfounded."[36]

In her response, Fredrickson said, "I've come to see sufficient reason to question the particular mathematical framework Losada and I adopted to

continued...

> represent and test the concept of a critical tipping point positivity ratio that
> bifurcates mental health into flourishing and human languishing." But she
> cited numerous studies she and others had conducted that supported her
> conclusion: "The data say that when considering positive emotions, more
> is better, up to a point ... and when considering negative emotions, less is
> better, down to a point."[37]
>
> We encourage readers to review Fredrickson's response, which is
> available online.[38] Regardless of the arguments made by Brown, Sokol,
> and Friedman, Fredrickson's research and that of her colleagues point
> compellingly to the benefits of a greater proportion (my word—Sandra)
> of positive to negative emotions. Thus, we agree with Fredrickson that
> enhancing a person's experience of positive emotions is absolutely warranted.

SONJA LYUBOMIRSKY'S RESEARCH ON WAYS TO INCREASE HAPPINESS

Sonja Lyubomirsky began her research work as a faculty member at the University of California, Riverside, where she is currently a professor of psychology. She and her colleague Ken Sheldon were awarded a large research grant (more than a million dollars) from the National Institute of Mental Health to study happiness. Her definition of a happy person was stated as "someone who frequently experiences positive emotions." Concurring with Diener and colleagues, she noted that "intense positive emotions do not predict happiness as well as low-grade but frequent positive emotions."[39]

She has authored two fine books on happiness, which you may wish to add to your reference library. *The How of Happiness* is a delightfully written, science-based guide for increasing the positive emotion of happiness.[40] In her more recent book, *The Myths of Happiness*,[41] she makes convincing arguments against powerful beliefs held by many people in Western cultures such as "I'll be happy only when I get married" and "I can't be happy when I don't have much money." She addresses what she calls "ten different adult crisis points beginning with relationships (marriage, singlehood, kids), moving on to money and work (job malaise, financial success and ruin), and ending with problems inherent to middle age and beyond (health issues, aging, regrets),"[42] adding that "these can be opportunities for renewal, growth or meaningful change."[43]

Lyubomirsky's stated research aim was to study what she calls the *architecture* of happiness and to discover how to help people permanently raise the level of happiness they experience day to day. She concludes, by the way, that the best assessor of happiness is the person, agreeing with Ed Diener in this regard.[44] Thus, she uses self-report measures of subjective happiness, global happiness, and mood. The four-item self-report Subjective Happiness Scale is reprinted at the end of this chapter; it is also available on her website, sonjalyubomirsky.com.[45]

To date, researchers have identified three broad factors that influence one's happiness.

1. *Genetics* accounts for about 50 percent of the variance explained when looking at why some people are happier than others.
2. *Life circumstances* account for only about 10 percent of the variance, contradicting what many people assumed before these positive psychology research findings were published. Beyond having enough money to be comfortable, more wealth does not make people happier. And living in certain countries with a stable government and safe streets does affect the level of happiness of citizens, but not as much as you might think.
3. Other factors, or the "we don't know yet" category as Sonja calls it, account for the remaining 40 percent of the variance.

A few comments about the genetics factor are worth noting. There seems to be a genetically determined set point, one that we are born with, that mediates a characteristic level of happiness for each person. Its heritability, determined by twin studies, is 0.40 to 0.50, about the same as for height.[46] Lyubomirsky affirms that this set point does exert an impact on the level of happiness that people experience. Nonetheless, she is quick to say that she does not agree with others who propose that happiness is primarily a personality trait consistent across situations throughout a person's life.

Lyubomirsky also notes that research shows evidence that humans adapt, over time, to positive life changes. This means that people (and this has been found across cultures) soon take for granted some change for the better in their life circumstances, whether as a result of things happening to the person or initiated by the person.[47] She recommends counteracting this trend toward *hedonic adaptation* by several means: varying the activities one engages in, to keep them fresh and invigorating; sharing them with others; ensuring "fit" of the activity with the person; encouraging the person to approach the happiness activity with the mindset that the activity will be helpful; and pursuing the happiness-increasing activity with effort.

You may wish to read about her "construal" approach to happiness research in one of two articles.[48,49] Both explain the studies showing that persistently happy people are pleased when others do well whereas unhappy people are likely to feel envious and upset. What is also particularly relevant to our coaching work are the findings that "having goals in and of themselves is strongly associated with happiness and life satisfaction."[50]

Lyubomirsky's research has focused on the "we don't know yet" factors, and on the effect of what she refers to as "intentional activities" on subjects' self-reported happiness. Her research outcomes have demonstrated that engaging in certain intentional activities does significantly increase subjects' happiness.[51] In later publications, she refers to the acts as "positive activity interventions."[52]

Lyubomirsky and her colleague S. Katherine Nelson have confirmed a number of factors were involved in the effective use of happiness strategies.[53] One, the positive reactions of important people in the person's life were important in how effective the activities were in increasing levels of happiness. Another was timing—for example, performing five acts of kindness in one day rather than across several days. Finally, if you as a coach need research evidence for the connection between happiness and success at work, and in relationships, and in health, we commend to you the chapter Lyubomirsky co-authored with Katherine Jacobs.[54] This excellent summary can assist you in making the case for your client to enhance their happiness through the well-researched methods described there.

THE BENEFITS OF ACTIVITIES INVOLVING THE EXPRESSION OF GRATITUDE

In one of her earliest studies, students were instructed to reflect on their blessings and write a brief summary of what they were grateful for.[55] Some subjects did this three times a week, while other subjects did so once a week. A third group did nothing, serving as a no-treatment control condition.

Those who counted blessings once weekly had significant increases in self-reported happiness. So did those who counted blessings three times a week, but their increases were not as great, leading to speculation that writing about gratitude more than once a week might have become tedious or boring. The control-group subjects actually showed decreases in self-reported happiness during the same period.

Lyubomirsky reasoned that thankfulness would reduce feelings of envy and serve as a coping strategy for refocusing on what was working in a person's life. Expressing gratitude for what is going well seems to help create a mindset incompatible with hate, greed, bitterness, and anger.

Based on numerous studies,[56] Lyubomirsky identified seven reasons that the intentional activity of counting blessings and expressing gratitude might boost happiness:

1. Grateful thinking promotes the savoring of life experiences by taking pleasure in what people already possess and are, allowing them to extract the greatest possible enjoyment from their current circumstances.

2. Expressing gratitude increases a person's sense of self-worth and self-esteem when reflecting on personal accomplishments or the good deeds or gifts of others. Also enhanced are confidence and the sense of being effective in the world.

3. Gratitude helps people cope with stress and traumatic events through the reinterpretation of negative life experiences by intentionally recalling those aspects that are still positive or are still functioning well in the person's life.

4. Expressing gratitude during difficult times may make it easier to accept a setback or loss and move on. The mechanism here may be a reassessment of what remains for the person—the capabilities, assets of personality, life experiences or talents that are still part of the person's identity.

5. Expressing gratitude may increase the person's propensity to engage in moral behavior, that is, being likely to assist others or to care for them, and to be less focused on materialistic motives.

6. Gratitude may help a person build social bonds through the enhancement of the feeling of connectedness with other people. Lyubomirsky notes that numerous studies demonstrate that people who feel gratitude towards others report having higher-quality, closer relationships with others. The mechanism here is thought to be the person's realization of the value of the relationship, which then leads to treating others better, because they matter.

7. Expressing gratitude seems to diminish the impulse to feel envy or resentment of what others have. In an early study conducted with her Stanford advisor, Lee Ross, Lyubomirsky reported: "We found that the happiest people take pleasure in other people's successes and show concern in the face of others' failures. A completely different portrait, however, has emerged of a typically unhappy person—namely, as someone who is deflated

rather than delighted about his peers' accomplishments and triumphs and who is relieved rather than sympathetic in the face of his peers' failures and undoings."[57]

RESEARCH ON ACTS OF KINDNESS

An early intervention focused on practicing kindness as a way of increasing happiness by becoming more involved with others.[58] In helping someone else, the person felt more generous and then made a better social comparison of themselves. Kind behavior also evokes reciprocity from the recipient, but not in a crass "tit for tat" way. Subjects were instructed to engage in five kind acts each week. These could be simple acts like saying thank you or helping someone else without putting oneself in harm's way, like donating blood. The students were asked to keep brief "kindness reports" describing their kindness acts.

This simple intentional activity led to striking results. The participants who practiced kindness experienced significant increases in their self-reported happiness, while the control group actually showed decreases in self-reported happiness during the same period.

Lyubomirsky's replications include research with students in a public school in Vancouver, British Columbia.[59] Other studies[60] found that the effects of this simple intentional act persisted when a person planned the five acts of kindness in advance; when activities were varied, so that they remained fresh and did not become a routine list of things to do; when the acts of kindness were meaningful to the person being kind; and when all five acts were done on the same day, once weekly.

Sharing gratitude directly with the person to whom one feels grateful is especially powerful, as Seligman noted in his early gratitude visit research.[61] Other researchers have found the same thing more recently.[62]

Since the publication of *The How of Happiness*, Lyubomirsky's lab has generated many studies that offer intriguing and potentially helpful applications that we can teach to our coaching clients. In a novel study, Lyubomirsky and colleagues compared behavioral outcomes and self-reported happiness and flow in Japanese employees working at the Hitachi engineering office in Tokyo.[63] Participants were randomly assigned to one of two groups. One group was asked to recall in detail three positive events that had occurred during the prior week and the feelings they engendered. The control group was asked to list their work activities, with no reference to emotions. To assess behavioral changes as a result of the intervention, all subjects wore a *sociometric badge* that measured movement throughout the day and time spent in interactions with others.

The employees who recalled the three positive events showed increasing self-reported happiness over time, compared to employees who simply reported their activities at work. With regard to movement, the results were intriguing. Subjects in the "three things" group moved about more than those in the control group; however, they interacted with others less often. As the researchers tried to make sense of these findings, they noted that their "social interaction finding may seem at odds with prior literature."

HAPPINESS-INDUCING ACTIVITIES FOR BUSINESS CLIENTS

So, how does this fit into coaching? Before you suggest to clients that they be kind or thankful more often, try these interventions yourself. We have discussed these research results with several of our executive coaching clients and then waited to see their responses. If a client expressed an interest in trying out one or more applications, we provided instructions and encouragement and later examined the results together. With several clients from non-US cultures where the individual pursuit of happiness is viewed less favorably, we have suggested these interventions with even greater caution.

However, we are seeing benefits for our business clients, usually subtle but sometimes profound, from counting blessings and practicing acts of kindness. These benefits can emerge even for people who are in workplaces characterized by cynicism and lack of collaboration. We note that Emotional Intelligence (EI) skills are likely to be involved here (to ponder the positive emotions research from another vantage point). We are reminded of Goleman's identification of empathy as a key EI skill.[64] In their book *The Leadership Challenge*, Kouzes and Posner write that "at the heart of effective leadership is a genuine caring for people."[65] And the issue of the caring (or kind) leader is taken up by several authors in the edited volume *Management 21C*.[66]

If someone seeks our coaching and we suspect that increased positivity might benefit that individual at work, we feel it important to at least introduce the topic. Not all will be receptive, but as long as we are alert to individual as well as cross-cultural differences, we consider exploring positivity techniques a more than appropriate coaching intervention. In Chapter 8 we describe several other interventions suitable for the workplace.

With Dr. Lyubomirsky's encouragement, in the following paragraphs we share several happiness interventions that we have found particularly valuable with our coaching clients. To begin, suggest to the client that they take time to notice what it feels like to engage in the interventions and how they feel afterward. You can mention the Subjective Happiness Scale[67] *(page 38)* as pre-post measure to track the impact of these activities on their level of happiness, preferably after using the technique for at least six weeks. You might also helpfully mention that research has indicated that recalling positive events at work makes employees feel happier.[68]

COUNTING BLESSINGS

Choose one day per week when you will pause and do this intervention. You can use the following words suggested by Lyubomirsky: "There are many things in our lives, both large and small, that we might be grateful about. Think back over the events of the last week and write up to five things that happened for which you are grateful or thankful."[69]

By the way, Lyubomirsky found that the impact of expressing gratitude is sustained by varying the ways that you express your thankfulness (to keep the strategies appealing and novel), and by writing about your blessings for some weeks and then, during other weeks, verbally sharing with others what you are grateful for. Working with a "gratitude partner" in an ongoing manner can boost the positive impact.[70] You may also want to consider expressing your gratitude directly, as Seligman suggests in his "gratitude visit" research, by writing a letter and presenting it to that person face to face.[71] With loved ones or other significant people who have passed away, this visit can be done symbolically, by imagining presenting the letter and carrying on a conversation with the person.

Drawn from his book, *Flourish*, here are the instructions for a gratitude visit.[72]

> *Close your eyes. Call up the face of someone still alive who years ago did something or said something that changed your life for the better. Someone who you never properly thanked; someone you could meet face-to-face next week. Got a face?*
>
> *Gratitude can make your life happier and more satisfying. When we feel gratitude, we benefit from the pleasant memory of a positive event in our life. Also, when we express our gratitude to others, we strengthen our relationship with them. But sometimes our thank you is said so casually or quickly that it is nearly meaningless. In this exercise ... you will have the opportunity to experience what it is like to express your gratitude in a thoughtful, purposeful manner.*
>
> *Your task is to write a letter of gratitude to this individual and deliver it in person. The letter should be concrete and about three hundred words: be specific about what she did for you and how it affected your life. Let her know what you are doing now, and mention how you often remember what she did. Make it sing! Once you have*

written the testimonial, call the person and tell her you'd like to visit her, but be vague about the purpose of the meeting; this exercise is much more fun when it is a surprise. When you meet her, take your time reading your letter.

PLANNED ACTS OF KINDNESS

For this kindness application, endeavor to identify five intentional kind actions that you can do all in one day without putting yourself or others in harm's way. These can be small acts of kindness and need not involve spending money. Examples can be providing babysitting or running errands for a new mother, holding the door for another, taking the time to acknowledge someone's good service by writing to their boss, or personally presenting a Thank You note to someone who has helped you in some way.[73]

SHARING HAPPIEST EXPERIENCES WITH TRUSTED OTHERS

Arrange a time with someone you trust who cares about your well-being. Deliberately engage in positive self-reflection and share aloud your happiest experiences, your strengths, and your cherished goals with this other person. Ask the person for feedback, support, and suggestions for how you could continue to flourish.[74]

IMAGINING YOUR BEST SELF

Imagine yourself in the future, after everything has gone as well as it possibly could. You have worked hard and succeeded at accomplishing all of your life goals. Think of this as the realization of your life dreams, and of your own best potentials. In all of these cases you are identifying the best possible way that things might turn out in your life, in order to help guide your decisions now. You may not have thought about yourself in this way before, but research suggests that doing so can have a strong positive effect on your mood and life satisfaction. So, we'd like to ask you to continue thinking in this way over the next few weeks, after writing about your ideal life in the future, outlining your ideal future life in as much detail as possible.[75]

RECALLING THREE GOOD THINGS AT WORK

Once per week spend about ten minutes writing on your tablet or laptop about three things that went particularly well for you at work. Use enough detail to describe why these events went well. Describe your feelings while the event was happening and at the present moment when you are recalling and doing your writing. Do this weekly for at least six weeks.[76]

Subjective Happiness Scale
(Lyubomirsky & Lepper, 1999) [77]

For each of the following statements and/or questions, please circle the point on the scale that you feel is most appropriate in describing you.

1. In general, I consider myself:

1	2	3	4	5	6	7
not a very happy person						a very happy person

2. Compared to most of my peers, I consider myself:

1	2	3	4	5	6	7
less happy						more happy

3. Some people are generally very happy. They enjoy life regardless of what is going on, getting the most out of everything. To what extent does this characterization describe you?

1	2	3	4	5	6	7
not at all						a great deal

4. Some people are generally not very happy. Although they are not depressed, they never seem as happy as they might be. To what extent does this characterization describe you?

1	2	3	4	5	6	7
not at all						a great deal

Note. Item 4 is reverse-coded.

Character Strengths, Virtues and Talents:

Deliberately Putting Your Best Foot Forward

In this chapter we dive into what excites so many about positive psychology: enhancing success by understanding our talents and strengths (we define the distinction between these two terms later in this chapter). We will consider how humans function at their best by examining Peterson's and Seligman's research on virtues and character strengths. Then we will learn about how people identify their talents, and how, with coaching, those talents may be developed into strengths. This chapter will also focus on two assessments: the VIA Survey and the StrengthsFinder 2.0.

The idea of using strengths to enhance well-being and leadership is widely proposed in the positive psychology literature, from bestselling books[1,2,3] to peer-reviewed research.[4] We will build on this literature by integrating the research and sharing our practical coaching approaches.

KNOWING YOUR STRENGTHS INCREASES SELF-CONFIDENCE, PRODUCTIVITY, INCOME, AND HEALTH

Research shows that when you help your clients understand their talents, develop those talents into strengths, and use those strengths more effectively, they will achieve higher income, greater productivity, and improved health and fitness. However, we want to emphasize that our focus is on helping coaching clients deploy the optimum amount of a particular strength at the right time. We do not claim that increasing strengths is a panacea. For example, although a person can be too passive for a situation, they can also become too assertive for a situation. We like to tell our clients that it is important to understand the "volume" of a particular strength and what level is "just right" for the situation at hand.

Studies indicate that self-confidence grows when people increase understanding of their key strengths. Moreover, self-confidence is related to higher income and better health. Research also suggests that increased knowledge of one's strengths boosts self-confidence. The wise and balanced use of strengths helps boost subjective well-being, and employees' overall engagement and productivity at work. In *Strengths Based Leadership: Great Leaders, Teams, and Why People Follow,* Tom Rath and Barry Conchie assert: "Over the past decade, Gallup scientists have explored in much more detail the mechanism through which a strengths-based approach influences our lives. These studies revealed that people experience significant gains in self-confidence after taking the StrengthsFinder (a Gallup assessment tool) and learning more about their strengths. This increase in confidence at an individual level may help explain how strengths-based programs boost an organization's overall engagement and productivity."[5]

A landmark study by Tim Judge at the University of Florida studied the evaluations of 8,000 men and women who were in their early twenties in 1979. They were followed for twenty-five years, with a focus on their income, career, success, and health. Higher self-confidence in 1979 predicted higher income levels and satisfaction twenty-five years later, in 2004. The group with high self-confidence made an average of $13,000 a year more, and their incomes continued to increase each year, more so than the other group.[6]

The health effects were surprising, too. The people who had lower self-confidence in 1979 had three times as many health problems at that time. Almost unbelievably, the group with high self-confidence in 1979 had *fewer* health problems in 2004 than they had had in 1979. The benefits of understanding and utilizing your strengths accumulate with each passing year.

It's important for us to help leaders understand and leverage their own strengths, and for leaders to help their employees uncover their strengths as early in their career as possible. Helping your clients use their strengths well, and at the right time and place, will help them thrive. In addition, the discovery and enhanced use of your clients' strengths has the potential to help their organization flourish more than other organizations, for many decades to come.

CHARACTER STRENGTHS AND VIRTUES

Martin Seligman assembled a team of fifty-five prestigious social scientists (including Donald Clifton, Mihalyi Csikszentmihalyi, Chris Peterson, Ed Diener, Kathleen Hall Jamieson, Robert Nozick, Daniel Robinson, and George Valiant) to produce the VIA Classification of Character Strengths,[7] originally to study positive youth development, with the support of the Mayerson Foundation. The VIA Classification is now considered a wealth of information for other endeavors related to studying or optimizing human development. Well-known Harvard professor Howard Gardner called the 816-page *Character Strengths and Virtues: A Handbook and Classification* "one of the most important initiatives in psychology of the past half century."

The research team studied and discussed the major writings of religious and philosophical traditions, including Confucianism, Taoism, Buddhism, Hinduism, Judaism, Christianity, Islam, Socrates, Plato, and Aristotle. They found that there was common recognition and praise for the same six virtues: wisdom and knowledge; courage; love and humanity; justice; temperance; and spirituality and transcendence. Seligman and Peterson developed a classification that resulted in a list of twenty-four character strengths, based on the following criteria. A character strength:

- is widely recognized across cultures
- contributes to individual fulfillment and satisfaction
- is morally valued
- does not diminish others and is admired by others
- has a negative opposite

- is trait-like: generally stable and present over time
- is measurable
- is distinct from other character strengths
- has paragons (is present in a striking way in some individuals)
- has prodigies (present to a high degree in some youth)
- may be missing altogether in some people
- is deliberately promoted by some social institutions.

Each of these twenty-four character strengths is associated with one of the six core moral virtues. This classification of character strengths is the foundation for the VIA Survey (*formerly know as Values in Action Inventory of Strengths*),[8] which we describe below.

PETERSON AND SELIGMAN'S TWENTY-FOUR CHARACTER STRENGTHS

Strengths of Wisdom and Knowledge: cognitive strengths that entail the acquisition and use of knowledge.

1. **Creativity (originality, ingenuity):** thinking of novel and productive ways to conceptualize and do things.
2. **Curiosity (interest, novelty-seeking, and openness to experience):** taking an interest in ongoing experience for its own sake; exploring and discovering.
3. **Open-mindedness (judgment, critical thinking):** thinking things through and examining them from all sides; weighing all evidence fairly.
4. **Love of learning:** mastering new skills, topics, and bodies of knowledge, whether on one's own or formally.
5. **Perspective (wisdom):** being able to provide wise counsel to others; having ways of looking at the world that make sense to oneself and to other people.

Strengths of Courage: emotional strengths that involve the exercise of will to accomplish goals in the face of opposition, external and internal.

6. **Bravery (valor):** not shrinking from threat, challenge, difficulty, or pain; acting on convictions even if unpopular.

7. **Persistence (perseverance, industriousness):** finishing what one starts; persisting in a course of action in spite of obstacles.

8. **Integrity (authenticity, honesty):** presenting oneself in a genuine way; taking responsibility for one's feeling and actions.

9. **Vitality (zest, enthusiasm, vigor, energy):** approaching life with excitement and energy; feeling alive and activated.

Strengths of Humanity: interpersonal strengths that involve tending to and befriending others.

10. **Love:** valuing close relations with others, in particular those in which sharing and caring are reciprocated.

11. **Kindness (generosity, nurturance, care, compassion, altruistic love, "niceness"):** doing favors and good deeds for others.

12. **Social intelligence (emotional intelligence, personal intelligence):** being aware of the motives and feelings of other people and oneself.

Strengths of Justice: civic strengths that underlie healthy community life.

13. **Citizenship (social responsibility, loyalty, teamwork):** working well as a member of a group or team; being loyal to the group.

14. **Fairness:** treating all people the same according to notions of fairness and justice; not letting personal feelings bias decisions about others.

15. **Leadership:** encouraging a group of which one is a member to get things done while at the same maintaining good relations within the group.

Strengths of Temperance: strengths that protect against excess

16. **Forgiveness and mercy:** forgiving those who have done wrong; accepting the shortcomings of others; giving people a second chance; not being vengeful.

17. **Humility/modesty:** letting one's accomplishments speak for themselves; not regarding oneself as more special than one is.

18. **Prudence:** being careful about one's choices; not taking undue risks; not saying or doing things that might later be regretted.

19. **Self-regulation (self-control):** regulating what one feels and does; being disciplined; controlling one's appetites and emotions.

Strengths of Transcendence: strengths that forge connections to the larger universe and provide meaning.

20. **Appreciation of beauty and excellence (awe, wonder, elevation):** appreciating beauty, excellence, and/or skilled performance in various domains of life.

21. **Gratitude:** being aware of and thankful of the good things that happen; taking time to express thanks.

22. **Hope (optimism, future-mindedness, future orientation):** expecting the best in the future and working to achieve it.

23. **Humor (playfulness):** liking to laugh and tease; bringing smiles to other people; seeing the light side.

24. **Spirituality (religiousness, faith, purpose):** having coherent beliefs about the higher purpose, the meaning of life, and the meaning of the universe.

We have asked two of the leading positive psychologists to tell us about their research on a particular strength that they have studied extensively. Roy Baumeister discusses willpower because of its strong role in enabling the coaching client to follow through on planned action steps. Robert Emmons discusses gratitude, a much-discussed virtue often included in coaching conversations by coaches who focus on helping clients have greater well-being.

Social psychologist Roy Baumeister's research suggests that the strengths of self-control and willpower can make a significant contribution to improvement of human welfare. In the best-selling book, *Willpower: Rediscovering the Greatest Human Strength*, he and co-author John Tierney emphasize how the use of willpower allows us to direct our lives and resist unhelpful temptations.

Are Self-Control and Willpower the Greatest Strengths?
—by Roy F. Baumeister

Self-control is a true strength and is among the most important ones in the human repertoire. It amounts to the ability to change yourself: to alter your thoughts, your emotions, and feelings, your actions and desires, and your level of task performance. It enables people to follow rules, which is essential for human civilization. Morality and laws would be useless without self-control, because what is the point of rules if people are not able to change their actions so as to obey them? Human free will, in whatever sense people have it, begins with self-control.

The benefits of self-control are legion. People with good self-control have myriad advantages over those with poor self-control. They perform better in school and work (earning higher grades and more money). They are liked better by peers and authority figures. People trust them more. They have more satisfying and durable relationships. They enjoy higher levels of happiness and lower levels of stress. They suffer fewer problems such as eating disorders and substance abuse. They commit fewer crimes. They manage their weight better. They treat others better. They even live longer!

Laboratory studies have found that self-control operates like a muscle (hence the "strength model" of self-control), in three respects. First, it gets "tired." That is, it seems to depend on a limited supply of energy, akin to the folk notion of willpower. In what researchers have come to call ego depletion effects, a person's level of self-control fluctuates, so that after exerting self-control, subsequent efforts are less effective than usual.

For example, after resisting a tempting plate of cookies, people give up faster on a difficult task.

Second, like a muscle, people start to conserve their strength when they have exerted it. Ego depletion does not mean that the brain is out of fuel. Rather, the body knows it has expended some energy and resists expending more. Third, just as a muscle can get stronger, self-control can be improved by regular exercise. Ego depletion is only a short-term effect, but in the long term, frequent exertion of self-control can improve one's willpower. This is what the Victorians called "building character." It works.

Willpower is tied in to the body's energy supply. Self-control is best when one has had adequate food and sleep, and even ego depletion can be counteracted to some extent by getting something to eat. Its link to bodily energy means, however, that self-control is affected by other processes. In particular, making decisions also requires willpower, so that after making many decisions, self-control is worse (and vice versa). When you are sick, your body uses its energy for the immune system, so your self-control suffers (you may notice yourself getting upset more easily than usual), and decision-making is impaired. Logical reasoning requires willpower. Even premenstrual syndrome appears to occur when the female body requires extra energy for its reproductive functions, leaving less to spare for self-control.

Psychology knows two traits that predict success in life across many different spheres. These are cognitive intelligence and self-control. Producing lasting increases in cognitive intelligence has proved elusive, but self-control (an ingredient of emotional intelligence) can be increased even in adulthood. That makes self-control one of the most promising vehicles for improving human life.[9]

Robert Emmons, the best-selling author of *Thanks!: How the New Science of Gratitude Can Make You Happier* and the editor-in-chief of the *Journal of Positive Psychology*, has conducted research highlighting that gratitude has a lasting positive impact on our life.

Is Gratitude the Greatest Strength?
—by Robert Emmons

Gratitude is a basic human strength, one of the five strengths that comprise the virtue of Transcendence in the VIA taxonomy. Groundbreaking research has shown that when people regularly cultivate gratitude they experience a multitude of psychological, physical, interpersonal, and spiritual benefits. Gratitude has one of the strongest links to mental health and satisfaction with life of any personality trait—more so than even optimism, hope, or compassion. Dozens of research studies with hundreds of diverse participants have revealed that the practice of gratitude leads to:

- increased feelings of energy, alertness, enthusiasm, and vigor
- success in achieving personal goals
- better coping with stress
- a sense of closure in traumatic memories
- bolstered feelings of self-worth and self-confidence
- solidified and secure social relationships
- greater generosity and helpfulness
- prolonging of the enjoyment produced by pleasurable experiences
- improved cardiac health—through increases in vagal tone, reduction in unhealthy cholesterol, and decreases in blood pressure
- a greater sense of purpose and resilience.

*What accounts for the power of gratitude? Consider the fact that it is other-focused. Most emotions are about the self—happiness, optimism, hope, pride, guilt—they are all about **us**. Gratitude takes us outside ourselves, where we see ourselves as part of a larger, intricate network of sustaining relationships, relationships that are mutually reciprocal. This explains the energizing and motivating force of gratitude. It is a positive state of mind* *that gives rise to the "passing on of the gift" through positive action. A grateful response is not complete until it has the following three elements: looking for the good, taking in or receiving that good, then giving back the good. Gratitude derives its full strength only when all three elements are present.*

In gratitude we become aware of our limitations and our need to rely on others. In gratitude we acknowledge the myth of self-sufficiency. We look upward and outward to the sources that sustain us. Becoming aware of realities greater than ourselves shields us from the illusion of being self-made, being here on this planet by right—expecting everything and owing nothing. The thankful person says that life is a gift to be grateful for, not a right to be claimed. This realization ushers in a grateful response to life. Gratitude is therefore the truest approach to life. We did not create or fashion ourselves. We did not birth ourselves. Life is about giving, receiving, and repaying. We are receptive beings, dependent on the help of others, on their gifts and their kindness. As such, we are called to gratitude. If we choose to ignore this basic truth, we steer ourselves off course.

In some respects this is a profoundly counter-cultural idea. Modern psychology has placed great emphasis on individual autonomy and self-sufficiency. Gratitude requires, however, that we affirm our dependency on others and recognize that we need to receive that which we cannot provide for ourselves. Until this dependence is acknowledged, gratitude remains a potentiality at best, and we are unable to capitalize on its promises and potential.[10]

If you want to become a more grateful person, the first step is to assess your current level of gratitude. This quick assessment will allow you to evaluate how grateful you are now and can serve as a starting place for coaching plans to increase one's gratitude.

HOW GRATEFUL ARE YOU? TEST YOUR GRATITUDE QUOTIENT

1 = strongly disagree	5 = slightly agree
2 = disagree	6 = agree
3 = slightly disagree	7 = strongly agree
4 = neutral	

_____1. I have so much in life to be thankful for.

_____2. If I had to list everything that I felt grateful for, it would be a very long list.

_____3. When I look at the world, I don't see much to be grateful for.*

_____4. I am grateful to a wide variety of people.

_____5. As I get older, I find myself more able to appreciate the people, events, and situations that have been part of my life history.

_____6. Long amounts of time can go by before I feel grateful to something or someone.*

Scoring instructions

1. Add up your scores for items 1, 2, 4, and 5.
2. Reverse your scores for items 3 and 6. That is, if you scored a 7, give yourself a 1; if you scored a 6, give yourself a 2; etc.
3. Add the reversed scores for items 3 and 6 to the total from Step 1. This is your total GQ-6 score. This number should be between 6 and 42.

Interpreting your score

40–42: Extremely high gratitude. People who score in this range have the ability to see life as a gift. For you, gratitude is a way of life.

37–39: Very high gratitude. Your life contains frequent expressions of gratitude, and you are able to readily acknowledge how others have helped you.

34-36: High gratitude. You are above average in gratitude and find it relatively easy to spend time reflecting on your blessings.

30-33: Average gratitude. You find it easy being grateful when things are going well in your life, but have difficulty maintaining a grateful outlook in tough times.

25-29: Below-average gratitude. You find it challenging to find reasons for gratitude in your life. Life is more of a burden than a gift. Perhaps you are just going through a downturn.[10]

THE SCIENTIFIC BASIS FOR FOCUSING ON STRENGTHS IN COACHING

Positive psychological interventions, in particular character strengths–based activities, have been demonstrated to lead to increased happiness, well-being, and in some cases, goal attainment, among both adults and youth.[11,12]

EFFECTS OF STRENGTHS AWARENESS ON HAPPINESS

In 2005, researchers Martin Seligman, Tracy A. Steen, Nansook Park, and Christopher Peterson came together to report on their fascinating six-group, random-assignment, placebo-controlled study testing five purported happiness interventions and a plausible control exercise. They found that three of the interventions lastingly increased happiness and decreased depressive symptoms. Interestingly, one of the most potent interventions involved strengths.

These researchers were interested in studying happiness. They examined three routes to the "good life": positive emotion and pleasure ("the pleasant life"); engagement ("the engaged life"); and meaning ("the meaningful life").[13] They contended that happiness is worthy of study in part because happiness is causal and brings many benefits beyond just feeling good. In view of the evidence that happy people are healthier, more successful, and more socially engaged, they developed interest in interventions that build happiness. In the previous chapter we discussed positive emotion and happiness. Now we focus more on an intervention that on the surface seems focused on happiness, but is intimately connected to our understanding of how to use strengths in coaching.

The researchers examined ideas all the way from Buddha through the human potential and self-help movements of the 1960s through the 1990s and found at least a hundred "interventions" claiming to increase happiness. They analyzed these and developed five hypothesized happiness-boosting exercises, as well as a control-group placebo exercise.

They studied the impact of the six interventions by measuring their effects on happiness and depression. They used a standard assessment to measure depression, the Center for Epidemiological Studies Depression Scale. To evaluate the week-by-week upward changes in happiness they hoped for, they created a new measure, the Steen Happiness Index. The index contains twenty items and requires one to reflect on the three elements of happy lives (the pleasant life, the engaged life, and the meaningful life): experiencing and savoring pleasures, losing the self in engaging activities, and participating in meaningful activities.

Participants answered the questions on a scale from most negative (1) to most positive (5).

- Most of the time I am bored.
- Most of the time I am neither bored nor interested in what I am doing.
- Most of the time I am interested in what I am doing.
- Most of the time I am quite interested in what I am doing.
- Most of the time I am fascinated by what I am doing.[14]

EXPERIMENTAL DESIGN OF THE HAPPINESS INTERVENTIONS

The study was conducted via the Internet, with the participants practicing their assigned exercise for one week. The exercises focused on building gratitude, increasing awareness of what is most positive about oneself, or identifying or using strengths of character. Using a randomized, placebo-controlled procedure, they compared the effects of these exercises with a reasonable control group: journaling for one week about early memories. The intervention lasted for one week but they tracked the effects for six months, measuring signs of both depression and happiness.

Study participants were recruited from people who visited a website created for Seligman's book, *Authentic Happiness*. The study was painted as an opportunity to help test new exercises designed to increase happiness, and 577 participants signed up.

After participants completed the initial questionnaires, they completed questionnaires to measure their happiness and depression levels. Then each was given a randomly assigned exercise. They were instructed to return to the study website to complete follow-up questionnaires after completing their assigned exercise. Participants completed the same measures of happiness and depression that were administered at pretest, and they also answered a question to assess whether they had actually completed the exercise as instructed.

Here are the exercises used in the study which were all performed in one week.

Placebo *(control exercise):* participants were asked to write about their early memories every night for one week.

Gratitude visit: participants were asked to write a letter of gratitude to someone who had been especially kind to them and deliver it in person.

Three good things in life: participants were asked to write down, each day, three things that went well that day and their causes.

You at your best: participants were asked to write about a time when they were at their best, then to review their story once every day for a week and to reflect on the strengths they had identified.

Using signature strengths in a new way: participants were asked to take the VIA Survey online and read about their top five ("signature") strengths, and then to use one of these top strengths in a new and different way every day of the week.

Identifying signature strengths: participants were asked to take the VIA Survey to identify their five highest strengths, and to use them more frequently during the next week (like the previous exercise, but without the instruction to use signature strengths in new ways).

RESULTS OF THE SIX PROPOSED HAPPINESS-BOOSTING INTERVENTIONS

The researchers found two exercises that significantly increased happiness and decreased depression for at least six months: *using signature strengths in a new way and writing three good things that happened that day.* Another exercise, the *gratitude visit,* caused large positive changes for one month. When participants continued their intervention activity past the prescribed one-week period, long-term benefits increased.

To increase happiness, the element of using their top strengths in *new and different ways* was essential to receiving those benefits, as opposed to the easier step of identifying and using their strengths more frequently. This point is often overlooked by strengths-based coaches.

Figure 1
The effect of the six interventions on happiness.

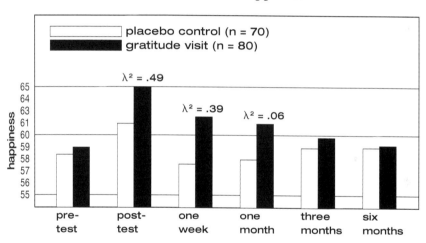

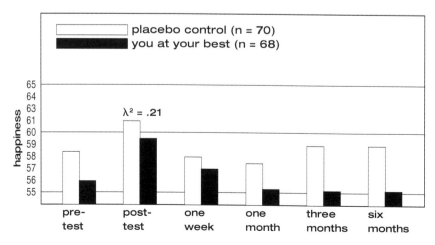

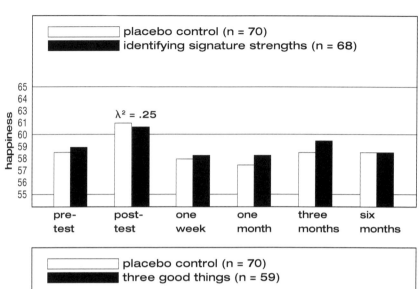

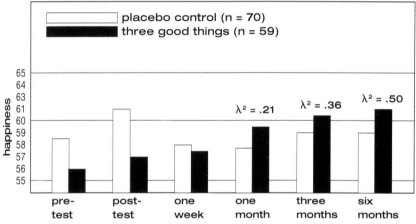

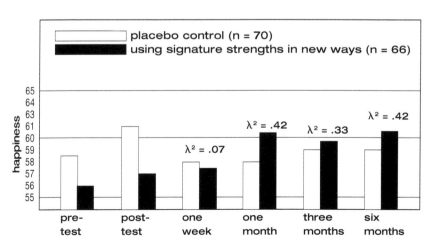

As Figure 1 shows, after one week of doing the assigned exercise, participants in the *gratitude visit* condition were happier and showed the largest immediate positive changes in the entire study. However, after three months, participants in this condition were no happier than they had been originally. Those who tracked *three good things* began to show beneficial effects one month following the post-test and reported higher residual happiness" at both the three-month and six-month follow-ups.[15]

Those who practiced *using signature strengths in a new way* exhibited immediate effects that were less pronounced than the result of the *three good things* condition. However, at the one-month follow-up and beyond, participants in the former group developed significantly more happiness than the participants who completed the *identifying signature strengths* exercise (that is, who did not use those strengths *in new ways*). Those participants who took part in the, *you at your best* assignment showed an effect only at the immediate post-test.

Many participants voluntarily continued to do some of the exercises, and the researchers hypothesized that continued practice of an intervention would mediate positive outcomes at later times. The outcome study showed that participants who continued the exercises had the biggest boost to their happiness.

After the researchers completed their study and reflected on the results, they came to the opinion that one week is not enough time for participants in the using *signature strengths in a new way* condition or the *three good things* condition to develop sufficient skill and experience to obtain significant benefit; with a little more time devoted to these practices, the results were positive and long-lasting. They concluded that these two interventions involve skills that improve with practice and are so enjoyable that they become self-maintaining.[16]

Coaching Tips
- Encourage your clients not only to use their strengths more (in situations where they are appropriate) but also to use them in new ways.
- When developing action steps such as these with your clients, remind your clients that the research shows that the benefits of actions may take time to kick in.
- Tell your client that the greatest benefits manifest over time, with consistent practice.
- Consider the personality of your client. Help them evaluate and choose which type of action steps fit best, not only with their situation and goals but also with their personality.

STRENGTHS, WELL-BEING, AND SELF-EFFICACY

Researchers Govindji and Linley investigated the theory that people who know their strengths, use their strengths, and follow the path that feels right for them (i.e. organismic valuing) will be happier.[17] They designed a study in which 214 college students completed measures of these variables as well as measures of self-esteem and self-efficacy. Analyses showed that the use of strengths and organismic valuing were significantly associated with well-being and vitality. The participants who used their strengths more were also higher in self-efficacy—believing that you are capable of achieving what you want to accomplish and that your actions make a difference. The questions the participants answered to evaluate their strengths were:

- I am regularly able to do what I do best
- I always play to my strengths
- I always try to use my strengths
- I achieve what I want by using my strengths

- I use my strengths every day
- I use my strengths to get what I want out of life
- My work gives me lots of opportunities to use my strengths
- My life presents me with lots of different ways to use my strengths
- Using my strengths comes naturally to me
- I find it easy to use my strengths in the things I do
- I am able to use my strengths in lots of different situations
- Most of my time is spent doing the things that I am good at doing
- Using my strengths is something I am familiar with
- I am able to use my strengths in lots of different ways[18]

Although this study only demonstrated correlations and does not prove that using one's strengths more leads to greater well-being, the findings suggest that questions designed to help a person identify their strengths, and use those strengths in specific new ways more frequently, are likely to bring positive results.

USING STRENGTHS IN NEW WAYS LEADS TO BETTER GOAL PROGRESS

Using one's strengths has been shown to be linked to subjective and psychological well-being, even when controlling for the effects of self-efficacy and self-esteem.[19] An interesting study of 240 college students used the VIA Survey to identify top strengths. Then the students were asked questions such as "How much have you used each of your signature strengths in working towards the first/second/third goal you identified for this semester?" The researchers found that the students who used their strengths more extensively made better goal progress, which was also associated with greater well-being.[20]

Coaching Tips

Here are some questions you can ask your clients related to leveraging their strengths:

- In what ways can you use your strengths more to help you achieve your most important goal this week?
- What are some new ways you can use your strengths that will be helpful to you?
- How will you use some of your strengths this week to achieve your goal?
- What strengths are you using today?
- How can you spend more time this week doing things that you are good at?
- What is the value, to you, for you to think about what your strengths are and how you could use them in some new ways to achieve your goals?

GROUP STRENGTHS-BUILDING APPROACHES

Some researchers in the United Kingdom were curious as to whether students who participated in character strengths–based exercises would show significant changes. The experiment consisted of 319 adolescents who were assigned to either the treatment group or the control group. The treatment group participated in the "strengths gym," a program of character strengths–based paper-and-pencil exercises. The goal of the program was to encourage students to build their strengths, learn new strengths, and learn to recognize strengths in others. The students took pre- and post-assessments to measure the impact of the intervention, including ones designed to measure life satisfaction, positive and negative affect, and self-esteem. The program included activities such as "spotting your strengths," where strengths were defined as "your best qualities." Each exercise included a definition of a character strength and exercises to build that strength, as well as a follow-up activity.

Participants were presented with the definitions of the twenty-four VIA character strengths and asked, "Which strengths do you think describe you best?" They were invited to pick five strengths from the twenty-four VIA character strengths.[21] These "strengths builder" and "strength challenge" exercises are similar to those suggested by Peterson, which were demonstrated to have long-term positive effects on happiness,[22] and to the Seligman et al. 2005 study, which showed that character strengths-based exercises have a beneficial effect on happiness and reduced depression.

CHARACTER STRENGTHS AT WORK

Positive psychological functioning is linked to valued work-related variables such as job satisfaction and work engagement. A recent study examined the relationship between strengths of character identified by the VIA Survey and work-related behaviors. Participants (887 women) completed the VIA Survey and the Work-Related Behavior and Experience Patterns questionnaire. The resulting strengths profiles show that individuals who had healthy work-related behavior differed from the strengths profiles of those that demonstrated burnout. Strengths of Zest, Persistence, Hope, and Curiosity were strongly correlated with healthy, ambitious, and engaged work behavior.[23]

LEADERSHIP IN UNDERGRADUATE COLLEGE STUDENTS

A study by Alina Black of Regent University explored the influence of strengths-based development on leadership practices among undergraduate college students while controlling for gender, years of leadership experience, and number of leadership courses completed using a quasi-experimental approach with a randomized control-group pre-test/post-test design. The sample included 95 student leaders (60 female, 35 male) with a mean age of twenty, with the majority being Caucasian (87%), from a Midwestern liberal arts university.

Participants in the study group completed six online strengths-based development learning modules, while participants in the control group completed traditional leadership development learning modules. The dependent variable was Kouzes and Posner's model of exemplary leadership practices, as measured by the Student Leadership Practice Inventory. Pre-tests and post-tests were administered for each dependent variable, with pre-test scores used as covariates in the statistical analyses.

Significant differences were found between the study and control groups. Student leaders who engaged in a six-week strengths-based development program showed significantly greater gains in the leadership practices of modeling the way, inspiring a shared vision, challenging the process, enabling others to act, and encouraging the heart, compared to the control group.[24]

STRENGTHS-BASED EXECUTIVE COACHING FOR LEADERSHIP DEVELOPMENT

A recent study of strengths-based executive coaching to enhance full-range leadership development provides an interesting example of how knowledge of strengths can be integrated into the coaching process. Derek Mackie, of Brisbane, Australia, designed a between-subjects waiting-list control-group study to explore the impact of strengths-based coaching on transformational leadership, as measured with a 360° (multi-rater) assessment. He assigned thirty-seven executives and senior managers in a nonprofit organization to either a coaching group or wait-list group. The coaching group received six sessions of coaching via a manualized coaching approach to ensure method consistency among the eleven executive coaches who delivered the coaching services. The manual outlined specific coaching activities to be used over the six coaching sessions during a three-month timeline.

Strengths were explored using the Realize2 Strengths Inventory, an assessment tool that measures sixty different strengths in individuals, such as curiosity, authenticity, and action.[25] An interesting component of Realize2 is that responses are categorized into realized strengths, unrealized strengths, learned behaviors, and weaknesses.[26] Mackie wanted to study leadership effectiveness as a core outcome of this coaching; he chose the MLQ 360 assessment to measure multifactor leadership theory, also known as the Full-Range Leadership Model.[27]

In the Mackie study, each executive received six ninety-minute coaching sessions, which followed specific strengths-based coaching approaches outlined in manual format. The coaching involved a strengths-based interview, as well as discussion of their MLQ 360 report and Realize2 inventory, using appreciative inquiry–style questions. The strengths-based interview asked about peak experiences and what energized them about their work. The coach provided structured feedback gained from the Realize2 assessment, such as realized strengths, unrealized strengths, strengths that were underutilized although known, learned behaviors (non-energizing competent behaviors), and weaknesses (characterized by low competence and lack of energy).

After reviewing their multi-rater assessment results, which included feedback on their leadership styles (which were characterized as transformational, transactional, or laissez-faire), the coach helped the coachee select three goals to focus on during the coaching, specifically including realized and unrealized strengths and a learned behavior or weakness. The coach and coachee then tracked progress on these goals, and the coachee committed to action steps congruent with their goals. During the midpoint of this study, the waiting-list control group began to receive coaching. Assessments were made prior to the onset of coaching, after the initial group received their coaching, and then again after the waiting-list control group had also received their coaching.

The results demonstrated significant increases, as measured by multi-rater feedback on transformational leadership behaviors after the structured, manualized strengths-based executive coaching, with the effect size in the intervention group more than three times that of the control group. Increased adherence to the coaching approaches described by the coach, and increased adherence to completing the coaching exercises described by the coachee, were significant predictors of the final transformational leadership scores.

In our individual executive coaching engagements, we prefer to have the coaching process and interventions more tailored to our client's personality and context than this manualized approach allowed. But we find Mackie's research findings intriguing, particularly for group coaching projects, which are common, especially for emerging leaders. We believe that Mackie's research should be replicated with a larger sample using randomization, while also assessing the impact of an additional relationship-building component between the coach and the coachee, and using a different measure of leadership behavior.[28]

GLOBAL CHARACTERISTICS OF CHARACTER STRENGTHS

Are particular character strengths more associated with life satisfaction than others? Peterson and his colleagues gathered a US sample of over 12,000 adults and a Swiss sample of over 400 adults. They completed surveys examining character strengths and life satisfaction. In both samples, the character strengths most highly linked to life satisfaction included Love, Hope, Curiosity, and Zest. The most commonly endorsed strengths in the United States were Kindness, Fairness, Honesty, Gratitude, and Judgment, and the lesser strengths included Prudence, Modesty, and Self-regulation. In the US sample, Gratitude was among the most robust predictors of life satisfaction, whereas Perseverance was among the most robust predictors in the Swiss sample. In both samples, the strengths of character most associated with life satisfaction were associated with orientations to pleasure, to engagement, and to meaning, implying that the most fulfilling character strengths are those that make a "full life" possible.[29]

Social intelligence is one of the twenty-four character strengths. Seligman and Peterson highlight that individuals that are high in emotional and social intelligence are particularly adept at perceiving emotions in relationships and have a keen understanding of how emotion affects relationships.[30] Here is an example of how one of our colleagues, executive coach and psychologist Dr. Relly Nadler, integrates the Emotional Quotient Inventory 2.0 with his client's strength in social intelligence.

Strategic Use of Strengths
by Dr. Relly Nadler

In **Leading with Emotional Intelligence**, *I write about how you can stretch your strengths further. This is not an obvious focus for most of us. We are drawn like a magnet to focus on our weakness rather than our strengths.*[31]

There are specific ways your strengths can be applied to beef up some other important competencies. Zenger, Sandholz, and Folkman (2004) describe how one competency can enhance another: "Leaders who scored in the top 10% on the differentiating behavior also tended to score very high on these supportive behaviors. We have called these supporting behaviors competency companions."[32] *They list mechanisms that explain this "competency companion" phenomenon:*

- Competency companions facilitate the expression of their competencies.

- Achieving excellence in one behavior helps develop a related behavior.

- One competency is a building block or main element for another competency.

- Developing a competency companion can change the skill level of a leader.[33]

When I work with a coaching client I always listen for their strengths. There are four steps that I focus on in order. The first step to improving emotional intelligence is to help the client identify their strengths and the

---

65

strengths of the employees that they are developing. The second step is developing a coaching plan. In the plan, the first action is to determine how they can stretch, redeploy, or build on their strengths. The third step is to identify any "fatal flaws" that could derail them if not attended to. If there aren't any derailers, then the fourth step is identifying competency companions, as part of the Option phase of the Auerbach GOOD Coaching Model. This is an artful coaching method to help our clients use their strengths strategically.

Below is the case example of Andrew. Andrew was a highly successful sales person of medical products. He wanted to be promoted to regional sales director and sought coaching to help accomplish this goal. One assessment that was helpful in this process was the Emotional Quotient Inventory 2.0. Andrew had strong scores in stress tolerance, optimism, problem solving, and self actualization on the Emotional Quotient Inventory. He had below-average scores in interpersonal relations, emotional expression, and empathy. Here is an excerpt from a coaching session where I helped him focus more on his leveraging his strengths.

Andrew: *I am really disturbed by these low scores; this is not what I expected. What can I do to bring them up? My boss is not going see this, is he?*

RN: *This assessment is confidential, and your boss won't see it unless you decide to show him. Let's first talk about these high scores and see if there is something about those that will help you with your lower scores. You are high in problem solving, optimism, stress tolerance, and self-actualization. These are great attributes that I think you could use to bring up your lower areas. You know how to solve problems, you are able to make plans for improvement, you can manage the stress this may involve, and you stay optimistic. What a recipe for success you have, and an arsenal of skills!*

Andrew: *Wow, I hadn't really put that all together.*

RN: *Yes, we often don't. So as we look at the areas you want*

> to develop—more empathy, interpersonal relations, and expressiveness—how could you use your key strengths to address these issues?
>
> **Andrew:** Well if I look at these as problems or areas that I want to improve, I would first establish the goal that I want to accomplish.
>
> **RN:** So what would that look like in regard to empathy, expressiveness, and interpersonal relations? They seem related, and you scored yourself lower on them.
>
> **Andrew:** Yeah, there are times that I am not putting myself out there and there are people I am not able to be there for. I am too busy and don't spent the time I need to with people.
>
> **RN:** So, as you use your problem-solving abilities, who are the people that would be the most important to have a better relationship with?
>
> **Andrew:** Well definitely my boss, one peer, and certainly my wife. I could improve my relationship with all of them.
>
> **RN:** What is one thing you could improve using your self-actualization skills, meaning your drive to improve yourself, that would have the biggest bang for the buck?
>
> **Andrew:** Definitely, listening. I am often distracted and often don't let others finish what they are saying.
>
> **RN:** Great. Let's use your strengths to come up with a strategy for you to focus on.

We continued to zero in on his listening skills and develop specific behaviors he could employ to improve his expressiveness, empathy, and interpersonal relations. Andrew developed a clear plan that emerged from his strengths.

The main benefits of focusing on strengths in coaching are that the client feels capable, motivated, and hopeful. A cornerstone of coaching is honoring the client's strengths and helping them expand and stretch what they are already good at.

VIA SURVEY

An effective way to begin a science-based positive psychology coaching approach for your clients is to first have your client take the VIA Survey, at www.viacharacter.org. This will give your client a list of their top strengths.[34]

The VIA Survey is intended primarily for adults. As it evolved through five different versions, it has been completed by over 350,000 individuals from more than 190 different nations. The questionnaire measures the degree to which respondents endorse items reflecting the twenty-four strengths of character, on a scale from 1 (very much unlike me) to 5 (very much like me). There are 10 items per strength, 240 all together. For example, Forgiveness is measured with items such as "I always allow others to leave their mistakes in the past and make a fresh start," "I believe it is best to forgive and forget," "I am unwilling to accept apologies" (reverse-scored), and "I hold grudges" (reverse-scored).[35]

IDENTIFYING A SIGNATURE STRENGTH

Once your client has obtained their list of top character strengths, assist them in determining which of those top scores would qualify as a "signature strength." You can ask them to what degree they feel the following statements are true about them to help differentiate between top-ranked strengths and their personally identified signature strengths:

- a feeling of "this is the real me"
- a feeling of excitement or invigoration when using the strength
- a sense of yearning to use the strength
- a feeling of inevitability about using the strength, as if it would be hard *not* to use the strength in that situation
- a feeling of intrinsic motivation to use the strength

Once the client has identified their signature strengths, the coach can use strengths-based questions. When a client is discussing a particular challenge or goal, the coach may ask:

- What is a new way to use one of your signature strengths to help achieve that goal?
- What is a strength you have not fully deployed that may help you, and how would you use that strength more with a particular goal?

Here is an example of how I (Jeff) assisted my client in using a signature strength. My client had a signature strength of Bravery, and he had previously discussed with me how he often observed that good ideas are brought up by people in meetings and other people shoot them down before they are adequately explored. I asked him, "What is a way you could use one of your signature strengths to help in this situation?" After some thought, he replied, "I will speak up in the defense of my colleague's good idea with some additional facts or observations, even if it means going against the majority."

Additional ways that coaches can use strengths in their coaching are to:

- Fine-tune the client's job with their strengths—discuss with your client ways they can use your strengths more, or in new ways, at work.
- Reflect on the value of strengths—discuss with your client what is especially valuable about their strengths. This will lead them to find ways to use them more frequently.
- Keep deployment of your strengths in balance—make sure your clients understand that using a strength too often in some situations can be a weakness. Discuss with your client what is the best intensity or "volume" of that strength in the particular situation they are concerned about.
- Ask the client a question that encourages them to identify an action step that uses their strengths: "What is a new way to use a strength that will be meaningful to you?"

STRENGTHS CAN HELP CLIENTS OVERCOME OBSTACLES

Using our character strengths and virtues helps us have positive experiences and emotions, as well as success in our relationships, work, and goals. Although the character strengths identified in the VIA-IS are relatively stable, they can be enhanced. The VIA-IS helps the coach launch a conversation with their client about strengths and virtues, helps the client increase their self-awareness of their character strengths, and opens up the conversation regarding how these strengths can be useful in accomplishing the client's goals. A major component of this conversation is discussing how these strengths may be deployed to help the client achieve goals and overcome obstacles in goal attainment. Moreover, the coach can help the client identify ways they can use their strengths to compensate for areas they are lacking.

For example, I (Jeff) had a client who was a coach in a private practice. The client told me, "I'm very uncomfortable with marketing. I don't want to come across as pushy, so I don't promote my coaching services." As a strengths-oriented coach, I replied: "I know that your top character strengths include social intelligence, love, and persistence. How might you use these strengths to help you in marketing your coaching services?" After reflection, the client replied, "I can use my strengths of social intelligence, love, and persistence to develop very strong connections with people (social intelligence), to communicate how much I care about their success (love), to stay in touch with them regularly as I continually improve my coaching skills (persistence), and to communicate my dedication to my development as a coach. In this way I believe I'll be building credibility and respect as a professional coach, which will help me obtain more coaching work."

IDENTIFICATION OF TALENTS WITH THE STRENGTHSFINDER 2.0

As mentioned in Chapter 1, we had the pleasure of knowing Donald O. Clifton, the father of strengths-based psychology and creator of the Clifton StrengthsFinder. By 1998, Don Clifton and a group of other Gallup researchers were deeply immersed in the benefits of developing people's strengths. Although Clifton died in 2003, his work has been vigorously advanced by the Gallup organization. As a result, the StrengthsFinder 2.0 assessment is a tool many coaches are familiar with. We use the StrengthsFinder 2.0 with our clients and believe you will find it extremely helpful.

Gallup's research on talents and strengths has been conducted over the past forty years in more than fifty countries. The StrengthsFinder assessment does not measure *strengths* per se but the presence of *talents* in thirty-four areas, which are also called themes. Talents are defined as recurring patterns of thought, feeling, or behavior that can be productively applied and that naturally exist within individuals. Strengths are defined differently—as the ability to consistently provide near-perfect performance in a specific task—but they must be developed, and are the product of developing and refining one's talents with skills and knowledge.

Another positive psychology coaching advocate, Robert Biswas-Diener, describes strengths simply as "pre-existing patterns of thought, feeling, and behavior that are authentic, energizing, and which lead to our best performance."[36] According to the Gallup organization, the sequence of each person's dominant themes is unique, like their fingerprints. They report that the chance that two people have the same five signature themes is one in 33 million. As of 2015, more than 12 million people in over fifty countries have completed the StrengthsFinder talent assessment.[37]

The first version of this assessment was described in *Now, Discover Your Strengths*. In 2007, Tom Rath, a primary member of the Gallup group, described a new edition of the assessment in his book, *StrengthsFinder 2.0*.[38] This assessment is described in its technical manual as an online measure of personal talent that identifies areas where an individual's greatest potential for building strengths exists. There are 177 item pairs that are based on the theory and research foundation from semi-structured personal interviews that had been used by Selection Research Incorporated and Gallup for over thirty years. The StrengthsFinder is intended for use as an evaluation to precede a strengths-based development process in either work or academic settings. After completing the assessment, you can receive an abbreviated report of your top five talent themes, or a more complete report that includes the top five themes, fifty Ideas for Action (ten for each of your top five themes), a Strengths Discovery Interview to help you examine your experience, skills, and knowledge with regard to building your strengths, and a Strengths-Based Action Plan form.

THE 34 CLIFTON STRENGTHSFINDER THEMES[39]

Achiever	Futuristic
Activator	Harmony
Adaptability	Ideation
Analytical	Includer
Arranger	Individualization
Belief	Input
Command	Intellection
Communication	Learner
Competition	Maximizer
Connectedness	Positivity
Consistency	Relator
Context	Responsibility
Deliberative	Restorative
Developer	Self-assurance
Discipline	Significance
Empathy	Strategic
Focus	Woo

The Strengthsfinder 2.0 assessment is copyrighted. This content is used with permission; however, Gallup retains all rights of republication.

USING STRENGTHSFINDER THEMES IN COACHING

Useful coaching questions for clients who have taken the StrengthsFinder that will help clients think more deeply about their dominant StrengthsFinder themes are:

- What can you do when you want to accomplish something?
- What can you do when you want to motivate others?
- What can you do to develop strong relationships?
- What can you do to understand situations better?

Reflection on these questions will help clients realize how they use their StrengthsFinder themes in their daily life. Next steps for the coach and their client are turning *talents* into *strengths* congruent with their most important values and applying those strengths to their most contextually relevant goals.

TIPS FOR STRENGTHS-AUGMENTED COACHING

Let's apply what we've learned from reviewing Seligman and colleagues' 2005 interventions study[40] and the Gallup research on identifying talents and turning them into strengths, adding our perspective that a strengths-based coaching approach generally helps managers and executives fine-tune their leadership style.

Consider these potential coaching questions for a balanced, strengths-augmented coaching approach.

- What talents could you develop further that would help you in your new role?
- What strengths could you use to help you in an area where you're struggling?
- What strengths could you use *in a new way,* to help you in an area where you're struggling?
- Reflect on strengths you rely on. What different part of yourself could you use in a new way to help you manage a weakness?

- What interpersonal strengths could you use more of to help you manage a difficult situation?
- What is a strength you sometimes might overuse, that you might benefit from dialing down in a certain situation?
- Who has a strength you don't have, who you would be willing to recruit to help you in situations where you have a weakness or a challenge?
- What are ways you can use your strengths more to develop others?
- What are ways to clearly explain expectations to your employees and help them decide what talents or strengths *they* have that could be leveraged to meet these expectations?
- How can you use your talents and strengths to better understand and motivate others?
- How can you do more of what you do best every day?
- What are ways you can help your team members do more of what *they* do best every day?
- What is a new way you can use one of your talents today? Tomorrow? And so on…
- What do you want to learn this week (or this month) to help turn your talents into greater strengths and that will help you accomplish one of your key goals?

Former Gallup Management consultant Erin Passons uses a coaching approach where she helps her client identify and understand his or her own unique combination of talents to maximize personal effectiveness and performance. Here is an example of this coaching approach based on a StrengthsFinder assessment.

StrengthsFinder Coaching Case: Emma
by Erin Passons, MBA

Emma has been in a leadership role for the last seven years and recently joined a growing start-up organization as a senior director, with a team of six direct reports. Emma's VP invited her to work with an executive coach to help her integrate into the fast-moving company, as well as to address some very specific communication challenges her VP had observed in her first ninety days.

Confident and self-aware, Emma was thrilled at the opportunity to work with a coach and evolve her leadership talents and capabilities. Emma took the StrengthsFinder assessment, which identified her top 5 signature themes as:

- Communication
- Strategic
- Activator
- Learner
- Individualization

She resonated quite strongly with her top 5 themes, and agreed that they described her to a tee—as she put it, "for better or for worse!" During the first coaching session she identified her primary goal as improving her communication style, specifically to become a better listener, to stop interrupting people, and to become an inspirational leader to others. Using the StrengthsFinder language, we were able to identify Emma's natural patterns of behavior and communication style, enabling us to understand where her challenges were coming from, and to help her redirect her talents to achieve more productive outcomes.

continued…

Coach: Tell me a little more about the challenge you're having with interrupting others.

Emma: It's such a problem. I know it really annoys people, and worse, it makes my team members feel like I don't care about them or I'm not listening, which isn't true at all. I try to control it and I just can't seem to stop myself when I'm in the moment.

Coach: Let's talk about your StrengthsFinder themes. Often the combination of Communication and Activator can be challenging because you know very clearly what you want to say and your mind is constantly formulating your next sentence.

Emma: Yes, that's exactly right! Also, I think the Strategic part causes me to naturally anticipate what the other person is going to say. So I think I know where they're heading and I want to insert my thoughts to guide the conversation.

Coach: Yes, I can see that. However, let's think about how you could use these three themes in a more productive way by leveraging your powerful talents of Individualization and Learner to balance them. How could you use those themes more when you feel that sense of urgency to interrupt?

Emma: Hmm, I'm not sure I use those themes when I'm talking with others. Maybe I could use my Learner talent to ask more questions before I jump in with my own perspective? I really am curious about what ideas my team members have to discuss, but when I interrupt them they seem to shut down. Perhaps my Individualization could get some practice by being more observant and watching how differently each person responds when I ask a question, rather than jump in with my answer? I think this could work!

Once Emma converted her Learner and Individualization themes into more purposeful talents, she was able to focus on being curious first, and assertive second. She continued to practice an inquisitive approach, asking

continued...

questions when she felt the need to interrupt, and she was amazed at how positively her team responded. Over time, she found the process easier, and it became more natural. She felt that all of her strengths were being maximized once she was using them in a more balanced and effective way.

SUMMARY AND CAUTION

For many coaches, the strengths-based coaching approach has become more than just a technique; it is an overarching coaching philosophy. Coaches who help clients use their strengths to deal with challenges and goals are helping clients achieve higher levels of well-being, resilience, and happiness, and are also helping them develop a lifelong formula of achieving goals and greater life satisfaction. In Chapter 10 we will caution against taking this approach too far, however, because in some situations, overuse of strengths can become a weakness.

CHAPTER 4   Coaching for Well-Being

Y ou now have a basic understanding of what positive psychology is and how important positive emotions are— plus an understanding of character strengths, virtues, and talents. In this chapter we explore well-being. First we'll review the impressive body of research on the subject, including studies, findings, and analyses by Gallup researchers, Chris Peterson, and Ed Diener. We'll examine Martin Seligman's theory of flourishing and how it relates to coaching, and we'll see a case study of coaching in action. Then, we'll present a seven-step process of coaching for well-being to aid you in applying this methodology to your practice.

Well-being coaching is an application of applied positive psychology. Well-being coaches are interested in helping clients achieve the highest levels of quality of life and subjective well-being—also called life satisfaction. Life satisfaction is not about just an individual's current feelings; it encompasses both the person's perceptions about how life has gone so far and his or her feelings about where it's headed. Life satisfaction is a measure of well-being that can be assessed in terms of mood, satisfaction with relations with others, satisfaction with achieved goals, and self-perceived ability to cope with daily life. In brief, well-being is a favorable evaluation of one's life as a whole rather than just one's current feelings.

Researchers have various definitions of the terms *life satisfaction, quality of life, happiness, subjective well-being,* and *flourishing.* In the positive psychology research literature there is vigorous discussion about how best to define and measure these constructs. There is also debate about whether some of the positive psychology research is too Western society–based, with too much emphasis on autonomy and individual goals, as compared to the greater emphasis on community found in many Eastern cultures.[1] As you work to understand your client's well-being goals, it is important to be sensitive to any contextual and cultural factors.

ADVANTAGES OF WELL-BEING, HAPPINESS, AND LIFE SATISFACTION

Fortunately, most people are generally happy. In psychological terms, this means that they would rate their moods and emotions in the positive range: somewhere above neutral. Personal evaluation of one's own quality of life, also called subjective well-being, is an important predictor of several aspects of life outcomes. On the personal side this includes health, longevity, and the quality of one's social life;[2,3,4,5,6] in our professional lives, job satisfaction, productivity, and success in the workplace; and from a societal perspective, desirable relationships with one's community.

Here are some of the interesting findings from such studies:

- Cheerfulness while in college is a predictor of later income.[7]
- Those who reported high life satisfaction were more likely than others to donate money to charity.[8]
- People who rated themselves as happy (high in positive feelings and low in negative feelings) in the previous month were more likely to donate blood and to give money to charity.[9]
- Happy people tend to be more popular and more likable.[10,11]

Psychologist Chris Peterson analyzed several studies of well-being and combined the data to show how various factors correlate with happiness and with life satisfaction. Table 1 is his summary of the findings of many studies, based on reviews by Argyle, Diener, Suh, Lucas, and Smith; Myers, Myers, and Dienger; and W. Wilson.[12]

Table 1:   Positive Correlations With Happiness
            And Life Satisfaction

Zero to small	Moderate	Large
Age	Number of friends	Gratitude
Gender	Being married	Optimism
Education	Religiousness	Being employed
Social class	Level of leisure activity	Frequency of sexual intercourse
Income	Physical health	Happiness of identical twin
Having children	Conscientiousness	Self-esteem
Intelligence	Extraversion	Test–retest reliability of happiness measures
Physical attractiveness	Internal locus of control	Percentage of time experiencing positive affect
Ethnicity (majority vs. minority)	Neuroticism (negative correlation)	

NATIONAL ACCOUNTS OF WELL-BEING

The measurement of well-being is being used by governments to improve their estimation of how well their country is thriving. National accounts of well-being have been created which complement common measures of economic well-being such as gross national product. Measurement of well-being provides leaders with information about quality of life in societies and can be used to identify what circumstances lead to high subjective well-being. Over forty countries have adopted recommendations to create national accountings of well-being.[13] Coaches trained in positive psychology play a pivotal role in creating and delivering programs that governments and organizations can implement on a large scale to increase subjective well-being.

MARTIN SELIGMAN'S WELL-BEING THEORY: PERMA

In his work studying happiness and life satisfaction, Marty Seligman describes how well-being is made up of five "building blocks":

- *Positive emotions.* Positive emotions make for a pleasant life.
- *Engagement.* This is the degree to which we're absorbed by the activities we engage in.
- *Positive relationships.* Positive social relationships are linked to many elements of well-being, including physical health, life satisfaction, career satisfaction, and even financial success.
- *Meaning*—the value we attribute to our activities, especially as they relate to self-actualization.
- *Accomplishment*—the happy result of achieving goals and meeting personal objectives.

Seligman refers to these five as the PERMA model. He emphasizes that the goal of well-being theory is to increase flourishing by increasing positive emotion, engagement, positive relationships, meaning, and accomplishment.[14]

You may be interested to know that reading this book may make you happier. Seligman argues that being involved in the positive psychology field, studying positive psychology, and interacting with others working with positive psychology all make people happier.[15]

GALLUP'S PERSPECTIVE AND RESEARCH ON WELL-BEING

Some of the most comprehensive research on this topic has been conducted by the Gallup organization, which has assessed individual well-being in more than 150 countries. The results of this research are reported by Tim Rath and Jim Harter in their book, *Wellbeing: The Five Essential Elements.*[16] They identified the "universal elements of well-being that differentiate a thriving life from one spent suffering" as these five distinct statistical factors:

- *Career well-being:* finding meaning in one's paid work
- *Social well-being:* having strong and positive relationships
- *Financial well-being:* maintaining sufficient, balanced finances
- *Physical well-being:* living a healthy life
- *Community well-being:* feeling engaged in one's community

Gallup's research indicates that, while 66 percent of the population fares well in at least one of these areas of well-being, only 7 percent flourish in all five areas. Fortunately, coaches can help their clients create specific well-being goals and develop greater overall life satisfaction in any or all of these five areas.

THE CONCEPT OF FLOURISHING, AND FLOURISHING AS A GOAL

The goal of well-being coaching is similar to Seligman's goal of positive psychology: to increase the level of flourishing in our clients. We mentioned in Chapter 1 that in the course of his work Seligman revised his early framework of positive psychology, which previously had only named positive emotions, engagement, and meaning as the make-up of well-being. After later adding positive relationships and accomplishments, Seligman revised the goal of positive psychology to "increasing flourishing" by enhancing functioning in all five PERMA elements. So, what did he mean by flourishing?

Flourishing is a combination of feeling good and functioning effectively on a subjective level: when a person feels life is going particularly well. Individuals who have a high level of flourishing— essentially those who have a high level of psychological well-being— tend to learn effectively, work productively, have strong social relationships, and make positive contributions to their communities; and they often have good health and life expectancy.[17]

Ed Diener and Colleagues' Eight-Point Flourishing Scale

Psychologist Ed Diener, widely recognized as one of the world's foremost experts on subjective well-being, developed with his colleagues the Flourishing Scale. This scale is a brief eight-item summary measure of the respondent's self-perceived success in important areas such as relationships, self-esteem, purpose, and optimism. This easy-to-use scale provides a single well-being score.

The Flourishing Scale measures eight features deemed to be components of flourishing by having participants rate how much they agree with the following statements, on a seven-point scale:

1. I lead a purposeful and meaningful life.
2. My social relationships are supportive and rewarding.
3. I am engaged and interested in my daily activities.
4. I actively contribute to the happiness and well-being of others.
5. I am competent and capable in the activities that are important to me.
6. I am a good person and live a good life.
7. I am optimistic about my future.
8. People respect me.

Scoring. Add the responses, varying from 1 to 7, for all eight items. The range of possible scores is from 8 to 56. A high score represents a person with many psychological resources and strengths.[18]

In 2009, researchers published results that leveraged the dataset from the European Social Survey, an academically driven cross-national survey of 43,000 adults from 23 countries designed to analyze flourishing in Europe. The most favorable results were found in Denmark, Sweden, Cyprus, Austria, Ireland, Norway, Finland, and

Switzerland, where at least 20 percent of the population claimed to be flourishing. On the other end of the spectrum were the Russian Federation, Portugal, Bulgaria, Slovakia, Ukraine, and Hungary, where less than 10 percent of the population claimed to flourish.[19] Their seven-element survey follows.[20]

The European Social Survey Flourishing Assessment

Using a five-point scale, where 1 indicates that you strongly disagree and 5 that you strongly agree, indicate how much you agree with the following statements:

1. *Positive emotions.* Considering all aspects of my life, I am a happy person.
2. *Engagement and interest.* I love learning new things.
3. *Meaning, purpose.* I generally feel that what I do in my life is valuable and worthwhile.
4. *Self-esteem.* In general I feel very positive about myself.
5. *Optimism.* I'm always optimistic about my future.
6. *Resilience.* When things go wrong in my life, it generally takes me a long time to get back to normal.
7. *Positive relationships.* There are people in my life who really care about me.

MEASUREMENT OF WELL-BEING, HAPPINESS, AND LIFE SATISFACTION

Several researchers have developed instruments for measuring well-being; we present five such instruments. The two Flourishing Scales listed above, and Diener's five-element Satisfaction with Life Scale which follows, will help start a coaching conversation. However, we often favor the Experience Sampling Method or the Auerbach Well-Being Satisfaction Scale, as these are more in-depth, providing specific information about the client's context, which makes them more useful for coaching.

Psychologist Ed Diener's Satisfaction with Life Scale is one of the most widely used tools for measuring well-being.[21]

Ed Diener's Satisfaction with Life Scale

This five-item instrument was designed to measure an individual's overall evaluation of life.

Instructions. Using a seven-point scale—strongly disagree (1), disagree (2), slightly disagree (3), neither agree nor disagree (4), slightly agree (5), agree (6), strongly agree (7)—assign a rating to each of the following five statements:

____ In most ways my life is close to my ideal.

____ The conditions of my life are excellent.

____ I am satisfied with my life.

____ So far I have gotten the important things I want in life.

____ If I could live my life over, I would change almost nothing.

Add up your ratings to calculate your total score.
Now, compare your total score to the following scale:

35–31 Extremely satisfied

26–30 Satisfied

20–25 Neutral

15–19 Slightly dissatisfied

10–14 Dissatisfied

5–9   Extremely dissatisfied

THE EXPERIENCE SAMPLING METHOD

The Experience Sampling Method, also referred to as the Daily Diary Method, was developed by Reed Larson and Mihaly Csikszentmihalyi. In their studies, beepers were used to contact subjects at random intervals, at which time the participants were to pause and record, right in that moment, their answers to questions such as "What are you doing?" "How much are you enjoying it?" "Are you alone or are you interacting with others?" We discuss this method in greater depth in Chapter 6.[22]

THE DAY RECONSTRUCTION METHOD

Daniel Kahneman developed the Day Reconstruction Method, which, combining features of time-budget measurement and experience sampling, assesses both how people spend their time and how they experience their various activities. Following procedures designed to reduce recall biases, participants systematically reconstructed their activities and experiences of the preceding day, rating their feelings—happy, depressed, worried, tired—for each activity.

Using this method, a 2004 study involving 900 Texas women found that its subjects' five most pleasurable and rewarding (positive) activities were, in descending order, sex, socializing, relaxing, praying or meditating, and eating. Also in the top ten positive activities were exercising and watching television or movies. Interestingly, compared to most other activities measured, caring for children was at the low end of pleasurable experiences.[23]

How do coaches introduce these various assessments into their own practices? Next, we show well-being coaching in action with a case study from one of our colleagues, Jonathan R. Aronoff. Later in this chapter, I (Jeff) present my step-by-step process for coaching for well-being, using the Auerbach GOOD Coaching Model™. That description will refer back to the case of Dr. North.

Case Study: Dr. North

by Jonathan R. Aronoff, PhD, PCC

Dr. North, a forty-six-year-old ophthalmologist, sought coaching to discuss what he could do to make his life more satisfying. He had been working with a psychotherapist for several years on personal issues and found the experience to be beneficial. However, he was unclear what to *do* now that he felt more centered and had a better understanding of himself. He believed that working with a personal coach would help him identify goals and strategies that would result in greater success, happiness, and satisfaction.

Dr. North selected a coach who specialized in well-being and wellness. In his first session, Dr. North was asked to identify his personal strengths and then provide examples of how he used these strengths in five areas of his life: career/occupation, social relationships, physical and psychological health, financial stability and use of finances, and community involvement. Through discussions with his coach, Dr. North concluded that these five areas contributed to his well-being and wellness. He also began to appreciate the positive affect his character strengths, when put into action, had on his well-being. What was still unclear was what exactly he needed to do to enhance his well-being, utilizing his strengths in each of the five life areas.

Dr. North was then asked to choose the one life area he wanted to enhance and focus on during his coaching sessions. Dr. North decided to focus on his career, because he believed that by increasing his satisfaction in this area he would eventually identify strategies to increase his happiness and satisfaction in the other four areas of his life. Using Auerbach's GOOD Coaching model, the coach began the process of assisting him to identify specific Goals, Options, Obstacles, and action steps to Do in order to achieve each goal. An example of the coach–client dialogue follows.

Coach: Since our last session have you given more thought to what you could do to enhance your career and ultimately increase your satisfaction working as an ophthalmologist?

Dr. North: Yes. I have to say I was very inspired by our last session. Thinking about ways to "jump-start" my career through the lens of what's in my best interest in terms of well-being freed me up from my fear and self-doubt.

Coach: That's great. What did you consider in particular?

Dr. North: For a long time I have been thinking about closing down my struggling rural practice and either purchasing an established larger practice or finding a location in the city to start a larger practice than the one I currently have in the country.

Coach: I'm sure there are many practical factors to consider, but I am interested in understanding how this change will enhance your well-being.

Dr. North: My practice in the country has been stagnant for years. It has felt like a weight on my shoulders that has become heavier every year. I think it has taken a toll on my physical and psychological health, my marriage, and my passion for doing "fun" things when I have free time. I realize that I have to change now and do something about my situation. If I can get past my self-doubt I imagine that by having a larger practice in the city I will have many more patients, make more money, create a motivated team of professionals—I wouldn't be working alone, have more time to be with my wife, and have more vacation time.

Coach: What are options you have to make this positive move to enhance your career well-being?

Dr. North: *Ideally, I would like to buy an existing practice from a doctor who wants to retire. I have been checking publications and the Internet for a while and there are often a few ophthalmologists trying to sell their practice. It felt daunting before, but now when I think about it as a necessary change for my personal health and well-being—I am motivated.*

Coach: *Your positive attitude is inspiring. What specific action steps do you need to take at this point? This will help us identify possible complications or obstacles that we might need to find solutions for as well.*

Conceptualizing his career changes through the lens of well-being, Dr. North was able to think optimistically about his future career Goals, consider a variety of Options, circumvent challenging Obstacles, and successfully Do productive goal-oriented action steps. His long-standing doubts receded into the background and no longer dominated his thinking or prevented him from taking positive action steps. Within a year, Dr. North was able to purchase an established practice from two retiring eye doctors in a nearby city, and in a timely fashion he closed his small practice in the country. Despite many challenges, and moments of feeling overwhelmed, Dr. North adapted to working with a new staff and used his combined affiliative and democratic leadership style to build a positive and thriving team. His character strengths (leadership, hope, love of learning, perseverance, honesty, and perspective) contributed to his success in changing this area of his life. Only when Dr. North was able to view his future happiness and success through the lens of well-being and wellness was he able to leverage his strengths.

Dr. North's motivation and gradual success working toward an enhanced career positively impacted the other four areas in his life. He did not need his coach in every instance to introduce another area of well-being. For example, midway in the process of acquiring his new practice, Dr. North informed his coach that he wanted to "tackle" his physical health problems, particularly medical problems due to his excessive weight. In coaching sessions, Dr. North considered possible strategies (options) to embrace in order to accomplish his physical health goal(s). Within a year, Dr. North lost over 75 pounds. He no longer had to take medication for his pre-diabetic condition, no longer had high blood pressure, and was permitted to stop taking medication for his high cholesterol. Dr. North exercised several times a week with a certified fitness trainer, sought consultation with a nutritionist, and prioritized time for rest. His increased energy, desire to "do more," and positive attitude about his physical image contributed to increased happiness associated with his increased physical well-being.

The combined impact of Dr. North's positive changes in his career and physical health also motivated him to spend more time with his wife, family, and friends (social well-being), and to take more time to use his finances with family and friends to have savoring experiences (financial well-being). Without his coach introducing the aspect of his life involving community, Dr. North sponsored a walkathon and a 10K runner's race through his practice. Everyone received a t-shirt and a water bottle bearing the name and logo of his eye care clinic. The fees to enter the races were donated to charities.

Coaching provided Dr. North with a framework to consider five areas of well-being that contributed to his physical and psychological wellness. The rewards from initiating and following through with activities increased his level of happiness in at least five areas of his life and contributed to his thriving and flourishing.

APPLYING WELL-BEING FINDINGS TO COACHING

Now that we've discussed the benefits of well-being, we will share how to apply these findings to coaching. To this end, we will share the step-by-step process for coaching for well-being, published in Jeff's *Well-Being Coaching Workbook*,[24] later in this chapter. Let's begin with the most important aspect of coaching: the client–coach relationship.

THE COACHING RELATIONSHIP

As the coaching field is relatively new, not much research yet exists on how to most effectively build a coaching relationship. However, the fields of both psychotherapy and consultation have much to say about strong counseling relationships, with guidelines focused on support, confidentiality, and goal orientation.

From the psychotherapy perspective, research has identified four factors essential to a beneficial counseling relationship:

- The relationship is positive. Psychotherapy research tells us that it is the *quality of the relationship* between the professional and the client, not the particular methodology used, which is most closely linked to an effective outcome.
- The client feels motivated and able to work collaboratively with the therapist.
- The therapist responds empathically to the client.
- The client and therapist agree on the goals of their work together.[25]

THE AUERBACH PROCESS OF COACHING FOR WELL-BEING

Now, with the importance of the coach–client relationship in mind, let's turn to applying the findings of well-being research to the coaching setting. To follow, we present the *seven*-step Auerbach Well-Being Coaching Process, the last *four* steps of which are the Auerbach GOOD Coaching Model™:

1. Establish the coach–client alliance
2. Assess life satisfaction and coaching goals
3. Create well-being vision
4. Determine well-being goals (G)
5. Explore options to move toward goals (O)
6. Consider and rehearse how to manage obstacles (O)
7. Commit to action steps: what the client will specifically do, when it will be done, and what support will be sought (D)

This process is designed to gradually guide the client from big-picture dreaming to taking the specific action steps that will fulfill that dream. As we proceed, we'll refer back, as appropriate, to Dr. North's story and how it applies to this process.

STEP 1: ESTABLISH THE COACHING ALLIANCE
Coaching Parameters

According to the core competencies determined by the International Coach Federation, establishing a coaching alliance begins with setting the parameters of the coaching agreement. The following elements address various practical aspects of the coaching relationship:

Location/logistics. Coaching sessions might be conducted via face-to-face meetings, videoconference, Skype, or simply by phone.

Schedule. While some clients might prefer a set forty-five-minute coaching session once a week, others might appreciate a different schedule or length of sessions, such as three seventy-five-minute coaching sessions a month.

Communication. Clarify how the client may contact you between sessions. We generally welcome clients to contact us at any time if the need arises; we find that clients appreciate this offer of support and rarely exercise this option.

Confidentiality. Clarify in your coaching agreement how you will handle confidential information.

Payment. Clarify the coaching fee and when and how it is to be paid. Generally, coaches prefer payment in advance of a session. Some coaches bill by the hour; we bill occasionally by the month, but more often have a set fee for a specific coaching duration.

Coaching Relationship Essentials

The International Coach Federation specifies that a coach must "establish trust and intimacy with the client" within "a safe, supportive environment that produces ongoing mutual respect and trust." The following behaviors build trust:

- Show genuine concern for the client's welfare and future.

- Continuously demonstrate personal integrity, honesty, and sincerity.

- Establish clear agreements and keep promises.

- Demonstrate respect for the client's perceptions, learning style, and personal being.

- Provide ongoing support for and advocate new behaviors and actions, including those involving risk-taking and fear of failure.

- Ask permission to coach the client [when addressing] sensitive, new areas.[26]

STEP 2: ASSESS LIFE SATISFACTION AND GOALS

Once the terms of the coach–client relationship have been established, the next step is to determine what the client wants to focus on in coaching. This begins with an assessment: essentially, where the client is now and where he wants to be. The client's "now" includes his subjective sense of satisfaction with life—his well-being baseline.

Where he wants to be is his preferred or target level of well-being.

Various assessment tools may guide you in this process, such as the Myers-Briggs Type Indicator, the VIA Survey, and the Strengths-Finder. To get things started, we often begin with the Well-Being Coaching Client Questionnaire and the Auerbach Well-Being Satisfaction Scale.

THE AUERBACH WELL-BEING COACHING CLIENT QUESTIONNAIRE

This questionnaire has a variety of general and personal questions that touch on Rath and Harter's "universal elements of well-being": career, social relationships, finances, community, and physical and psychological health. It was designed to serve two purposes: to provide coaches with a more complete understanding of their clients, and to hopefully pique the clients' interest, encouraging them to contemplate exactly what they want to get out of the coaching experience.

(The Auerbach Well-Being Coaching Client Questionnaire appears in the Appendix.)

THE AUERBACH WELL-BEING SATISFACTION SCALE™

I (Jeff) have used the Auerbach Well-Being Satisfaction Scale™ (see sidebar) with over a thousand clients. I find it to be useful in developing a coaching plan that emphasizes enhanced well-being. The scale is available at www.executivecoachcollege.com. Should you in turn use it to develop coaching agendas with your clients, we welcome feedback on how well it serves you (positive@executivecoachcollege.com).

The Auerbach Well-Being Satisfaction Scale consists of twenty-two paired items that survey the five areas Gallup has identified as statistically unique components of a comprehensive conceptualization of well-being. Respondents are provided the following directions to evaluate their current level of satisfaction with particular aspects of well-being, such as their physical well-being or their social well-being, and are then asked to indicate how motivated they are to make efforts in increasing their satisfaction in these areas.

> Here is a sample of the Well-Being Satisfaction Scale, showing the directions and seven of the twenty-two questions. This brief example is not for use with your clients, but it will help you understand the process should you choose to go online and use the complete scale.

AUERBACH WELL-BEING SATISFACTION SCALE™

Directions:

Please answer each question. The number 1 represents the lowest level of satisfaction and 7 represents the highest possible satisfaction. For the upper choice (row A), choose a number that represents how satisfied you are in that area (overall in the past week). Then for the lower choice (row B), choose your target satisfaction level, which includes a determination not only of your target level, but also how motivated you are to make changes in this area. These areas can become part of your well-being vision and your coaching agenda. What satisfaction number are you at now? And what is your target level? You may have target satisfaction scores that are the same, or different, from your current level of satisfaction. There are no right or wrong answers, this is entirely your choice—you decide what is important to you.

Keep in mind that some areas may not be that important to you right now. For example, let's say you are not interested in exercise in this chapter of your life. You might rank this area as a 6 because you are quite satisfied with this area of your life now, even if someone observing your exercise habits might rate you as lower. You are rating your satisfaction level, not other people's opinions. Let's say you are very interested in positive

---

relationships in this phase of your life. You might choose to rank this a 5 if you feel generally satisfied with that area of your life. Upon reflection, though, you may conclude that you feel particularly motivated to increase positive relationships from a 5 to a 7, so you would enter a 5 in the upper row and a 7 in the lower row.

Seven Example Questions from the Auerbach Well-Being Satisfaction Scale™

1. Meaning and purpose
The amount of meaning and purpose in my life now

A	1	2	3	4	5	6	7

Target satisfaction level

B	1	2	3	4	5	6	7

2. Positive feelings
The amount of positive feelings I feel about myself now

A	1	2	3	4	5	6	7

Target satisfaction level

B	1	2	3	4	5	6	7

3. Optimism
My optimism level now

A	1	2	3	4	5	6	7

Target satisfaction level

B	1	2	3	4	5	6	7

4. Resilience
The amount of resilience I feel that I have now

A	1	2	3	4	5	6	7

Target satisfaction level

B	1	2	3	4	5	6	7

5. Relationships
The quality of my relationships with others now

A	1	2	3	4	5	6	7

Target satisfaction level

B	1	2	3	4	5	6	7

6. Friend or partner
My feeling of closeness with a special friend or partner now

A	1	2	3	4	5	6	7

Target satisfaction level

B	1	2	3	4	5	6	7

7. Eating Habits
My eating habits now

A	1	2	3	4	5	6	7

Target satisfaction level

B	1	2	3	4	5	6	7

Integrating the Emotional Quotient Inventory 2.0 into Coaching for Well-Being

Another tool that can aid in establishing the goal, as well as assisting with other aspects of coaching, is the Emotional Quotient Inventory 2.0 (EQI2.0), which we often use to help clients develop and balance their emotional and social intelligence. The EQI2.0 is an assessment published by Multi-Health Systems that can contribute valuable information to the well-being coaching setting, especially its "well-being indicator."[27]

According to the Multi-Health Systems website:
Generally speaking, people with higher emotional intelligence scores were more likely to also report higher happiness scores, and vice versa. Given this trend, the decision was made to move happiness away from representing a component of EI to more appropriately represent a reflection of one's well-being. As a result, the Well-Being Indicator page of the EQI2.0 assessment was created. The development of the Well-Being Indicator included a detailed look into the relationship between one's level of happiness and all the other facets of emotional intelligence. A series of theoretical, practical, and empirical analyses identified Self-Regard, Optimism, Interpersonal Relationships, and Self-Actualization as key facets of emotional intelligence, with direct connections to happiness and well-being that can be developed by effective coaching practices.[28]

Once you've collected all your assessment materials, you move on to the next step: helping the client craft his or her well-being vision. The vision will help the client develop specific goals for the coaching work. These goals will be the backbone of your client's coaching agenda. Note, however, that the assessment data is largely meant to be a conversation starter. It's important that the *client* chooses the goals to focus on in coaching. Research findings indicate that holding the reins of their own futures empowers clients and enhances their motivation.[29]

Step 3: Create a Well-Being Vision

In this step, the coach helps the client imagine and describe what life would be like if the satisfaction targets were achieved. This is first explored in conversation, after which the client usually writes an Ideal Personal Well-Being statement.

Your Ideal Personal Well-Being Statement

Now that you've explored some of the details of where it is you'd like to be, we need to work to make that happen. This commitment requires imagining that you're living a life where your *target* well-being levels in fact *are* your current levels. In other words, create in your mind your ideal image of yourself with respect to these well-being practices and behaviors—imagine that you're actually *living* the life you've been envisioning. Then, write it down on the page to follow, describing your ideal well-being as vividly as you can.

As an example, let's say you'd like to develop your career and health—more specifically, you want to feel engaged in a deeply satisfying career and to live a healthy lifestyle in the broadest sense of the term. So, you'd want to imagine yourself two years from now doing just that, in which case you might write:

Whenever I talk about my work, people comment on how positive and enthusiastic I am about my job. I've become more peaceful as a person because I'm no longer frustrated that I'm wasting my time. My self-esteem has improved because I'm accomplishing things that make a difference to me. I eat healthy food, which I consciously enjoy sharing with my partner. I exercise three times a week, outdoors when I can, and often with a friend. I also make time to create and nurture important personal relationships, and I have lunch or dinner with a friend at least once a week.

Step 4: Determine Well-Being Goals

Now that the client has a vision, your next objective as coach is to help the client determine how to move toward that vision—essentially, what the client wants to accomplish through the coaching process. This is done by helping the client identify the principal goals to pursue in order to reach that vision, as well as identifying and building the motivation to pursue that vision and manage obstacles that might arise. (We noted earlier that it's the client, not the coach, who should decide the goals for the coaching sessions.)

In applying this process to Dr. North's story, Step 4 was the point when he decided that he would work to increase his happiness and satisfaction in his career, after which he hoped to address happiness and satisfaction in the other four areas of his life. In coaching Dr. North, coach Aronoff used the Auerbach GOOD Coaching Model.

The Auerbach GOOD Coaching Model™ and Well-Being Coaching

The Auerbach GOOD Model™ relates to Steps 4 through 7 of the larger process.

> G—Goal
> O—Options
> O—Obstacles
> D—Do

It is an easy-to-remember, practical roadmap to help the coach follow an effective coaching process. The client contemplates Goals, Options, and potential Obstacles before laying out what to Do in order to improve their well-being. The GOOD Model may appear similar to the GROW model, which speaks to Goal, Reality, Options, and Wrap-up. However, the GOOD model goes a step further in that it acknowledges and addresses an all-too-common occurrence: how often clients' optimistic work toward a goal can get derailed by obstacles. Such setbacks can be difficult to overcome. We believe that it is helpful to discuss potential obstacles in advance so that the client can have a plan to maintain their momentum if an obstacle arises.

This coaching model helps the client execute the client's well-being plan. During the coaching process the coach asks prompting questions that are, ideally, integrated into a natural conversation, one characterized by active listening, empathy, and support. Regardless of the exact phrasing, the principal question at each step should in essence ask:

G. What are the most important *goals* you want to work toward in our coaching together?

O. What *options* are available to help you move forward with these goals?

O. What *obstacles* might get in the way of your progress? What can you do to manage them if they arise?

D. Now, what specifically are you going to *do*, and when are you going to take action?

So, in the Goal phase, you might ask the client:

- What is a goal you want to focus on?
- When you are successful with your goal, what will it look like?
- Can you tell me more about your goal? What makes it important to you?
- What goal do you want to work toward today?
- How does this goal fit with your vision or purpose for the emerging chapter of your life?
- What outcome would you like?
- How would you like to feel?
- What is important for you to accomplish today? This week? This month?
- What type of change would make your life even better?

Motivational Interviewing as an Aid to Well-Being Coaching

So, how do we help clients identify what motivations will help them pursue their goals? In this task we can again benefit from research findings, this time regarding motivational interviewing. This is a well-researched behavioral intervention that has gained popularity in public health due to its proven efficacy in addressing multiple behaviors, health risks, and even self-management of illness. (Promising experiments include studies of physical and mental health[30] and chronic care management, addressing self-efficacy and perceived health status.[31])

Initially developed by clinical psychologists William R. Miller and Stephen Rollnick, motivational interviewing attempts, in a nonjudgmental and nonconfrontational manner, to increase a client's awareness of the potential problems caused, consequences experienced, and risks faced as a result of a particular behavior. In other words, the approach seeks to help clients think differently about their behavior—and ultimately to consider what might be gained through changing that behavior.

For example, a coach might ask:

- What are the good things about keeping things the way they are?
- What are the not-so-good things about staying the same?
- What are some of the best things about moving forward on this goal (or making this change)?

The case study "vignette" (see sidebar) demonstrates motivational interviewing in action.

continued...

Motivational Interviewing Coaching Vignette
by Lynn K. Jones, DSW, PCC

Casey, a thirty-five-year-old human resources executive, sought coaching to decide whether to seek a promotion. As she worked to determine a goal for the coaching engagement, it became clear that Casey had a lot of ambivalence about accepting more responsibility at work. Casey already felt guilty about not giving her family enough attention, and she and her husband were considering having another child. On the other hand, Casey had invested a decade at her job, had worked hard to get where she was, and was concerned that not accepting a promotion would put her career on hold.

Casey had actually been working on "creating more work-life balance" for the past six months, through reading and some workshops, and was disappointed that she'd not been able to make any progress. What became clear as we talked was that she was already so overwhelmed by juggling all the demands of her job and her family that the prospect of anything more was paralyzing.

To help Casey work through her ambivalence, I posed some motivational interviewing questions. These were helpful because they facilitated her weighing her options as we worked through the GOOD Coaching Model.

LJ: What would be the good things about staying the same and not taking the new job?

Casey: I am pretty much maxed out and just keeping my head above water; but, we are managing. In my current job, I have some flexibility: if something comes up at home, I can work it out to be there. My boss and I are talking about my switching to a schedule where I can work at home one day a week, which would really make things a lot easier for me. My boss and I are also talking about me moving in the direction of coaching at my organization, which is what I really want to do.

LJ: What would be the downside to not taking the new job?

Casey: My career might stall a little bit. I would give up the chance for

continued…

the prestige that accompanies a promotion. It's hard for me to feel as though I can't move in the direction I've been working so hard for. I would feel resentful of my family and my husband for holding me back.

LJ: *What would be the downside of taking the new job?*

Casey: *I am already so stressed. I'm having trouble with my back. I'm so tired by the time I get home at 7 PM that I only have the energy to put my kids to bed. My kids need more attention from me than that. My husband, who is working from home, is doing the lion's share of the childcare and managing the household, and he feels resentful that I can't do more. We hardly ever see each other, because he ends up having to work until 2 AM and then I get up at 5 AM to work-out before I head out for my hour commute. I can't imagine how I could possibly take on more responsibility. On top of all that, my husband really wants to have another child.*

LJ: *What would be the good things about taking the new job?*

Casey: *The way things are now, I can't imagine any good things. I am realizing that the way we are living our lives now is not sustainable. Adding anything more, like a bigger job or another child, really can't be a consideration before we stabilize our lives.*

What Casey realized by working through her options this way was that there was a major obstacle blocking her from making a decision purely based on what was good for her career: that her current life was not "sustainable." She agreed that she needed to make it sustainable before she could realistically consider adding more responsibility to her job, adding another child to her family's already frenetic environment, or both.

This resulted in her determining what she would **do**: "get back to basics," where both she and her husband would focus on eating better, getting more sleep, and getting more help with the household, before adding a new variable. Lightened by her realization, Casey looked forward to a night out with her husband when she would share her thoughts with him.

The conversation would continue over a brief vacation with family.

Once Casey's life stabilized and became less overwhelming, she felt more able to make decisions about her career and her family, and with less worry. Most importantly, she felt a sense of hope that she could get her family members' lives back on track—and was once again excited about their futures.

Readiness to Change

One of the benefits of motivational interviewing is that it recognizes that clients approach counseling or coaching at different levels of readiness to change their behavior (see sidebar). Now, it's easy to think that, if a person seeks some sort of guidance and support, they'd of course be ready to change some behavior in order to act on the counsel offered. But consider, for example, if the coaching had been mandated: the client may never have thought of changing the behavior in question. Another client may be just in the beginning stages of contemplating her situation, and not yet really willing to pursue anything tangible—willing to *think about* a change, but not to make a change. Some might think that just attending coaching will be sufficient, that no active work is called for outside the consulting office. Others may have been unsuccessful in previous attempts to actively change certain behaviors.

STAGES OF READINESS TO CHANGE

Precontemplation: no perceived need for change.
"I don't have a problem."
Contemplation: thinking about making changes.
"Something is not quite right. Maybe I am using too much, but even if I am, I am not ready to do anything about it."
Preparation: preparing and feeling motivated to change.

> "I don't like how I feel or act, and I got suspended from school. Maybe I should consider reducing my use or stopping it altogether—maybe I'll try stopping next week."
>
> *Action:* actively making changes and modifying behavior.
>
> "I have stopped using and it is not as bad as I thought."
>
> *Maintenance:* maintaining the change over a period of time.
>
> "I still think about it and it was hard when I went to that party, but I am doing OK without it—I feel better about myself."[32]

Step 5: Explore Options to Move toward Goals

In the Options phase of the GOOD Coaching Model, the coach helps the client identify the specific behaviors—action steps—that will help them achieve the selected goals. Ideally, within this process, the coach works as much as possible to draw the answer out of the client, so that the client can own both the inspiration and the impetus of the action steps. It's best that the coach offer specific suggestions only after having first mined the client's resources and ideas. This is the preferred approach for two reasons. First, clients often know best which action steps suit their opportunities and challenges. Second, research findings show that "the self-directed person" perceives goals as "opportunities of the future," which "become more important determinants of his action than do events of the past."[33] It's not that coaches don't have knowledge of potent options a client might take; they do. It's that when the client identifies the next steps by themselves, they may be more likely to follow through on them. At times the coach will offer suggestions, but we prefer to do that only after the client has exhausted all of their own ideas.

To help draw out next steps from the client, the coach might ask prompting questions such as, "What are several options available to you that could help you move forward on this goal?" Taking a more pointed approach, one might ask: "What actions can you take this week that will help?"

Here are some sample questions for the Options phase of the GOOD Coaching Model:

- What are some ways this could be done?
- Tell me about how you've accomplished something similar in the past.
- What ways have you seen your mentors approach such a task?
- What are five or six actions that you could take to achieve your goal?
- If you choose not to take some of these actions, what will the impact be?

In the case of Dr. North, Jonathan Aronoff suggested: "Let's think about the options you have to make this larger ophthalmology practice in the city a reality." To this Dr. North replied: "Ideally, I would like to buy an existing practice from an ophthalmologist who wants to retire. I have been checking the newspapers and the Internet for a while and there are always a few eye doctors trying to sell their practice." Working to break down the plan into even more specific action steps, Aronoff continued: "Okay, so what could you do next to pursue this goal?"

Again, the idea is to prompt the client to drum up next steps. Only once all client ideas have been aired would we offer a direct suggestion, ideally phrased along the lines of: "Would you like to hear a suggestion of an activity that might help?" Occasionally, you may want to follow up your suggestion with a concise rationale (in just two or three sentences), including appropriate evidence proving the efficacy of a particular technique, and then wait for the client's reaction. And though we may suggest an activity, we don't require that the client accept it. We are careful to not take over the coaching session—it is up to the client to choose what to do or not do.

Step 6: Consider and Rehearse How to Manage Obstacles

In Step 5 we discussed the process of clients brainstorming *options* to help them move toward their goals. Sometimes clients will run into *obstacles* when trying to execute their plan. Sometimes these obstacles are external. For example, in the first week she'd planned to go to the gym for an hour before work, the client is informed by her boss that she must come in early. Sometimes the obstacles are internal, as when a client cancels his meeting with a financial planner for fear he won't get his paperwork ready in time. So the next step in the GOOD model is the important phase of exploring obstacles that might arise in pursuing a goal, and then mentally rehearsing how to manage them.

Mental rehearsal, a technique often used in sports, involves *mentally* practicing a task rather than actually performing it. We combine mental rehearsal with scenario planning to help a client have a back-up plan for these possible obstacles. So, for example, if the client might be unable to go to the gym as often as she'd planned—and, knowing her boss, anticipates that her fitness goals might be difficult to actualize—she can mentally rehearse that. She can decide that, should her before-work plans be stymied, she can fit in her sixty minutes with a brisk walk at lunch and time on her stair-stepper just before dinner.

Here are some coaching questions useful during the obstacles stage:

- What could get in the way of your moving forward on this step?
- What external challenges—originating outside of you— might interfere with your achieving your goal?
- What internal challenges—originating within you—might interfere with your achieving your goal?

- Who can you get support from to help you overcome that obstacle?

In the case of Dr. North, as much as he wanted to imagine his new practice, his pessimistic mindset discouraged him from thinking that he could successfully complete the steps necessary to pursue his goal. So his coach helped him to think more accurately, and the client realized that most of his worries were unfounded. Dr. North mentally rehearsed effectively arranging the purchase of the practice and then building a viable team to support that practice.

Step 7: Commit to the Action Steps they Will Do

After clients have identified their goal, brainstormed action steps, and planned how to manage obstacles, it is time for them to clearly state what they will do. In this phase the client states what specifically they are going to do, and when. At this stage we also help clients set up an accountability process and a support system to aid their success:

We often ask this specific three-part accountability question:
- Now that you have discussed your goal, your options, and how you'll manage any obstacles that might arise, what specifically are you going to do?
- When are you going to do that?
- How will I know how you are coming along with that?

This provides accountability, which many clients find an especially helpful element of the coaching process. Most clients are highly likely to follow through on their action steps when they have made such a declaration to the coach.

Here are some coaching questions useful during the Do stage of the Auerbach GOOD Coaching Model:
- What specifically are you going to do?
- What are you going to do, and when are you going to do it?

- What strategies or actions are you willing to take to achieve your objective?
- When and how will I know how you're coming along with that?
- It looks like you have an initial plan: your goals, several actions for achieving your goals, plus strategies to compensate for the obstacles. Now, what steps are you going to take?
- You have now outlined your steps. What is your prioritization of these steps and your timeline for completion?
- What is the most immediate action you're willing to take to put your goal into action this week?
- What step or steps will you accomplish this week?
- Which of those steps has first priority, second, etc.?
- How much time will each step require?
- When will you complete each step?
- How will I know you have completed these steps?
- What will you do today to make this happen?
- What step are you going to do before you _____ [some particular activity, such as *go to sleep tonight* or *start work tomorrow*]?

SUMMARY

Numerous studies have demonstrated coaching's efficacy in enhancing well-being in individuals, helping them achieve higher performance and fulfilling their personal goals. As beneficial as this is on the individual level, there are even wider implications for society as a whole. Marty Seligman stresses these reasons we should help people increase their well-being: it is an antidote to depression, it increases life satisfaction, and it assists with learning and leads to more creative thinking.[34] Furthermore, an individual's progression toward their important life goals is associated with increased well-being.[35] Goals usually represent an individual's interest in achieving some type of personal change, enhanced meaning, and purpose in life.[36] In short, coaching increases well-being, hence it increases flourishing.

Seligman articulated in his book *Flourish* that a long-range mission for positive psychology is for 51 percent of the world population to be flourishing by the year 2051. Coaches conducting well-being coaching will be doing their part to facilitate this goal, actively contributing to enhanced health, improved relationships, and higher productivity worldwide, and hopefully more enhanced societal well-being on a global scale.

| CHAPTER | Coaching for |
| 5 | Accomplishment |

How to Help Clients Develop Competencies as Well as Strengths

In Seligman's PERMA model (introduced in Chapter 4), there is a fifth element important for well-being: accomplishment. Note that Seligman makes a distinction between accomplishment "in its monetary form" and "the achieving life, a life dedicated to accomplishment for the sake of accomplishment." He asserts that both are important. He doesn't prescribe what people should pursue to feel they have accomplished or achieved something. It could be a hobby, an avocation, or any activity of interest that captures the person's attention, like his own pursuit of playing what he calls "serious duplicate bridge."

He notes that accomplishing something of value can be for its own sake and not necessarily be tied to meaning or the experience of positive emotion. Nevertheless, this is a key element in his updated theory of well-being.[1] What can we do to help our clients realize their accomplishments to deepen their sense of well-being? Our personal experience aligns with the research findings: deliberately identifying and deploying one's strengths can nurture our well-being. We've observed first-hand that clients who deploy their strengths at work are more likely to experience engagement, even flow, on the job. And this has an additional benefit: a higher level of engagement may enhance performance, which is likely to be reflected in improved performance assessment by coworkers and superiors, which is an achievement by most standards. We are also convinced by Seligman's assertion that accomplishment and achievement are important elements of well-being.

THE IMPORTANCE OF COMPETENCIES AS WELL AS STRENGTHS

This seems to suggest a simple progression: leverage your strengths and you will achieve your goals. However, we are persuaded by the research, and our clients' actual functioning at work, that this formula is incomplete.[2] We are convinced that significant achievement requires addressing competencies as well as strengths. We are concerned that coaching around the topics of skill, competence, and achievement may be shortchanged, given the emphasis on the pursuit of strengths in the positive psychology domain.

This chapter presents the research demonstrating why developing competencies is so important. We offer a case study demonstrating how we apply this research when coaching the pursuit of any achievement or accomplishment, be it seeking promotion at work or mastering a musical instrument.

First, a few words about the language used in the research. Currently, the leadership-development and talent-management literature tends to define the term *competency* much as Michael Lombardo and Robert (Bob) Eichinger do: as a measurable characteristic of a person that is related to success at work.[3] This measurable characteristic can be a behavioral skill (e.g., making timely and high-quality decisions, or developing and sustaining a broad network of relationships with peers), a technical skill (e.g., establishing and monitoring budgets for large development projects, or accurately calculating distances between waypoints in navigation models), an attribute (e.g., above-average verbal intelligence), or an attitude (e.g., a sustained focus on delighting customers, or consistently expressing the desire to work collaboratively with coworkers).

Competence is a state of being capable and demonstrating capability in some characteristic. Since all competencies are measurable, they are often called *skills*—we ourselves did so above—even though, strictly speaking, the two words are not exactly synonymous. Skill is defined as "the ability to do something," whether deriving from "training, experience or practice."[4]

It's important to specify that, while one can possess various degrees of skill in any one ability, typically competencies indicate abilities that have been learned or practiced to the level of mastery, expertise, or the full command or understanding of a subject. In the research literature, the term *mastery* or *skill* refers to a state in which competencies are demonstrated at the right time, with the right intensity and frequency, with the right people, and with successful results. That is, a person displaying mastery in a *competency* does it at just the right level, neither overusing nor underutilizing that competency. We note the distinction between a competency *learned to mastery* and a *strength*. A competency developed to the level of mastery would be observed by important others as being skillfully deployed with intended positive outcomes. A strength can be viewed as a competency that one person has developed better than most people, but it is not usually evaluated in terms of the *skill* shown by the person possessing that strength.[5]

A well-known framework of competencies for the workplace was established by Mike Lombardo and Bob Eichinger, the founders of Lominger, during their time at the Center for Creative Leadership (CCL) in Greensboro, North Carolina.[6] During the early days of CCL's now famous studies of leadership in US corporations, these two men figured prominently among the thought leaders writing in the 1980s and 1990s. Having conducted a content analysis of expert sources,[7] Lombardo and Eichinger ultimately selected sixty-seven competencies that comprise the Leadership Architect competency framework, the foundation of the Lominger talent management library. In recent years, seven international focus areas have been added, based on the authors' experience and additional research.[8]

Many of you who do executive or other business coaching are familiar with the appraisal of competencies using so-called 360° feedback. Eichinger, Lombardo, and Dave Ulrich have made a compelling case that 360° feedback is more appropriate for development than for performance appraisal or the selection of internal candidates for positions.[9] Other researchers have observed that a person's self-assessment of competencies in isolation can be inaccurate when compared to the results of multi-rater feedback for that person.[10] Research shows that people at work often rate themselves more generously than their bosses or peers rate them.[11]

When organizations' leaders (with, in some cases, the help of their HR executives) identify their strategy (e.g., Mayo Clinic's strategy is "creating a caring service environment while ensuring that individual differences are valued at every level of the organization"), they determine which competencies are crucial for the successful implementation of that strategy. These are often called *mission-critical competencies.* Since all of the organization's job descriptions are derived from this strategy, it stands to reason that the competencies required for an organization's success are the same as the competencies required for an employee's advancement in that organization.

FINDINGS FROM THE COMPETENCY RESEARCH AND WHY THEY MATTER

A consistent finding from the competency literature is that most successful leaders possess a number of competencies which they deploy in building a successful career. Typically, they demonstrate five to seven of the most important competencies necessary to perform successfully, and at least an average capability in the remainder of the competencies deemed critical for their role. In the majority of large US organizations, senior-level jobs require skill in ten to fifteen competencies for the person to be successful.[12]

When we summarize the competency literature, we find a key conclusion regarding strengths versus competencies. While everyone is found to possess some number of strengths, these strengths *may* be, but just as likely *may not* be, those required for successful performance in a particular job. To accurately determine this, an assessment must be done that compares a person's level of mastery in designated competencies with others' skill in those same competencies which are required for that identical job or an equivalent type of work.[13]

Many coaches assume that all competencies are equal, but research has shown otherwise. Competencies differ with regard to the level of developmental difficulty, that is, how hard they are to learn. Strategic thinking (or "strategic agility" in Lominger terms)[14] is a very complex set of competencies with high developmental difficulty. Another difference concerns opportunity: how likely the employee is to get the chance to learn them. Innovation management is a case in point. Opportunities to learn this competency can be limited (and the level of developmental difficulty is also high).

TYPES OF COMPETENCIES

Lominger's work with thousands of managers and leaders led to the grouping of competencies into three types, or tiers.[15] At the most basic level are the "price-of-admission" competencies—those necessary to have a chance at being successful in a role. These are integrity and trust; ethics and values; intellectual horsepower (being intellectually sharp and capable); functional/technical skills for that role; action orientation (enjoying hard work and seizing opportunities for action more than most others); perseverance; customer focus; standing alone (accepting personal responsibility and willing to be the only champion for an idea or position); drive for results; and problem-solving ability.

Since everyone seeking a position of responsibility is presumed to have them, price-of-admission competencies are not a differentiator of talent. When coaching business clients regarding their goals, we inquire about their current level of skill in the price-of-admission competencies.

To create their 2006 norms, Lominger analyzed their client database (results from 2,060 employees in thirty-five different North American organizations). They found little difference between North American and non–North American data in the price-of-admission competencies. Other research indicated no significant gender differences in what was deemed important to compete at a basic level at work.[16] Both men and women must demonstrate competence in ethics and values, know the business, show that they are dedicated to their company's customers, be action oriented, and deliver on their commitments.

To advance, employees must develop competencies in a second tier, those that differentiate leaders from followers. Lominger identified eight "competitive edge" competencies highly correlated with success for managers and leaders. These "critical differentiators" of effectiveness are dealing with ambiguity; creativity; strategic agility; innovation management; managing vision and purpose; planning; motivating others; and building effective teams.

It is not surprising that few candidates for promotion, regardless of their level in an organization, demonstrate all eight of these competencies. Although Lominger's research found that six of these eight competencies were consistently correlated with high performance ratings, only 1.6 percent of the managers and executives in the sample demonstrated at least five of these eight critical skills. A vast majority—66.7 percent—demonstrated *none* of them.[17]

In a third tier are the competencies that are specific to a level or management rank in a company. That is, as one moves up in an organization—from individual contributor to manager to executive— these are the competencies required to meet job challenges at that particular organizational level.

THE SIGNIFICANCE OF ORGANIZATIONAL LEVEL AND COMPETENCY DEVELOPMENT

Different experts have developed different guidelines for advancing in one's career. In the classic text *The Leadership Pipeline*, the authors identify six levels of leadership required to reach the top of an organization. These are: manage self (individual contributor); manage others (first-line manager); manage other managers of others; functional manager (a leading position in HR, finance, etc.); business manager (usually a general manager or group manager who is in charge of several functions); group manager (managing the portfolio for several businesses); and enterprise manager (chief executive of the company).[18]

Similarly, Arthur Freedman proposed that an organization's top rung could be reached via a model of five primary pathways. The five pathways are individual contributor, supervising manager, single business manager, executive manager of several businesses, and institutional leader.[19]

Freedman identified a critical point about the competency/ growth continuum. To navigate the transition required to advance to new managerial positions, a person must continue to demonstrate established competencies, learn new competencies, and let go of competencies no longer appropriate in the new, more senior role. For example, consider Tatum, transitioning from individual contributor to supervising manager. To succeed as a supervising manager, Tatum must reprioritize her skill set. She must let go of focusing on being a technical expert and instead rely on the people who report to her to share their expertise. She will need to develop as an effective manager who demonstrates the emotionally intelligent behaviors of listening, engaging others, inspiring others around a common organizational purpose, and ultimately creating and sustaining a high-performing team.

COACHING FOR COMPETENCY DEVELOPMENT AS WELL AS LEVERAGING STRENGTHS: THE CASE OF KEN

Here I (Sandra) present a case to illustrate how an executive coach can assist a client in the development of their competencies. Ken[20] is a thirty-year-old employee of a large (50,000 employees worldwide) global telecommunications firm headquartered in Europe. When we began the coaching, he was the supervisor of a product development team. As such, he was a first-line manager. He had worked in that position for eighteen months. Here are his replies to my preliminary queries about his so-called *current state* at work.

Trained for promotion? No, but mentored by boss.

Previous position: Technologist in a revenue-contributing business unit and successful individual contributor.

Advancement prospects: "Demonstrated promise as a company leader"; eligible for the organization's high-potential development program.

Sought coaching from Sandra for: Never coached before but interested because his boss had found coaching valuable and was willing to sponsor Ken's coaching.

In preparation for his organization's high-potential program, Ken completed a Voices® 360° survey to aid him in plotting his learning agenda.

Lominger competencies relevant to Ken:
- Sixteen central to the organization's strategy
- Five critical for success in a line manager role: organizational agility, building effective teams, delegation, customer focus, decision quality

Voices ratings were collected from:
- Ken himself
- Two direct reports
- His boss
- His boss's boss
- Three peers
- Two internal customers (business-unit leaders)

KEN'S VOICES® DATA

On the five Lominger competencies critical for success in the manager role, Ken rated himself as competent in customer focus and decision quality, as he applied his technical knowledge to new product development initiatives; other raters observed his capabilities here, with a high degree of inter-rater agreement.

Ken's self-ratings were lower than all his other raters in delegation and building effective teams. His direct reports found him to be more competent in delegating, commenting that he was very clear in communicating his objectives and providing considerable oversight for their results. However, all his raters agreed that he was less skilled in building effective teams—because, they observed, he engaged his reports on a one-to-one basis rather than building their synergies as a collective group. Although he stated concisely the results the team needed to deliver, Ken was not creating with his reports a shared mindset toward common organizational goals.

His top five strengths on the Gallup StrengthsFinder were:[21]

- Deliberate (being careful, vigilant and private about one's life)
- Discipline (needing the world to be predictable)
- Input (being inquisitive and a collector of information)
- Intellection (enjoying mental activity)
- Learner (drawn to the process of learning)

CONCLUSIONS FROM THE RATINGS AND IMPLICATIONS FOR DEVELOPMENT

To maintain the anonymity of his Voices® 360° report, Ken provided his boss with only a verbal summary of the findings, noting that he and all raters observed low competence in organizational agility. This made sense to Ken; in his earlier roles he had not needed to understand how organizations functioned as entities. Ken also realized that he had not focused on cultivating strong relationships across the organization. They agreed that his first step in developing organizational agility should be to learn more about the culture and practices of the company. Another significant finding was that Ken did not seem to be creating with his direct reports a shared mindset of pursuing common organizational goals. Here was a coaching opening for him: to become aware of the value of helping team members recognize their individual contribution to the team effort and understand how their individual contributions had an impact on the organization's success.

As Ken considered the best way forward, he recalled that his Gallup strengths Input, Intellection, and Learner could help him develop the five core competencies necessary for success as a manager. He and I also agreed that his Deliberate and Discipline strengths no longer served him, as he needed to foster open dialogue among his team members, building strong morale and team spirit. Finally, Ken would receive formal training in management, including theory and practice in delegating and managing teams. He would also consult *For Your Improvement.*[22]

THE COACHING PROCESS: SANDRA AND KEN

Ken and I worked for six months, expanding on the productive discussions he'd had with his boss. Through our conversations, he came to understand that not only did he need to continue to be clear and concise in stating his objectives, he also needed to step back and allow others to complete the activities he'd delegated to them.

We explored how Ken's micromanaging tendencies possibly resulted from overusing his Discipline and Deliberate strengths. Ken realized that these strengths were probably based on a deeply held value around the importance of holding oneself accountable. In acknowledging how critical accountability was to him, he realized that his sense of its importance might well be inhibiting the development of accountability—and even autonomy—in his team members. Ken came to see the benefit of delegating important, meaningful tasks, as well as routine ones. In addition, he would immediately begin spending more time coaching them and supporting their ideas about how to effectively complete their responsibilities.

I encouraged Ken to study *For Your Improvement's* suggestions for building effective teams and then discuss them with his boss. They agreed that Ken could leverage his Gallup strengths of Input and Intellection while creating a climate of innovation and experimentation with his group. Ken came to see how establishing a common cause around the team's overall purpose tangibly advanced the organization's strategic goals—and how engaging the team in setting their own objectives would help increase their sense of ownership in the organization's success.

In our discussions of Ken's development planning, he agreed that he needed more on-the-job responsibilities to develop in place projects and assignments that would add scope (greater responsibility) and scale (involving managing a greater number of people). To this end, Ken and his boss initiated his participation in a start-up acquisition.

As our coaching came to a close, Ken commented that he appreciated that he could leverage his Gallup strengths in his development journey while also focusing intently on the competencies critical to his future success. He commented that at first he had believed that using his strengths should be his sole focus. He then came to appreciate that he was overusing one or more of them. He also realized the importance of developing mission-critical competencies to ensure his success in more senior roles.

When we had a post-coaching follow-up conversation six months later, Ken reported that his team had become a more cohesive working group that was meeting or exceeding all of its key targets. Ken's boss had commented favorably on his new routines for developing his direct reports through increased delegation of significant responsibilities, regular biweekly one-on-one meetings to assess progress and to offer coaching, and beginning a rudimentary succession plan with the assistance of Ken's HR business partner. Ken and his boss reported that Ken was becoming a spokesperson for how the organization's strategy was expressed in the work of his team, raising their visibility in the organization and finding opportunities to share their successes outside their immediate circle of Ken's peers and their teams.

IMPLICATIONS OF THE RESEARCH FINDINGS FOR OUR COACHING

The case of Ken was just one of many in which we saw that exploring competencies as well as strengths exponentially benefits those seeking advancement. Here are our suggested guidelines for incorporating leadership findings into your coaching practice:

1. *Help assess which price-of-admission competencies are applicable to your client's current position.* You can support clients in making certain that they are demonstrating skill in the competencies associated with success in their current position. They can refer to their job description and seek expert advice from their HR business partner.

2. *Determine to what degree your client demonstrates these competencies.* Performance reviews, when available, are an excellent resource for data on your client's competencies. A more thorough assessment, of course, would result from a 360° feedback survey.[23] Ideally, for this process, employees select raters who have known them for at least a year and have regular opportunities to observe them on the job; these may include subordinates (direct reports and support staff), peers, bosses, and even customers.

3. *Help your client improve in any lower-rated competencies.*

4. *Assess your client's goals for advancement. The following questions can be useful in facilitating this discussion of future goals:*
   - Based on your organization's current strategy, what type of work do you want to do in three years' time?
   - If you can imagine disruptive forces changing your company and your industry, what might your future role be like, and how could prepare now?
   - What kind of organization would you want to be a part of?
   - What ultimate level of leadership do you aspire to, and in what size of organization?

5. *Encourage your client to explore the mission-critical skills required for success at their desired level.* If your client was granted a 360°

feedback survey, identify the technical competencies specific to their organization's success. Even without a survey, much could be gleaned from your client's researching company information online, or even conducting informational interviews with others in the enterprise. Encourage the client to explore whether there are specific technical competencies they must acquire for success at their desired level in the organization, as well as the leadership competencies needed for success. The leadership research points to a formula for most effectively developing competencies:

- Seventy percent of development should be on-the-job-learning, through shadowing others who are skilled and through job assignments that stretch a person beyond their comfort zone. This on-the-job-skill acquisition is also called learning in place.
- Twenty percent of development should come as a result of coaching or mentoring that encourages the learner's taking actions that will promote acquisition of key competencies.
- Only ten percent of development should involve formal training at work or education outside of work.[24]

At its core, this development formula is about learning through experience on the job. We recommend that your client's action plan for development reflect the 70-20-10 formula. The client could initiate conversations with their line manager, HR business partner, formal mentor, or senior leaders to explore what projects, rotations, task forces, or other responsibilities could help them make significant gains in their leadership competencies.

CHAPTER 6

Time and How We Spend It:

Helping Clients Increase Engagement, Flow, and Meaning in Their Lives

MIHALY CSIKSZENTMIHALYI'S WORK ON HOW WE SPEND TIME

Does how we spend our time affect our well-being and experience of satisfaction at work and in our lives? Researchers say yes. Mihaly Csikszentmihalyi's research is especially relevant. He investigated the quality (or, we could say, the positivity) of how we spend our time. His findings will help you in helping your clients spend their time in ways that are personally meaningful.

Mihaly Csikszentmihalyi is a professor of psychology and management at the Drucker Graduate School of Management at the Claremont Graduate University. There he helps oversee the Quality of Life Research Center, which focuses on positive psychology topics, including a multi-nation study of happiness. He and Martin Seligman are long-time collaborators; they have even explored the conditions that might help create world peace. They joined forces as guest editors of the January 2000 Special Issue on positive psychology of the *American Psychologist*, the flagship publication of the American Psychological Association.[1]

Csikszentmihalyi is regarded as an intellectual powerhouse in the positive psychology movement. He takes a special interest in the quality of human experience, and has concluded that the excellence of daily life depends upon not just what we do but *how* we do what we do. In his book *Good Business: Leadership, Flow, and the Making of Meaning* he speaks of *human* or *psychological capital*.[2] This psychological capital is the "psychic energy" that we employ when we devote ourselves to a person, a task, or a pleasurable pursuit.

He notes that William James, one of the first American psychologists, spoke of a person's selective attention as one of the factors influencing how we experience our lives. This attention—this *bandwidth*, or capacity for cognitive processing—is limited, so we can pay only so much attention at any given time. Therefore, *what* we pay attention to, throughout our waking hours, becomes an important variable in how we experience time and the quality of our lives.

Csikszentmihalyi concludes that the greatest rewards in life derive from consistently choosing goals that lead to personal growth and what he terms "social synergy," or contributing to the greater good. Such goals involve our taking on ever-increasing challenges, developing skills useful to ourselves and to others. Not surprisingly, he expresses concern regarding how much attention we "waste" on activities that do not contribute to our satisfaction with life. He is particularly concerned regarding how much time Americans, particularly teens, spend watching TV or viewing entertainment online. He believes that we squander our psychological capital worrying about what others think of us (beyond developing a sound reputation for our work and our personal character), or acquiring things to impress others.

THE EXPERIENCE SAMPLING METHOD

He developed a real-time measurement technique called the Experience Sampling Method (ESM).[3] In a typical ESM study—which might span weeks or even months—several questions are posed to subjects regarding how they are spending their time at that moment, how meaningful the activity is, and how engaged they are in it. Csikszentmihalyi asserts that ESM is a more reliable and accurate method than a diary, which is retrospective and relies on memory for the reconstruction of daily activities. In the most well-funded of his early research studies, subjects carried a pager that beeped at random intervals. This signaled the subjects to stop whatever they were doing and record their responses to the ESM inquiries:

- At this moment, what are you doing? And with whom are you doing it (or are you alone)?
- How happy are you?
- How much are you concentrating on this activity?
- Are you feeling good about yourself right now?
- How motivated do you feel as you engage in this activity?

Numerous studies done in the United States and other countries in the developed world have found three classes of activities in which people spend their waking hours:

1. *Productive activities*—working to earn a living; studying; discussing a problem or talking more casually with others at work; daydreaming about projects while at work; driving and commuting. (We add volunteering to this list.)

2. *Leisure*—of which there are two types: passive and active. This distinction is an important one for Csikszentmihalyi. Active leisure includes hobbies, sports, socializing, cooking (especially with others), playing musical instruments or singing, and attending live theater or music concerts (which are deemed more mentally engaging than watching musical performances on TV, or viewing movies or other online content). Passive leisure he defines as watching TV or movies, hanging out, resting, or being idle. (To this category we add mindless Internet surfing or excessive routine online chat.)

3. *Maintenance activities*—grooming, shopping, cleaning, waiting in line, and mindless food preparation.

In earlier work, Csikszentmihalyi and his colleague Reed Larson found that most teens spent a lot of time watching TV or "hanging out," or talking but not saying much, by their own self-reports.[4] These teens stated that they did not feel challenged at school or in their lives generally. They seemed less happy and satisfied than the smaller percentage of their peers who reported being more challenged by their studies. Teens in this latter group spent more time with their families and played sports or a musical instrument.

For adults, Csikszentmihalyi's research results showed what he called "the paradox of work." Work was the source of greatest satisfaction for some adults, while many others said that they despised their jobs and went to work only because they had to. With respect to others, a person can be:

- in a public space at work, around strangers in some public place, or with casual friends or acquaintances
- with family, close friends, or significant others
- alone

His results show that, in terms of being with others in the public space, people felt either the greatest satisfaction or the greatest strain while at work (if bosses were difficult and/or coworkers were not cooperative). Being with family was also either enjoyable, especially for men (taking into account cultural differences), or unpleasant. Being alone was the most difficult of all. Csikszentmihalyi documented that a person who is alone on weekends and away from work may experience thoughts that become increasingly negative. This person is more likely to notice their aches and pains.

The most adverse and trying situation for a person was being alone with nothing to do, without resources like money and social support from family or friends. Without people around us, and a focus, life is not only less meaningful, it feels profoundly difficult.

FLOW

Csikszentmihalyi notes that without a focus, the mind is in chaos. Unless a person learns to control their attention, that is, to concentrate and engage in goal-oriented activity, their thoughts scatter and become negative. He concludes that it is much easier to focus our psychic energy when we have goals, especially goals that require that our skills be highly deployed and that the means for reaching our goals commands our attention. *Flow* is the term he coined to name this physical/mental/ emotional state, described as:

- Feeling like effortless action.
- Where a person is pursuing goals that demand specific responses and where clear, relevant feedback is available. That is, the person will know almost immediately whether their actions are successful.
- Involving activities that require high levels of skill and concentration.
- Generating what he termed the "paradox of control." This he described as feeling sometimes nearly on the edge of being out of control, while simultaneously feeling exhilarated at the completion of the task because the person is able to maintain control over their physical movements or the environment.
- Losing self-consciousness. By this he means that the person is so focused on the activity that they are no longer distracted by others' opinions or judgments about what they are doing.[5]

Examples of flow are reported by those who sail, kayak, river-raft, and rock-climb, where the demand for skillfulness is high and the feedback is instantaneous. Doing brain surgery is also reported to be a flow experience by talented surgeons working with skilled teams in operating rooms. People can experience flow while gardening, creating art, making music together, or weaving. Hunting is also reported to be a flow activity in some of the cross-cultural studies, along with engaging in traditional crafts, and singing and storytelling with members of one's clan or tribe. Examples of flow as a cognitive activity include engaging in lively conversations and debates, and doing crossword puzzles alone.

APPLYING ESM WITH COACHING CLIENTS

If we make the effort to evaluate how we are spending our time, that precious and limited commodity, our observations can be revealing. The ESM data can be useful in examining what is occurring in our daily lives. The data can inform decisions regarding what we would like to have happen more often. We can ask our clients how they might create the conditions that enhance their engagement at work or even lead to an experience of flow, on the job and elsewhere. ESM findings may also assist the client in approaching their maintenance activities so they are less onerous and time-consuming.

We use the ESM method with clients to discover their allocation of precious commodities, their time and psychic energy—by identifying where they are putting their attention during the day. The results can be startling, so we prepare the client for the ESM assessment by normalizing the experience of perhaps being surprised, even unsettled, by what is uncovered. After this preparation, we coach them in using the data to make different choices in the future if the results are perceived as disappointing or undesirable. While it does take time and effort to collect ESM data, we recommend this exercise as a worthwhile assessment for both business and personal coaching clients.

CASE EXAMPLE USING ESM DATA

One client, whom I (Sandra) will call Laurent, was indeed surprised by his ESM results. This thirty-six-year-old, never married, software design project manager sought coaching because he was unhappy—not depressed. (We carefully interview any prospective client to make certain that coaching is more appropriate than therapy.) In this case, he attributed his unhappiness to his dissatisfaction at work, a family-owned software company in a major French city. He had returned to this city, where he was born, to create his own family at some point in the future and to be near his parents and cousins. After earning an MBA at a top US business school, he worked in Boston and Brussels, enjoying considerable recognition in the multinational companies that employed him.

To begin the ESM, I called him at random times on his cell phone over the course of the first two days. Thereafter, he set his watch alarm to alert himself. He collected data for two weeks, a time frame that most of my business and other clients have found not too long or tedious. When he reviewed his data, what really upset Laurent was how little focus he had during most of his hours at work—a troubling realization for someone who, in former times, took pride in being able to concentrate intensely and get things done. He was also dismayed by how seldom he engaged in the active forms of leisure that he had loved—before he became so caught up at work—even though he had friends and the time and money with which to do these activities. The data also showed that after he spent time with his girlfriend he would go home alone and begin ruminating in an extremely negative manner—about her real or imagined shortcomings, his lack of career success, his uncertain future, his despicable boss, and on and on.

We used the ESM data to guide us in generating more positive emotions and restructuring how he spent his time. He was also unsettled and a bit sad to discover how seldom he felt that he behaved like a leader at work, given his past track record. We then explored ways he could redirect his focus and rediscover the rewards of behaving like a leader even when his boss might take no notice.

SETTING UP THE ESM ASSESSMENT WITH CLIENTS

In the coming two weeks, try the ESM for yourself for at least seven consecutive days or preferably two weeks. Set your smart phone or other device to prompt you during waking hours to notice what you are doing and jot it down. Then quickly answer the ESM questions below, which we have modified for use with our clients.

1. At this moment, what are doing and with whom (or are you alone)?

2. How satisfied are you right now? Use a scale from 0, "not at all satisfied—I'm bored," to 10, "I am completely satisfied with what I am doing."

3. How much skill is required for this activity?
   - No skill is needed. A child could do it.
   - Some skill is needed.
   - A moderate amount of skill is needed.
   - The level of skill needed requires me to "stretch" in order to do this activity.

4. Describe your level of motivation as you engage in this activity.
   - I'm doing this because I have nothing else to do.
   - I'm doing this because someone else is making me do it.
   - I do this activity because I know I have to do it.
   - I'm doing this activity because I want to do it.

5. How challenged do you feel by this activity? Use a scale from 0, "this activity presents no challenge whatsoever; I could do it on autopilot," to 10, "this activity presents an extremely demanding challenge for me."

6. How much are you concentrating on what you are doing at this moment? Use a scale from 0, "I am completely distracted and paying no attention at all," to 10, "I am completely absorbed and engaged in what I am doing and cannot think about anything else."

Once you have collected your data, notice what percentage of time you engage in the four types of activities (productive, active leisure, passive leisure, and maintenance), and with whom. Notice how often you experience a state of flow, if at all, and look for activities that could potentially lead you into flow.

These sorts of observations would then become topics for a conversation with a coach peer if you wish to reflect further on the data with a thought partner. In discussion, the two of you could explore your use of time overall, and how satisfied you feel with the discoveries that emerged from your data. You could also explore the implications for change that you see as potentially valuable in enhancing your engagement at work and elsewhere and how you might increase your experience of flow on the job or while engaged in other activities.

WHEN TO USE AN ESM ASSESSMANT

In our experience, the ESM assessment is most useful for coaching clients who are curious or even upset about how they are spending their time, or for those who report that work is unhappily taking up most of their time. We introduce the ESM activity after establishing rapport and trust with the client, but early enough in the coaching process for the data to be informative for our conversations. We decide what method of prompting is best and the range of daytime hours during which the client will collect data. We encourage collecting data during weekends as well as weekdays. We tailor the questions to suit the client's needs, keeping in mind that too many queries may be cumbersome.

We support the client's discovery of which activities require the highest level of skill, are the most personally meaningful, and are important because of with whom the client does them. We encourage the client to reflect on what activities provide the greatest positive challenge, compel the most intense focus, and are the most enjoyable and rewarding. As with Laurent, we are alert for what is missing from a client's experience of their life. For a particular client, it may be time with friends and family, time spent meaningfully alone, time to just relax, or time spent traveling or discovering new aspects of the client's environment.

We look for activities that lead to the experience of positive emotions, including the pleasure that most people report when they describe being in a flow state. The overall objective of the ESM assessment is for clients to discover ways they can rebalance excessive time doing maintenance activities, and to find greater satisfaction in how they spend time overall. We certainly want to help them enhance their sense of flourishing by planned involvement in well-being activities in the different domains of their lives, such as volunteering, exercise, cultural pursuits, or travel.

We explore the results and their overall meaning with the client. Since we know that a client may express surprise, dismay, or relief when delving into their data, we sensitively discuss their responses and their implications, and inquire about what changes they wish to embark on.

Many of our clients find useful Csikszentmihalyi's distinction between active and passive leisure. We have found that some clients insist that passive leisure has its place in how they spend time, providing the space and hours to simply "do nothing" or to read online content that others might not consider particularly worthwhile. Often clients want to spend more time with loved ones or friends, or pursue a creative endeavor. We support the client in designing an action plan and embracing new activities such as learning photography, taking a class in painting, joining a book club, professional association, or charitable organization, or pursuing membership in a church, synagogue, or mosque.

Some of our clients are keen to take up or return to a sport that involves skill and concentration and might lead to flow states, such as distance running, kayaking, or scuba diving. Other clients have discovered that flow might emerge for them in leisure activities that require initial lessons and then extensive practice, such as chess or bridge. A few of our clients decide to spend passive leisure in ways they determine would be more constructive, such as watching TED talks or participating in online discussion groups on a topic important or fascinating to them.

We then look at our clients' productive activities and ways they can increase their satisfaction, focus and concentration, enjoyment, motivation, and even flow, at work. We discuss how they might enrich their jobs through online classes provided by their employers, executive education courses, or technical training related to their role.

We suggest that they talk with their line manager or possibly members of the human resources team about such possibilities.

Other clients have shadowed a seasoned colleague in another function to gain a broader understanding of the company; taken on a short-term assignment in a different division or in another country; or transferred to another line of business in the organization. Obviously, resigning is an option, at least in some cases. However, a number of our clients have found that by pursuing develop-in-place activities they could enrich their experience at work and perhaps be promoted by demonstrating to their bosses their interest in doing more.

INTRINSIC AND EXTRINSIC MOTIVATION

We explore the distinction between intrinsic and extrinsic motivation and see if there are ways that the client can become more self-motivated and internally driven by their job. We encourage our clients to ponder how they might become more focused on their work activities by deliberately deploying their strengths more each day, using their VIA or StrengthsFinder results. We also explore whether our clients might feel more satisfied by becoming more deeply engaged, by aligning what they do at work with the strategic goals of their company or nonprofit. We suggest that our clients take notice of what activities at work compel them to use their existing skills and to stretch beyond their current level of competence.

In some cases, it is important for the client to look at how to better manage time away from work and more effectively juggle the responsibilities of parenting and running a household. In these conversations, we ask whether some tasks can be delegated to other family members, or outsourced if the family budget allows. We may also discuss how to complete errands in an efficient way, using lists and planning the most direct route from one store to another.

For clients overwhelmed by clutter, hiring a reputable professional organizer may bring much-needed order if their ESM data reveals hours wasted on looking for things or moving piles from one place to another. Sometimes setting up a personal work space like a writer's garret or art studio can support the client's efforts to pursue meaningful goals outside of work.

Some clients' data indicates what we would determine is overwork, given a high percentage of time spent in productive work in their jobs. In this case, we might ask their permission to discover what this might mean in terms of how time is spent during weekends or evenings after work.

We realize that work may be perhaps the primary source of worth for some clients, and for others perhaps a possible substitute for close relationships. We know that it is crucial to discern with the client whether the ESM data has revealed a short-term phase of overtime that they find not at all motivating; or perhaps the overtime represents a newly found reengagement with work by devoting long hours to a project about which the client feels excited or challenged.

As coaches, our own ESM or other self-assessment data may enable us to perceive more clearly how we are spending our time in our work. Our ratings of satisfaction with particular activities, the skillfulness required, our level of motivation and concentration, as well as how challenged we feel during our activities, may provide us with insights regarding how absorbed we are in what we are doing. As we review how we spend our leisure time, we may conclude that it is engaging and stimulating, or perhaps it is less invigorating than we wish it to be.

We encourage you to use your own data to help you understand how to better assist your clients.

THE IMPORTANCE OF FOCUS AND PURPOSE

Without a focus, our thoughts scatter, often turning negative, and our level of productivity, to be sure, is lower. Peak performers such as effective business leaders and Olympic athletes know that setting clear goals is crucial to competing well, whether in the marketplace or on the playing field. Sharing our goals with others may likewise enhance our enjoyment of the process of goal pursuit. For an individual high-performer, like an elite athlete, these clear goals are paramount in committing to the training regimen that is necessary for success.

We often facilitate conversations with our clients to reflect on the larger purpose that underpins their goals. For *ownwork*, we often recommend that clients write personal mission statements for their work and their overall lives.

For coaching clients who wish to be more focused at work, here are some tips drawn from the performance-enhancement research and time-management literature:

- Identify a physical threshold or boundary where you enter your workplace. Imagine that, as you cross that threshold, you make a clear separation from home/personal life to focus on work life. You can do the same for home life, creating a threshold at the front door. Crossing that line, endeavor to make a mental separation of home from work life, to the extent that is possible, so that you can focus on your loved ones.
- Before leaving work, organize your workspace. Prepare a to-do list for the next day for yourself, and do this with key direct reports. Return phone calls that must be made before the end of the current business day.
- To create time in your company for projects that need your individual time and focus, check with your boss about creating signs that say, *I'm very busy right now—please do not disturb,* and ask coworkers for their cooperation in observing those times, and scheduling team meetings at other times.
- Take time to imagine, while on your way to work, the workday unfolding as you wish it would.

CHAPTER 7

Applying the Latest Research on Goal Setting and Mindset

HEIDI GRANT HALVORSON'S SUMMARY OF THE NEW RESEARCH ON GOALS

As coaches, we are well versed in the importance of setting goals. Goals are crucial to feeling engaged by what we do. Goals are crucial to our succeeding, as noted by many who are influential teachers of coaching as well as positive psychology researchers such as Seligman, as he describes in his book, *Flourish*.[1]

Most of us coaches have thought for years that all outcome goals specifying the *what*—"I will do this" or "I want this"—were equal. (We are making a distinction here between outcome goals and *performance goals*, which in sport psychology specify the *how* of performance.) Most of us would agree that outcome goals, to be helpful in our pursuit of desired end results, need to be specific, observable, realistically achievable, and measurable. What got us taking notice and thinking differently about setting goals is a research summary described by Heidi Grant Halvorson in her book, *Succeed*, published in 2010.[2]

She cites the results from her own research and those of other investigators[3] and concludes that our *motivation* (our reason for setting goals) leads to two quite different tracks. Thus, not all outcome goals are created equal, or to be more correct, not all goals produce effects in the same way. To succeed in what we wish to accomplish, we need to understand whether we are motivated by wanting *to be good at something* or by wanting to *get better at something*. As we read the first chapters of *Succeed*, our initial reaction was to wonder whether this distinction between being-good and getting-better motivations was significant. We already knew that the distinction between intrinsic and

138

extrinsic goals was very important in a person's pursuit of a goal. After reflecting upon her descriptions of the two types of motivations for goals and then taking her assessment to see which was more true for us, it's fair to say that each of us was impressed by how crucial these differences in motivation actually are. When we know what motivates a client, as Halvorson suggests, we coach them differently, as you will see in this chapter.

One key difference between the being-good and getting-better motivations has to do with time. Getting-better motivated goals are pursued over a long period of time, like months or years. Being-good motivated goals are pursued for days or weeks. Another key difference has to do with what a client does when the going gets tough. Depending on whether a client is motivated to be good at something or to get better at something, there is a striking difference in how they react when encountering obstacles. This has implications for how we effectively coach clients when they feel fatigued or blocked in their goal pursuit. We invite you to try Halvorson's assessments to see for yourself what motivates you. She, her editor, and her publisher all granted us permission to share these assessments with you. We think you'll find your results revealing and perhaps even surprising.

HALVORSON ASSESSMENTS FOR GOAL SETTING
Which Goals Are You Good at Reaching?

Answer the following questions using this scale:

1	2	3	4	5
Never or seldom		Sometimes		Very often

1. How often have you accomplished things that got you "psyched" to work even harder?
2. How often did you obey the rules and regulations that were established by your parents?

---

3. Do you often do well at different things you try?
4. I feel like I have made progress toward being successful in my life.
5. Growing up, did you avoid "crossing the line," to avoid doing
things your parents would not tolerate?
6. Not being careful enough has gotten me into trouble at times.

Promotion Goals score: Q1 + Q3 + Q4 = _____

Prevention Goals score: Q2 + Q5 + (6 − Q6) = _____

What Motivates You: Being Good at Something or Getting Better at Something?

Using the scale below, rate how much you agree with each statement, that is, how true this is of you, in general.

1	2	3	4	5
Never or seldom		Sometimes		Very often

1. It is very important to me to do well at school or work compared to my classmates or co-workers.
2. I like having friends who can teach me something about myself, even if it isn't always positive.
3. I am always seeking opportunities to develop new skills and acquire new knowledge.
4. I really care about making a good impression on other people.
5. It's important to me to show that I am smart and capable.

6. I strive to have open and honest relationships with my friends and acquaintances.

7. I strive to constantly learn and improve in school or at work.

8. When I am with other people, I think a lot about how I am "coming across" to them.

9. I feel good about myself when I know that other people like me.

10. I try to do better than my coworkers or classmates.

11. I like to be in relationships that challenge me to change for the better.

12. In school or at work I am focused on demonstrating my ability.

Add up your scores from numbers 1, 4, 5, 8, 9, 10, and 12. Divide this total by 7. This is your Being Good at Something score.

Add up your scores from numbers 2, 3, 6, 7, and 11. Divide this total by 5. This is your Getting Better at Something score.

IMPLICATIONS OF THE ASSESSMENT SCORES

Which score is higher for you? If you are like most people, you pursue both kinds of goals to some extent, but one of them more often than then other. If someone is more motivated, more of the time, by a desire to be good at something, this suggests that they are driven by the aspiration to show that they are smart, capable, or talented, or able to outperform others and outdo the competition. The desire to be good at something is tied to attaining *external* validation for one's worth.

Examples of "being good at something" goals are getting good grades, getting accepted into a prestigious graduate program, hearing yes when you ask someone attractive to spend time with you, meeting revenue targets at work, coming in first in the beauty contest, winning a contract by outselling three competitors, losing the weight you gained during the holidays to fit into your fantastic new outfit, or beating out the other contenders for a job.

Successfully reaching goals motivated by the desire to be good at something is linked to a feeling that we possess *traits* like intelligence, beauty, or an almost innate capacity to attract others. Students and employees with being-good motivation often *do* get the best grades or are the highest performers. The desire to be good at something is all about the perceived competence of the person as judged by others. The person with this type of motivation will be eager to demonstrate how competent they are by actually reaching the desired outcome. It's about proving oneself.

HOW DIFFERENT GOAL MOTIVATIONS AFFECT RESILIENCE IN THE FACE OF DIFFICULTY

What happens when a person motivated to be good at something encounters difficulty when striving toward the desired end result, or experiences setbacks or failures along the way? When this person does not reach the goal, they are likely to conclude that they are not smart or not capable, in an all-or-nothing way. The person is making an attribution about failure that is tied to traits that they are likely to regard as unalterable and immutable. The person can then experience insecurity or feel disinclined to try again. This attribution and overall negative self-assessment can lead to feelings of anxiety or to diminished self-esteem, lower self-confidence, and even reactive depression.

When the going gets tough, the person may stop putting forth so much effort, which may lead irrecoverably to falling short of the push needed to succeed. If failure is the result, it confirms the person's negative self-appraisal regarding not having enough smarts or talent in the first place. We find very compelling Halvorson's clear description of the linkage between self-worth and a person's being motivated to show that they are very capable and able to outdo others. However, when the going gets tough, this person is *more* likely to give up.

If your client is more motivated by being-good goals, what are the implications for you as a coach?

Halvorson notes that the research suggests that most people in developed countries, particularly the United States, are motivated in this way. This type of motivation is the best type for putting forth the effort to earn the grades to get into graduate school, to sustain the intense study at a law school that "weeds out" its underperforming first-year students, or the persistence to compete for a new job or promotion. It should be said that this type of drive is externally referenced and extrinsically motivated. As a result, motivation can wane when others' feedback is not supportive.

In contrast, there is a smaller group of people motivated primarily by the desire to *get better* at something. That is, they are motivated more by learning new skills and developing themselves over time than by what they have to prove to others in the present moment or immediate future. With this group, we are talking about the pursuit of *mastery goals* by engaging in daily or weekly activities or practices over a long period of time while remaining focused on the end result and sustaining a disciplined approach.

Examples of this second type of goal pursuit would be mastering the piano; learning to play golf well enough to accept invitations for foursomes in social or business situations; or becoming cross-culturally competent in work settings. Other examples include building an enduring, persistently successful coaching practice earning a specified amount per year; publishing your book; maintaining your weight within a certain range, say five pounds if female; exercising regularly (again, one needs specificity—e.g. at least three times a week for thirty minutes); or engaging in positive communication with your spouse or partner at least twice a day.

When motivated to learn complex competencies, people judge themselves in terms of their observable skill acquisition or progress toward their personal or professional development over time, rather than in terms of beating the competition. Getting-better motivated folks chalk up poor performance to not yet having learned or mastered a given skill and are likely to seek out more experienced people to learn from. When the going gets tough, they are *less* likely to give up. Instead, they apply more effort, which is likely to be helpful. When stuck, or aware that they are not performing skillfully, they ask others for advice. They are also more likely to cooperate with others in working toward common goals over time than those motivated by being good at something.

Being driven to be better at something is about intrinsic motivation. The desire for the outcome comes from within, and so does the validation of how well the person thinks they are doing. The person with getting-better motivation may be less affected by criticism and rebuke from others. They are less likely to engage in social comparison, and as a result they are less distracted by how others are performing. But they still benefit from social support and hearing others' tips for managing themselves when the going gets tough.

So, which kind of motivation behind goal seeking is better? Halvorson maintains that "it depends" on the nature of the reward for achieving a goal and whether people are pursuing goals in areas that are complex or unfamiliar, or where there are known obstacles. When the performance is relatively straightforward or even easy, or the content manageable even if onerous (like all the memorization required to pass the Bar or the CPA exam to practice law or accounting), those motivated by being good at something may find that this serves them better. When the activity involves highly skilled, complex behaviors that a person will use over time, getting better at something is the more helpful motivator.

To summarize other key findings regarding goal pursuit: motivation theorists have found that, on average, people who *believe* they *will* do well actually will do better than those who predict that their performance will fall short. And it turns out that believing you will do well works better for people who are motivated primarily by getting-better goals. This is because they will be less daunted by difficulties and obstacles and will demonstrate greater persistence in their efforts toward learning and mastery more than those who typically are motivated by being good at something.[4]

This happens because the getting-better motivated folks tend to believe that they will reach their objectives if they keep putting forth the effort, so they remain resolute in the face of obstacles. They also see value in learning from the efforts they expend, even if success will be very hard to achieve in the long run. Ultimately, as Halvorson states, "When the task is difficult and persistence is the key to higher achievement, get-better mastery goals have the clear advantage" over the being-good goals.[5]

It's important to stop and note here that the desired outcome might be the same for people with either motivation. What differs is how people think about the desired end result and frame their approach, particularly when the pursuit is challenging and great effort is required. For example, performing well at work may be about mastery and development over the long-term course of one's career; or it can be about besting one's peers in reaching targets in the third quarter and getting a bigger bonus than they do.

IMPLICATIONS FOR POSITIVE PSYCHOLOGY TECHNIQUES IN COACHING

Given that a basic tenet of positive psychology is using optimistic thinking to bolster motivation, we might assume that optimism is the right way to push for whatever goal we are seeking. The latest research and new summary of older findings show that this is not always true. Why? To answer this question, let's recap the primary distinctions between *being good at something* motivation and *getting better at something* motivation.

When you are striving to be good at something, you are being competitive—you need to beat someone else for the best grades, the top scores, the highest quarterly revenue; to be the first to own the newest customized gadget or possess the trendiest information; or to win over the most attractive mate. Here we are talking about extrinsic motivation and pleasing and impressing others. It's about using personal characteristics such as intelligence and attractiveness to get what you want. It's also the best way to motivate yourself when you must outperform others.

However, when the going gets tough, someone trying to achieve a being-good goal is likely to feel like giving up and may falter in their efforts much too soon, often just when a strong push is needed to get to the finish line. Your client will benefit from you, their coach, cheering them on, reminding them that their characteristics or traits are sufficient and that their activities around preparation, study, and optimal performance can make the difference in attaining the goal. You can urge them to stay focused on this shorter-term, more tactical outcome with exhortations like "I know you can do it!" This goal pursuit tends to be more private for the person. This means that the client is not likely to want to share their disappointments with others. They will not be inclined to ask for support or guidance.

On the other hand, when a client has a getting-better motivation, you coach them quite differently. When the going gets tough, you remind them of the long-term benefits of making changes related to enduring well-being, or acquiring skills they can deploy for many months or years. You can invite them to brainstorm on what other social support, additional information, or training can help them move through a challenging time. You can encourage them to think of experts they can shadow to better learn complex skills, or whose mentoring might give them a boost.

When coaching a client motivated to get better at something, you can explore whether they would like to use social media to gain support by going public with their goals. Tips, war stories, and ways to overcome obstacles can all be shared experiences, from which the client can glean valuable insights. Sharing tales with others along the way can help the client gain perspective and insight regarding how to overcome challenges. Tough times can be understood as normal phases that most people experience when putting forth an effort over a period of many months or even years. Clients can come to understand that others have been there too, and gotten past the tough times. Getting-better goals tend to be intrinsic, self-referenced, and have more staying power.

PROMOTION-FOCUS VERSUS PREVENTION-FOCUS GOALS: HALVORSON'S SUMMARY OF THE SECOND TYPE OF MOTIVATION

Halvorson also describes extensive research that demonstrates that there are goals with a *promotion focus*, which is distinct from a *prevention focus*.[6] Promotion-focus goals concern things we would like to do and involve our maximizing gains when we put forth effort. (Note that promotion-focus goals include *both* being-good and getting-better goals.) With promotion-focus goals, we hope to acquire a new skill or to attain something desirable—attention, accolades, or someone's love. When we are motivated by promotion-focused goals, we are seeking achievement, accomplishment, and positive outcomes. We are operating in approach mode. In contrast, the aim of prevention-focus goals is to avoid mistakes, thwart or fend off problems, and protect ourselves from losses. Prevention-focus goals are oriented toward fulfilling duties and obligations, in order to avoid shame, embarrassment, or disapproval. We pursue prevention-focus goals to stay out of harm's way—as Halvorson puts it, we are trying to keep our lives "free of negatives."[7] Doing things the right way helps us avert trouble and feel safe and secure.

What is important to note here is that the desired end result can be the same—for example, wanting to do well at work. Given the type of motivation driving us, we may strongly wish to avoid being criticized by our family and friends for not doing well on the job. Or, in contrast, we may be motivated by a desire to perform optimally in order to feel satisfied and to enjoy the perks (praise from the boss, bonuses) that doing well at work will bring.

Thus, our perceptions and subsequent approach will be different, depending on whether we have a promotion or a prevention focus. We can frame these two different types of motivations in terms of gains and losses. Halvorson maintains that each of us has a "dominant focus," either promotion or prevention. Understanding our client's dominant focus can be helpful in deciding how best to apply positive psychology techniques in our coaching.

So, how does being optimistic about gaining something or receiving positive feedback have an impact on promotion focus versus prevention focus? The person with a promotion focus is highly invested in succeeding. They care a lot about reaching the goal. Staying motivated and persisting in their efforts are enhanced by receiving positive feedback. As Halvorson puts it, "the more you seem to be succeeding, the more motivated you become. Increasing confidence heightens your energy and intensity [toward goal pursuit]. Negative feedback ... dampens your eagerness. Feeling like you might fail saps your motivation."[8]

But for a person with prevention focus, motivation does not feel like an eagerness to pursue the desired end result. Instead, as Halvorson comments, prevention-focus motivation feels like "vigilance, a desire to stay clear of danger. Vigilance actually increases in response to negative feedback from others or doubting yourself. There's nothing like the looming possibility of failure, the very real likelihood of danger, to get your prevention juices flowing."[9]

Sensing failure, those with a *prevention* focus will feel *more* motivated; they will try harder and put forth greater effort. In the same situation, those with a *promotion* focus will feel *less* motivated and may slow down their pace, or abandon altogether their pursuit of the goal.

The point here for us as coaches applying positive psychology techniques is that these motivational distinctions are real. This means that the kind of feedback we give may diminish our client's motivation if they are prevention-focused. We would be mistaken if we assumed that optimism should always be offered or that positive feedback is always the best way to support our clients in making progress toward goal attainment. Halvorson's research shows that it is not so simple. In what may seem counterintuitive but has nevertheless been demonstrated by the research, people with a prevention focus are motivated by *criticism*. Those with a promotion focus are motivated by *applause*. This empirical finding has important implications for us as coaches.

COACHING THOSE WITH A PREVENTION FOCUS

For those with a prevention focus, successful goal pursuit is enhanced by suppressing optimism and curbing enthusiasm and confidence. Remaining vigilant requires the person not to get too positive about reaching the outcome, but rather allowing uncertainty to stimulate more effort. Learning from negative role models can be helpful. Citing Barbara Ehrenreich,[10] Halvorson makes the case for "vigilant realism" for those with a prevention focus, in contrast to the optimistic outlook helpful for those with a promotion focus. Those with a prevention focus will be soothed by conditions and actions that enhance security, such as lifetime warranties, robust insurance policies, anticipating and planning for emergencies, and yielding to a more conservative bias by saying no more often when considering risky situations.

Those with a prevention focus will benefit from coaching that helps them cope better with others' rejection or exclusion, which is likely to prompt them to withdraw. They will also be aided by coaching that teaches them how to manage their anxiety and even panic when something goes wrong and how to refocus on what they can actively do to keep an upsetting event from happening again in the future.

COACHING THOSE WITH A PROMOTION FOCUS

Those with a promotion focus will be energized by ideas like "nothing ventured, nothing gained" and by taking greater risks. Their propensity to be more exploratory can be supported and celebrated by us as coaches. Because their motivation tends to wane over the long haul, they will be aided by coaching that helps them build on each small win and leverage what they have achieved. Keeping them thinking that the goal is within reach can be beneficial in sustaining their effort. Those with a promotion focus can be reminded to increase their approach actions in order to successfully pursue the attention of the desired other.

HALVORSON AND HIGGINS: "DO YOU PLAY TO WIN—
OR NOT TO LOSE?"

In a fascinating piece that appeared in the *Harvard Business Review*,[11] Halvorson and E. Tory Higgins elaborated on her work in *Succeed*. The provocative title captured a fundamental difference in being motivated by a prevention focus versus a promotion focus.

In illustrating the two types, the authors noted, "Promotion-focused people see their goals as creating a path to gain or advancement and concentrate on the rewards that will accrue when they achieve them. They are eager and play to win.… Prevention-focused people, in contrast, see their goals as responsibilities, and they concentrate on playing it safe.… They are vigilant and play not to lose, to hang on to what they have, and to maintain the status quo."[12]

Halvorson and Higgins encourage their readers to create what they call *motivational fit* between co-workers—that is, to match the boss's style of feedback with the employee's predominant motivational focus. They further suggest that this fit include the way in which goals are discussed and set and how incentives are offered and negotiated. Even role models and the type of messages can fit well or not so well. They note, "The promotion-focused are more engaged when they hear about an inspirational role model, such as a particularly high-performing salesperson or uniquely effective team leader. The prevention-focused … are impressed by a strong cautionary tale about someone whose path they shouldn't follow, because thinking about avoiding mistakes feels right to them."[13]

Just as the authors indicate ways to maximize the fit of motivation style between boss and employee, we can learn from this research and apply it to our coaching. We find that paying attention to our clients' preferred focus—whether promotion or prevention—can guide us in aligning our feedback and queries with their perspective on the world. We believe that we have become more effective coaches as a result of identifying this motivational preference.

We also appreciate the insight from Halvorson and Higgins that job fit is influenced by motivational preference. In roles where the employee helps a company remain compliant around regulations and state and federal requirements, prevention-focused folks are likely to be better suited. This is also true for roles in which a person's job is to enhance safety by reducing risky practices and enforcing proper procedures in industries, such as oil and gas, where the consequences of mistakes are dire—think Exxon *Valdez* and the BP oil spill. Prevention-focused employees can serve an organization (and feel well suited to doing so) by helping anticipate hazards, assessing risk, and providing oversight of daily safety practices.

Promotion-focused folks are better suited for "green fields" or "blue sky" thinking—for visioning, imagining, innovating, and helping define the high-level strategic direction an organization would benefit from taking. Their promotion focus aids them in sales and in managing other sales professionals, whose optimism must be sustained in order to close deals. If you are seeing some interesting themes here, the research indicates that they are real differences. If we understand these motivational differences in our clients, we can better tailor our coaching work.

WRITING A CLEAR ACTION PLAN

Whether it's being-good versus getting-better motivation or prevention versus promotion focus, Halvorson reminds us that *all* goal seeking is enhanced by writing a clear, definitive plan that states the specific outcome (the *what*) and the timing (by *when*). The steps in reaching the goal (the how) can be usefully put into if-then statements that guide action. For example:

- If it's Monday, I exercise at the gym for forty-five minutes.
- Only if it's after 4 PM on weekend days or holidays can I enjoy six ounces of wine.
- If I'm ever offered a cigarette, I will say no.
- When I see Mary in our photography class, I will say hello and get a conversation going.
- If I'm the lead on our team's pitch to the client, I will prepare the first draft of our materials within three days and give it to the group to review within twenty-four hours.

The other key reminder from Halvorson is that imagining reaching the goal is not enough to ensure that you will attain it. Anticipating all the obstacles and planning how to overcome them is a second critical activity in succeeding.

As a peak-performance expert, I (Sandra) would add to these two steps an assessment of current skills to identify what may be missing that is critical in reaching the desired end result, regardless of the underlying motivation. The coachee then can address any skill deficits first. Or, if the skill is present but the coachee is not deploying it (a performance deficit situation), then the conditions or reasons for this can be explored and addressed. Of course, this information may come up in the listing of obstacles. I recommend that skill assessment be part of the up-front planning, in addition to listing and finding ways to manage impediments to attaining the goal.

THE IMPORTANCE OF MINDSET IN GOAL ATTAINMENT

As she tells it, one of the major influencers in Heidi's early career was Carol Dweck. I (Sandra) had the pleasure of hearing Carol present her work on mindset at the 2011 annual APA convention in Washington, DC. She was a faculty member in psychology at Columbia, Harvard, and the University of Illinois before joining Stanford University's Department of Psychology in 2004, where she still is at the time of this writing. She has been focused on social psychology and theories of the origins of intelligence.

She became well known to the general public after the publication of her book *Mindset: The New Psychology of Success* in 2008.[14] In this book, Dweck explored the differences in people's attribution about their intelligence, whether they perceived it as innate and unchangeable—a "fixed mindset" or a "growth mindset." In a growth mindset, people believe that they are not restricted by innate limitations and that their efforts can lead to success. In a 2008 interview, Dweck said:

In a fixed mindset, students believe their basic abilities, their intelligence, their talents, are just fixed traits. They have a certain amount and that's that, and then their goal becomes to look smart all the time and never look dumb. In a growth mindset, students understand that their talents and abilities can be developed through effort, good teaching and persistence. They don't necessarily think everyone's the same or anyone can be Einstein, but they believe everyone can get smarter if they work at it. Those with a growth mindset believe that their performance can be improved with effort and that [they] are not bound by fixed, immutable traits.[15]

We encourage you to explore Dweck's work through her book *Mindset*, her YouTube videos, and her website.[16] Some of you who are parents may find useful advice to give your children about the importance of effort in their academic achievement. Of particular relevance to our coaching is a quote taken from her website which captures essential points from her research:

> *Whether they're aware of it or not, all people keep a running account of what's happening to them, what it means, and what they should do. In other words, our minds are constantly monitoring and interpreting. That's just how we stay on track. But sometimes the interpretation process goes awry. Some people put more extreme interpretations on things that happen—and then react with exaggerated feelings of anxiety, depression or anger. Or superiority.*
>
> *Mindsets frame the running account that's taking place in people's heads. They guide the whole interpretation process. The fixed mindset creates an internal monologue that is focused on judging: "This means I'm a loser." "This means I'm a better person than they are." "This means I'm a bad husband." "This means my partner is selfish."*
>
> *People with a growth mindset are also constantly monitoring what's going on, but their internal dialogue is not about judging themselves and others in this way. Certainly they're sensitive to positive and negative information, but they're attuned to its implications for learning and constructive action: "What can I learn from this?" "How can I improve?" "How can I help my partner do this better?"*

What does this research have to do with our coaching? These findings have important consequences. We can encourage our clients to develop a growth mindset by explaining to them the importance of the belief that their efforts can make a difference in the present, regardless of what they are convinced are their innate or genetic endowments. We can call on Dweck's research findings as we encourage our clients to keep trying in a skillful way and to continue to put forth effort as they persist toward their goal.

We can encourage the use of the VIA strength of curiosity and of learning for its own sake to support our clients in continuing to push out of their comfort zones to acquire new skills and to put themselves in situations that are new and challenging for them.

We can coach them about the futility of praise for being "really smart" or the like. Instead, we can steer them toward a pursuit of persistent effort and help them coach themselves with statements like, "You worked really hard at that. Keep it going and you will reach your goal." We can remind them that the brain can actually adapt, truly change, when we attempt new things and push ourselves to acquire new knowledge.

We think that coaching has a lot to do with a growth mindset. We honor the work of Carol Dweck and we hope you will share it with your clients.

A Case Illustrating Halvorson's Research on Motivation

Since becoming familiar with the value of using Halvorson's assessment in identifying motivational preference, I (Sandra) have used it to good effect with nearly all my clients. When a new client, Nan, was referred to me for coaching to help her with her nonfiction writing, I asked her to complete Halvorson's assessment and the VIA Survey.

Nan's motivation scores revealed that she was highly driven to "get better at something," much more than "being good at something." At age thirty-four, this did not surprise her. She had completed a degree in literature, with honors, at a top-tier state university. She had been hired from a pool of fifteen candidates for a prestigious editor's-assistant job with a publisher in a major East Coast city. She had married the man she believed was her soul mate, and they were raising twin girls in their first home in the suburbs. She commented to me that she felt she had "already competed" well in her field after earning outstanding grades and had won the heart of someone she and her friends thought was special.

When I asked her to reflect on earlier instances when she had demonstrated that she was becoming better at something, she paused and thought for several minutes. "You know," she said, "I was developing long-term practices when I decided to stay fit after graduating from university. I joined a gym and went regularly three times a week. I decided to eat well, no matter what happened, when I took a challenging job in publishing. I helped my boyfriend, who became my husband, develop some healthy habits for eating. I think I also became better at parenting after finding out, to my shock, that we were having twins. There was no family history. I resolved after leaving the doctor's office that I'd better become twice as good at being a mother than I might have been otherwise. I asked my own mother and extended family to teach me about good mothering. My husband and I went to parenting classes. We stayed in touch with the other students, some of whom became our friends. I organized play dates and exchanges of chores so all of us new mothers could benefit from our common desire to be good parents and to help each other do that."

When Nan called me, she was ready to take a year off and pursue her own writing. What surprised her was that she felt uncertain about whether she could focus on her own work after years of evaluating others' manuscripts. She did not know whether she would demonstrate the discipline needed to pursue this interest during her leave of absence from her job. She was used to functioning optimally as a key employee who was hard-charging, exceptionally productive, and often praised by the head of the firm. She had been promoted twice and was paid well among those in her field.

We contracted for ten hours of coaching and signed our agreement. Her primary short-term goal was to establish a writing practice within three months. A more distal goal was to create an outline and three sample chapters for the fiction book she was imagining by the end of six months. A further goal was to secure an agent to send the manuscript around to publishers (other than her employer, whose focus was on nonfiction and children's literature). Nan hoped that her agent would be able to help her find a home for her work, win her at least a small advance, and negotiate a suitable contract for her.

She was clear about all these objectives and believed that the timeline was reasonable. However, she was fretful in a way that was unsettling for her. We explored the intensity of her motivation and found it was strong. When we looked at obstacles that might impede her progress, she exclaimed she'd had an "epiphany."

Nan: *That's it! I have been worrying about all the things that could get in the way of my doing this. I'm also concerned about not having structure to my day like I'm used to at work. I might just waste time, and I really wouldn't like that. It would bother me a lot to be unproductive.*

SF: *So, let's first think together about the obstacles. What do you imagine will make it difficult to create this writing practice?*

Nan: *There is no place in the house currently that is really mine. So where would I do my writing? The children attend school until two-thirty, but then I need to pick them up and I want to be with them for the rest of the afternoon. We've had a nanny for too long. Now I'm eager to spend more time with them while they're in elementary school. So, my writing needs to happen primarily while they are not in the house. I'm sure of it. My husband makes a good living but also likes having my salary. Obviously, we won't have that. I can't promise when or if my writing will make money. He says he's supportive, and I believe him, but I guess I need to be sure.*

SF: *You describe yourself as someone who is excellent at problem solving. I'm wondering how you can use that well-developed skill here to tackle each of these obstacles so you can move forward.*

Nan: *That's a great approach for me. I enjoy working through problems that seem daunting and making things happen. Let me think about what I can do here.*

As we harnessed her problem-solving skill, she became more animated. She said she felt less worried, as she systematically identified each impediment and found a solution. She secured a babysitter and took her husband to dinner at their favorite restaurant. She thanked him for all the support he'd given her as a working mother and for being her best "cheerleader" for her career. She then shared her concerns that he might feel less enthusiastic about her writing and not earning a salary for a year. Nan told me that he was stunned. He was genuinely happy that she was now turning her attention to her own writing. They had managed their money well, and they were "ready" for her to take time off as she had done during their twins' first year. "Go for it!" he told her. "You have my total backing for this."

Nan was relieved and pleased to hear his commitment. They then brainstormed on where in the house her "writer's garret" could be. They liked their family room, but they could rearrange things to use their formal living room more often than they normally did. Nan and he went shopping for the office furniture she needed, and he helped her upgrade her computer with more advanced software. The family room soon became her writing space.

She and I laid out her writing schedule, having explored when she thought she would be most likely to get immersed in the process. She decided to dedicate 9 AM to 2 PM every weekday to her writing practice, while the children were at school. She felt that this dedicated time would allow her to have fun with her children each afternoon and give her sufficient time in the morning to drive them to school and to run at least one brief errand on her way home. Her husband agreed that he would take on more of the shopping on the weekends. He added two household chores to his current list.

SF: *So nicely done. You've tackled the obstacles one by one. I think your approach embodies what Stanford researcher Carol Dweck calls a growth mindset. It's about seeing learning as positive. It's also about seeing that, through our efforts, we can become more skilled at something we did not originally think we could do very well.*

Nan: *That's right. I saw her YouTube video on raising kids to have a growth mindset and really was impressed. I hadn't thought it could apply to me as well as my girls.*

SF: *Yes, indeed, it can. Now, what else will support your practice?*

Nan and I discussed her joining a writers' group where she could read her drafts to the other budding writers. She asked for and secured her boss's agreement to assist her in finding an agent, providing the schema for the book proposal, and reviewing the outline and sample chapters.

I suggested a resource to Nan as a new fiction writer. She had never written a plot and had expressed concern about how best to map out her story. I referred her to the website for Martha Alderson, who is well known for her *Blockbuster Plots* manual, workshops, and telephone consulting.[17] Nan checked out Martha's work and was excited about using the advice in her own writing and perhaps enlisting Martha's consultation as she initially mapped out her story.

SF: *What strengths did you discover in the VIA that you can bring to your writing practice?*

Nan: *I liked doing the VIA assessment. I clearly can apply my Creativity, Persistence, and Curiosity strengths to my writing practice.*

SF: *How do you think that you can leverage these strengths as you take on this new phase of your life?*

Nan: *I do experience myself as a creative person and see my writing practice as an expression of that. I think I will post quotes on the wall from my favorite fiction writers to remind me I am joining their cohort and bringing my creative process into the world as they did. There are many examples of my being persistent when I think back to my days at university, when I was a mother of infant twin girls, and when I dealt with tight deadlines in my job.*

SF: *How can you remind yourself of those times when you exhibited the strength of persistence?*

Nan: *I am very visual. I will put pictures of the girls and my favorite photo of me on my desk in my writing space. I have a letter of commendation from my boss that I treasure. I'll put it in a beautiful frame and hang it where I can see it when I am writing.*

SF: *One of the things that Halvorson reminds us from her research is that "getting better at something" motivation involves engaging in practices for the long haul, over a period of months and even years. She reminds us that there are times when we will feel tired, discouraged, and like we might want to give up. These are the times, when we are understandably faltering, that remembering to call on sources of social support can be incredibly helpful. Halvorson mentions using social media, chat rooms of like-minded folks, and other groups of people to keep us going with their cheers, their tips for managing through the rough spots, and their encouragement. As you hear about her suggestions, what could you do when the going gets tough, as it will for most of us, in doing something important for the long haul?*

Nan: *These are great ideas and help me be ready for those challenging times. I think the writers' group I'll be joining will definitely be one source of support. I'll ask my husband to cheer me on. I might call Martha Alderson for consultation or get involved with her workshops to see what ideas they provide for keeping going, as well as for writing great plots. This has been a really helpful conversation. Thank you.*

CHAPTER 8

Applying Positive Psychology for Productivity and Well-Being at Work

T his chapter offers our perspective and a number of tools useful in the application of positive psychology to the workplace. If you are an internal coach in an organization, we think you will be inspired by the front-lines report from contributor Geraldine Haley. She introduced strengths-based approaches and created the infrastructure and momentum to sustain their use with key employees of Standard Chartered Bank, high-level bankers. You may be prompted to consider replicating her success in your company. You'll also read about how to create trust in organizations and within other groups using Judith E. Glaser's elements of Conversational Intelligence.

Behavioral scientists and leadership development researchers have created a body of knowledge and best practices from which you can draw, whether as an external executive coach or as an internal coach inside a company. Positive psychology aims to enhance both the productivity and the well-being of employees, and these both have effects on the profitability of an organization. In this chapter, we speak about techniques suitable for individual clients and teams, and approaches and methods that could have an impact at the organizational level.

GALLUP'S RESEARCH ON WELL-BEING IN THE WORKPLACE

Research conducted by Ed Diener and colleagues provides evidence regarding the connection between happiness and workplace success.[1] Likewise, the Gallup organization has been involved in the study of organizations that shape their environment and their performance-management practices to enhance the well-being of their people.[2] Results of such interventions include desirable employee behaviors such as coming to work on time and taking less sick leave. At the aggregate level (referring to the whole organization), private-sector companies that demonstrate higher employee well-being have better business outcomes at the business-unit or division level, higher reported customer satisfaction, and a better bottom line (higher profitability).

When you unpack the Gallup research to understand what specific interactions made a difference, you see good results from some startlingly simple behaviors. Of particular note is the highly positive impact on employee well-being when a manager paid attention to a subordinate and took interest in that person's job activities and their life outside of work.

This beneficial effect was even greater when the manager focused on the employee's strengths and how the employee could use these capabilities, talents, and virtues as they carried out their daily responsibilities. Likewise, when employees spent time around other happy employees, this positive emotion seemed to be contagious and multiplied the beneficial aspects for those "exposed" to positive emotions. And when employees reported having fun at work or working in an atmosphere that was fun, they also reported higher levels of well-being.

In the Gallup research, having a best friend at work corresponded to that employee's being seven times as likely to feel engaged by their job, being more engaged in serving customers, having fewer industrial accidents and injuries, and reporting greater levels of well-being than employees lacking this significant relationship in the workplace.[3] Another finding was that employees who rated their career well-being as high (reporting high satisfaction with their career to date) were at least twice as likely to be thriving in their lives, compared with employees who rated their career satisfaction as low. Happier employees are more likely to help customers in an engaged way. This may account for Gallup's finding of higher customer satisfaction scores for companies whose employees report higher well-being.[4]

HAPPINESS AT WORK AND ITS MANY BENEFITS

Sonja Lyubomirsky and her colleague at the University of California, Riverside, Julia K. Boehm (now at Chapman College), evaluated a broad range of studies[5] involving three different research designs: longitudinal (research that looks for evidence of temporal order—that is, this factor or state preceded another—but cannot address causality); cross-sectional (research examining the evidence for correlations and the existence of relationships between variables); and experimental designs—in this case the authors note that "induced positive or negative emotions via random assignment provide the strongest evidence for causality."[6] Boehm and Lyubomirsky's review of studies investigating happiness and success at work is impressive in its scope and the overall sample sizes. This helps us as coaches be confident about extrapolating the study's findings to the real-world work situations in North America in which our clients spend their time. Internal coach-employees working in the United States and Canada should thus be well armed with data supportive of positive psychology interventions in their workplace. The essential findings across a variety of work settings indicate "that happiness is not only correlated with workplace success but that happiness often precedes measures of success and that induction of positive affect leads to improved workplace outcomes."[7]

Specific outcomes suggest that employees who experience high positive affect describe their jobs in positive terms; express greater job satisfaction; report a higher degree of autonomy in carrying out their work activities; are rated more highly by their managers on objective metrics; are likely to display more "good corporate citizen" behavior in protecting the company's assets and reputation; work in a more conscientious manner; are perceived as more cooperative with colleagues; and are more likely to participate as a volunteer in outside projects.

Employees who experience positive emotions are more engaged with their work and less inclined to manifest withdrawal behaviors such as burnout, absenteeism or leaving their company. They may manage conditions of organizational change more effectively than their less happy counterparts. The findings suggest that feeling happier at work is related to feeling and behaving in ways that demonstrate greater commitment to the job and to the employer.

What can we do as coaches to apply these findings? We can begin our coaching conversations by sharing the research findings regarding why it's so important to help create a climate at work in which all employees can experience more positive emotions. We suggest that those of you who work as external executive or business coaches consider discussing with your clients their network of relationships at work. We also suggest that you explore how well they feel their teams are functioning and how cooperatively their peers and leaders share information and support one another across organizational boundaries.

We ask our clients whose goals are work-related to reflect on who might become their best friend in the workplace, citing the possible benefits of cultivating such a relationship. We explore with them who is a trustworthy, "friendable" colleague with whom they have things in common and can imagine spending time over lunch or coffee or walks around the organization's site.

We ask our clients about the mood they characteristically bring with them to work. If the client tells us it is less than positive throughout the day, we explore the possibility of entering the workplace with an intention to be more engaged with others, beginning with saying hello and taking a few minutes to chat, and asking them a bit about their lives outside of work (without becoming too intrusive, of course). As we coach clients who manage others, we explore how that person can do their part to pay more attention to their direct reports and allocate time to help them cultivate and deploy their strengths on the job. There is strong evidence that devoting time to positively focus on subordinates and peers can raise employees' level of positive emotions in ways that can favorably impact a unit's or even an entire company's bottom line.[8]

In our conversations with managers who came for coaching to address problems with their direct reports, we remind them of the most recent Gallup survey regarding why most people leave their jobs.[9] The number-one reason employees quit is because they report to a "bad boss." We encourage our coachee managers to look at what they can do to enhance their relationships with direct reports and share with them the benefits of creating a positive climate as part of the changes they are considering.

Positive Psychology within Standard Chartered Bank
—by Geraldine Haley

In this section we share with you the positive impact of systematically deploying strengths-based approaches at a large global bank. We are so pleased that Geraldine Haley agreed to contribute this report from her "front lines" HR work for a global financial institution.

In 2000 Dr. Tim Miller joined Standard Bank as the group head of HR, and a series of strategic people decisions were made to support the organization's development at a pivotal time in its history. In essence, there was optimism that this organization could grow significantly and fulfill its strategic ambition to be the best international bank in its chosen markets of Asia, Africa, and the Middle East. In particular, it was recognized that creating a senior cadre of leaders who could quickly reach their potential and create outstanding performance for themselves and their teams was going to be critical to future success.

In thinking about the top one hundred leaders who could have a significant impact, it was decided that a significant shift to a positive psychology approach would re-energize leadership energy around people and performance and move from deficit-based to strengths-based development conversations. We partnered at the time with the Gallup organization and embarked on a very interesting journey, not only to adopt a strengths-based approach to development but also to survey and create an understanding around staff engagement.

Before going into the detail, it is worth reflecting now on the impact of these decisions. This organization has delivered record profits over the last ten years. Profit grew from USD 1,262 million in 2002 to USD 6,876 million in 2012, and the employee base expanded from 29,000 to 89,000. Our leadership development practices are now signature processes for us.

The original thinking on leadership effectiveness focused on:

- Self-awareness, which helps to create new responses and adaptiveness
- The ability to reflect and learn from experience (to build skills, knowledge, and new behaviors)
- Exceptional performance through playing to strengths and leveraging excellence from your team
- Attracting talented people and inspiring them to do exceptional things
- Influencing broadly throughout the organization, both formally and informally
- Focusing on longer-term goals; balancing the important with the urgent
- Recognizing integrity and authenticity as personal values and as highly congruent with organizational values

- Managing and prioritizing time and energy toward clear life goals
- "Being" rather than doing

These principles have stood the test of time. They underpinned the interventions outlined below and have evolved into the future-focused set of leadership capabilities described in Figure 1.

Fig. 1: Leadership Capabilities at Standard Chartered Bank

SCB Leadership Framework — *What the future outcomes might look like:*	
SUBJECT MATTER EXPERTISE ("A GIVEN")	
SENSING THE FUTURE	The world is changing very quickly. We need to encourage leaders to obsessively scan what is out there, see how new patterns and trends are forming and work out how that impacts markets, customers and our people. *Our leaders are intensely curious, they are intrigues by external events and always open to new possibilities. This is in the spirit of tremendous hope and ambition for our future. Focused on the long-term health of the Bank in the context of a sustainable world agenda.*
WHOLE PERSON	People who are self aware, authentic, ethical and skillful are best equipped to handle the challenges of the future. This means attending to our physical, mental, emotional, and spiritual intelligence, while being politically and culturally aware. *Personal humility. The ability to engage the right brain and engage in non-linear, nonOrational, divergent thinking. Able to explore alternative models of the organisation — for example seeing it as a human system as opposed to a machine. The ego maturity to hold complexity and create conditions where others can also handle uncertainty productively.*
DISTRIBUTED INFLUENCE	In a matrix organisation we need influential leaders who think win-win, value engagement and collaboration and through this build the right climate for leadership at all levels. *Our leaders are impactful and passionate. They influence with a strong sense of values to do what is best for the long term health of the Bank, putting the collective agenda before their own agenda.*
INTEGRATED EDUCATION	Amidst competing demands we need to focus on the right issue and execute with drive and tenacity but with an appreciation of the whole value chain and the knock on effect of our actions and how the performance in the short term earns mid term options. *Our leaders swoop and soar. They see talent management as a source of genuine competitive advantage and demonstrates this at micro-level (in the attention they pay to their teams) and macro-level in strategic talent resourcing, development and deployment decisions.*

Looking back, we believe that a key element of our organizational success has been the quality of leadership and our ability to accelerate outstanding performance through a strengths-based approach. So how does this work?

CONDUCTING A STRENGTHS -BASED INTERVIEW

During the selection process we start with a strengths-based structured interview. This is conducted for us by the Gallup organization and provides a qualitative understanding of the strengths and talents of the individual as compared to around 60,000 leaders in their global database. This information is usually introduced between the initial and final-stage interviews so that a more comprehensive understanding of the individual can be quickly gained and the final discussions can focus on organizational fit with our culture and stated values. More importantly, in an environment where talented individuals may be courted by many banks at the same time, a personalized approach that focuses on strengths and the difference the candidate can make in the context of Standard Chartered Bank is a significant motivator.

On one's joining the organization there is significant attention during the first ninety days, with the help of an internal Leadership Effectiveness Facilitator, who partners with Gallup to provide detailed feedback to the individual on their leadership strengths. This enables them to build their self-awareness and understand how they can quickly build stakeholder credibility within the organization. Potential derailers are also discussed and understood. Some core facilitation questions are:

- What do you understand to be your core strengths that will be identified and respected quickly in this role?
- How will these align to the expectations of high performance?
- How can you leverage these to build credibility with your team and your stakeholders quickly?
- Let's also think about what could derail you and how you

can leverage the resources around you to mitigate against these risks.

- How do your strengths align to the organizational values so that your team and peers will perceive you as a role model?
- What adaptations or behavioral choices do you know you will need to make to strengthen this alignment?
- What enables you to be at choice so that you can create positive energy for yourself and others?
- Who provides you with positive energy at work that you can harness?
- Who are the role models that you know you can learn from as you think about the adaptations you want to make and the capabilities you want to build?

There is also facilitation support for a twelve-month period, which typically would involve three or four face-to-face team meetings, bearing in mind that these teams are geographically dispersed. A particular focus is given to the initial meeting, where rapport, understanding, and trust need to be built quickly between the team and their new leader. This is done through appreciative inquiry, exploring and understanding each other's strengths and key motivators both at work and outside work. In fact, during a 2.5-day intervention the first half-day is dedicated to in-depth sharing of "personal storyboards" and the use of StrengthsFinder data. StrengthsFinder is a very simple tool from Gallup which explores an individual's energies and particular interests.

Collectively reviewing the team's StrengthsFinder data enables conversations about how individuals will bring their unique strengths to the performance of the team quickly and can harness a reshaping of individual priorities based upon strengths. The other key advantage to this approach is that in a global setting, cultural differences and nuances within teams can be easily explored and harnessed. All of this is hugely energizing and motivating and creates a climate for the leader to create aspirational goals and performance levels more effectively.

As the team matures, bespoke (customized) facilitated interventions will be required, but again in the spirit of sharing, exploring, and learning, rather than assigning blame or criticism. "Courageous conversations" was a phrase that was quite well known for a period where leadership teams were encouraged to use the facilitation to have those difficult conversations that were being avoided but could have a significant impact on the performance of the team or the function that they were leading. A leader moving into a new role would be given similar support, and as their tenure matures, during say the second year, a Leadership Effectiveness Facilitator may still work with them, though less frequently, to ensure that they are refreshing their understanding about themselves and how their strengths and limitations are impacting others.

Our global leaders are also developed together through a core suite of leadership development programs. The design of these programs centers on experimenting with provocative specialist external faculty, interwoven with facilitated peer coaching so that a new frame of reference on self-awareness and collective leadership can be explored. Individuals are invited to share both their personal and their professional journeys and to reflect on how these interrelate closely with their aspirations and the underlying purpose of the corporate "Here for good" brand and at the individual legacy level. We are fostering a leader-led learning approach to our work, where leaders bring their own life stories to others through storytelling, with self-disclosure linked to values, and share in the everyday realities of taking group-wide ownership of the key adaptive challenges we face.

More radically, we are taking a multi-level approach, developing our top leaders alongside the talent of the future in our growth markets (such as China and India), with a powerful combination of cross-cultural mutual mentoring, experiential field research, and focused project work. While we benefit from a highly diverse population of leaders, there is a real appetite for taking inclusive leadership and emotional intelligence to the next level through shifting our mindsets and dialogue. "Many come to China to change China, but leave being changed by China," said a Chinese mutual mentor.

It is unusual to have a team of internal Leadership Effectiveness Facilitators, and we are often asked why we do this. In essence, the real advantage is that these individuals have organization context and can therefore quickly assimilate and understand the total environment in which leaders are operating. Particularly for teamwork, they are therefore able to support and challenge the content as well as the process, and this enables them to be exceptionally valuable organizational development resources. We do use external resources in a selective way, identifying tutors, coaches, mentors and other specialist help and targeting specifically what an individual may need. We induct all our external resources to understand a positive psychology and strengths-based approach so that they can work within this framework to align with ours.

A senior leader in the organization said:

I understand that as a strengths-based organization we are all seeking to become the best we can possibly be. The facilitation I receive enables me to seek further understanding on how I can grow, where I can perform at my best, and how I can assist my team to succeed. This can be done by leveraging the strengths I have and building on them to benefit me, the employees, and ultimately the organization. It is also through this development work that I can recognize my areas of weakness, which are important as I need to manage around these and ideally leverage the resources around me to compensate.

I see the main benefit of this strengths-based approach as the huge positivity it creates. Individuals understand how they can use their strengths to full advantage in their role and therefore be successful quickly. Positive energy is created through achievement and drives people to do more to further broaden and take on bigger challenges. In leadership roles this helps create a motivated and engaged group of employees who see the benefit of working hard to gain success. Employees feel empowered to achieve and drive themselves, without waiting for direction. An organization which has a positive culture, lives real values, is high-energy, and is focused on maximizing strengths is a great place to work.

SHIFTING FROM A DEFICIT APPROACH TO AN ABUNDANCE APPROACH AT THE ORGANIZATIONAL LEVEL

We expect that some of you work in organizations as internal coaches or HR professionals and want to help the entire organization shift to a more positive climate. We have identified certain themes that may be of interest to the leaders of companies, even CEOs and the executive boards of large global organizations, if these changes are tied to possible increases in productivity and enhanced profitability.

One of the most articulate proponents of positive psychology is Alex Linley, who founded the Centre of Applied Positive Psychology in Coventry, England. He is English, a prolific writer, and passionate about bringing strengths-based approaches to organizations in their performance management, leadership development, and recruiting activities.[10] In his edited volume, *Oxford Handbook of Positive Psychology and Work*, Linley makes a thoughtful argument for helping organizations transform their thinking from a deficit, problem-oriented framework to what he terms an "abundance approach."[11] As we think many of you will agree, most companies have traditionally followed a deficit model when solving problems they faced. Linley explains cogently that "in contrast, an abundance approach starts from a differing fundamental assumption: that the role of the manager and the organization is to embrace and enable the highest potential of both the organization and its people ... [by] identifying, understanding, enabling, and sustaining the highest potentials of what people, both individually and collectively, have to offer."[12]

Linley urges consultants and others who work in organizations not to be deterred by any initial lack of acceptance manifested by leaders when presented with new theories and possibilities. Given the number of leadership development trends over the last thirty years, it's understandable that a company's leadership would wonder whether positive psychology is just another "flavor of the month." Being able to justify this approach with sound research is truly helpful when proposing changes to leaders. Linley comments in his introductory chapter, "Don't assume that just because deficit models are the status quo that they are the right ... or the only solution. Increasing evidence points to the value and efficacy of adopting abundance approaches to organizational performance and development."[13]

A VIEW TO CREATING A POSITIVE ORGANIZATION

Another English consultant, Sarah Lewis, lays out the following activities as key to the growth of a positive and inspiring workplace:

Create a workplace that feels good; play to everyone's strengths; recruit for attitude [that is, look for potential employees who are focused on their strengths and interested in making a positive difference]; encourage positive deviation; build social capital [the value within social networks in an organization, as evidenced by positive interpersonal relationships in a workplace]; make sense together [that is, collectively examine events and issues through dialogue and attempt to make meaning of them as a group]; be an authentic leader [defined as owning one's personal experience and acting in accord with one's true self, as well as exhibiting behaviors such as acting ethically, morally and with transparency]; create conditions for change; create reward-rich environments; and be appreciative.[14]

In her book *Positive Psychology at Work*, Lewis describes the conditions that companies can aspire to as a way of building positive organizations. She notes that the interest in "positive leadership" by some positive psychology researchers has led to the exploration of "authentic leadership," found in other writings on leadership development. She also uses a phrase that you will see in other literature, "positive deviance," and comments, "a positively deviant organization is one that is flourishing, benevolent, generous and honors people and their contributions. It is focused on creating an abundance of good and positive things."[15] Here, "deviant" refers to being different in focus from that of most organizations, which are oriented toward "preventing bad things from happening and narrowing the deficit gap."[16]

APPRECIATIVE INQUIRY: ITS ROLE IN CREATING A POSITIVE ORGANIZATIONAL CLIMATE

We take particular note of Lewis's involvement with David Cooperrider's recent work in her emphasis on being "appreciative" and referring to herself as an "appreciative leader." Many of you have some or even a great deal of familiarity with *Appreciative Inquiry* (AI).

One reason AI has become included in the theories and methods of positive psychology is its focus on strengths as the "engine" that will drive engagement of people in organizations.

In the *Thin Book of Appreciative Inquiry* (a succinct AI summary), author Sue Annis Hammond explains AI's basic principle: "Appreciative Inquiry suggests that we look for what works in an organization. The tangible result of the inquiry process is a series of statements that describe where the organization wants to be, based on the positive moments of where they have been, because the statements are grounded in real experience."[17] She comments on a key difference between change management theory in its traditional approach to identify and diagnose a problem and then fix it, versus the focus in AI on what an organization does well so that it can leverage its successes.

Cooperrider and his colleague Diana Whitney write that "AI theory states that organizations are centers of human relatedness, first and foremost, and relationships thrive where there is an appreciative eye—when people see the best in one another, share their dreams and ultimate concerns in affirming ways, and are connected in full voice to create not just new worlds but better worlds."[18] At its essence, AI is about valuing the best of what is currently happening in an organization, imagining what could be happening in the future, inquiring with a small group of others as to what ought to be occurring, and then taking action to create the desired state.

The term *Appreciative Inquiry* was coined in 1980 when Cooperrider was a graduate student in the Organizational Behavior Program at Case Western Reserve University, in conjunction with his dissertation advisor, Suresh Srivastva. Cooperrider is now a professor at the Weatherhead School of Management. He sees his approach as a substantial departure from the customary focus on correcting deficiencies in workplace interactions. He has dedicated his career to helping organizations become strengths-based and far more effective for having done so. You may wish to consult his recent publications.[19]

Cooperrider and Whitney outlined the now famous 4-D Model

of appreciative inquiry in their 2005 book.[20] They believed that the overuse of "problem solving" as a model was often limiting discussion of new organizational models. Cooperrider, Srivastva, and Whitney took a social-constructionist approach, arguing that organizations are created, maintained, and changed by conversations, and asserted that methods of organizing were limited only by people's imaginations and the agreements among them. The College of Executive Coaching pioneered the use of AI applications in coaching in 2000 with our first Appreciative Inquiry and Coaching classes, taught by our colleague Robert Voyle, PsyD.

AI involves discovering what is working well and what the strengths are in an individual, team, or group, and applying those to creating and implementing a vision of a future that excites, engages, and motivates employees. There are four stages to the 4-D AI approach:

- Discovery: identify strengths, assets, and wishes
- Dream: identify the dream or vision as an expression of strengths in the future
- Design: determine a plan to realize the vision
- Destiny: take action toward the vision

In coaching, the AI approach includes ongoing support for actions toward the vision and involves the whole system as much as possible. This means handling any internal issues (such as assumptions or objections) that are in the way of achieving the vision, as well as continuing to learn about and build on strengths. Sometimes it is necessary to revisit or refine the vision as new information or opportunities become available.

HOW WE USE APPRECIATIVE INQUIRY WITH OUR INDIVIDUAL CLIENTS AND TEAMS

We find the AI focus and inquiry immensely valuable in our coaching. Particularly at the outset of executive and business coaching, we use AI-oriented questions to help our clients develop the mindset of success. We ask questions such as:

- Who are you when you are functioning at your best?

- Tell me about a peak experience when you were functioning at your very best without worrying about how others would approve or evaluate you, knowing you were doing your very best work. (I, Sandra, find this question very similar to the "success review" query used in sport psychology to facilitate an athlete's imagining their best performance in order to recreate that state at will, with its emotions, underlying motivation, associated level of arousal, body sensations, posture, facial expressions, thoughts, and images.)

- What factors allow you to be most successful, and how can you create these circumstances?

- What is your personal mission for what you want from coaching?

- What have you already learned that you can leverage and amplify?

- What in your past successes provides the information that will help you be even more successful/creative/wise/powerful in the future?

- How can you bring your full attention and skills to examining this issue [sometimes we use the client's word, *problem*] so that you can imagine an array of solutions, and find among them one really good one to try?

For teams, our experience tells us that creating energy and a mindset oriented toward solutions and action is likely to be very useful to the group as they discuss a challenge or problem.

We recognize the value of clear-eyed analysis of root causes and the importance of drilling down into metrics that describe the current state of the enterprise. We also know that an insightful analysis of competitors' strengths and weaknesses is crucial in strategic planning at the organizational, business unit, and team levels. At the same time, we value Cooperrider's work in focusing on the individual and collective strengths of the team. As we exhort the team leadership and members to cultivate and sustain a future-oriented mindset of success, we apply an AI approach with the following kinds of questions:

- What are our past successes that we can leverage to meet this current competitive challenge, marketplace issue, or missed targets?

- [If things seem particularly difficult at present, we ask:] What are we doing well right now, even as the data tells us we need to do more or make some shifts?

- When we think of our current success factors, however insignificant they might seem at times, how could they lead us forward?

- What can we learn from this setback that can reenergize us?

- What are the lessons from this incident that can remind us of who we are when we are at our best?

- What can each of us individually do differently and better, starting right now, as a result of our discussion?

- What did each of us do well today, and what did our team do well in this meeting?

We also know the importance of welcoming, acknowledging, and learning from any skepticism expressed by team members. We encourage the sharing of such skepticism, while always focusing on how it might lead us to a solution or action plan. Sometimes innovative ideas are expressed *in the form of* skepticism. When we hear such comments, we want to capture the spark of creativity in them and not try to sell group think or absolute consensus. We hope you have found this section on AI helpful and that you feel inspired to further explore this approach. In the sidebar, we offer a case study using AI principles, authored by Patricia Schwartz, a senior faculty member of the College of Executive Coaching.

Attitude Adjustment
by Patricia Rachel Schwartz, MA, PCC

I was contacted for a coaching engagement because of my strengths-based/appreciative inquiry approach. Paul was a senior manager in his forties working in the headquarters of a fast-paced international company. He had been with the firm for five years. He had always been a peak performer, working with high-end clients, who consistently gave him high ratings. He managed his project teams and collaborated with other senior managers. His relationships with colleagues were generally decent to good.

The company wanted help for Paul because over a short period HR had received unsolicited negative feedback from three of Paul's seven direct reports. HR was concerned about his behavior and its effect on morale. The feedback expressed was that Paul was micromanaging, that he sometimes overreacted, and that he was overly curt.

For background, the VP of HR told me that the company's headquarters had recently undergone numerous staffing changes as part of an organizational restructuring. As a result Paul had an almost completely new team, which he had not been significantly involved in hiring. In addition, Paul had earlier asked to transfer to an emerging international region, but this had been denied because of his importance to national clients.

The four goals for our coaching, determined in a three-way conversation with HR, Paul, and myself, were greater self-control, a more positive attitude, modeling leadership, and increased positive interactions with Paul's team and its members. Success measures included: specific examples of positive feedback from team members and HR; significant reduction in negative feedback; and for Paul to cite daily examples of effective and

continued…

positive interactions with his team.

I integrated the Auerbach GOOD coaching model (Goals, Options, Obstacles, Do) into my coaching framework. My first step was to create a positive coaching environment, which would lead to working with the goals and developing some options with the client.

My first in-person session with Paul was set for half a day. I learned that Paul's closest colleagues were no longer working in the same office, and that he was uncomfortable with the new office culture that had formed while he was frequently out working on other projects. He said he was upset about the feedback he had received from HR. He was offended, and he said it wasn't valid. He told me he had asked to open a new region because he felt he needed a new challenge and wanted to assemble his own team. He also stated that he hadn't been able to take much time off from work for several years; he worked long hours and was heading toward burnout.

Paul and I agreed to initially focus on increasing his positive emotions to help him feel better, think more clearly, make better decisions, and improve his interaction with others. This would enable him to handle larger issues.

When we began our first session, Paul was hesitant. However, by the end of that session he was talking about how surprised he was that we did not begin by focusing on his problems. Instead, I began by using an appreciative inquiry technique. I asked him to recall a positive work experience. "Tell me about a best experience; a time when things were going very well on a team you were on or leading, when you were all pulling for the same goals and you were on top of your game, motivated, excited about your work and your team, and were feeling great. Who was involved, what was going on?" It took him a minute to get over the shock of this inquiry. Once he did, he gave me two examples of past great team experiences. After sharing these stories he was much more relaxed. He smiled and was clearly moved by recalling his past peak experiences.

One of his stories was particularly relevant to his current situation. It was related to a football championship game; he named it the Sugar Bowl story. After he told the story, I asked him what feelings he had had while he was telling it. He answered, "It felt really good to remember it."

I probed further to elicit a more specific description of those feelings. He identified a sense of calm, as if he were in a protected zone in the middle of chaos. It provoked a feeling of trust between himself and the other team members, as well as confidence, competence, and a feeling of happiness. He got a little choked up as he identified these emotions and said he had not felt these feelings in a while.

I noted for him that he felt the feelings when he remembered the story; therefore, he could re-experience them anytime, just by remembering the story. He was initially skeptical about this, but later realized that these positive feelings resided inside him, and therefore he could access them whenever he wanted.

I told him about the research on how positive emotions help open our minds to possibilities. Then I gave him some homework. I asked him to set his smartphone to remind himself four times a day to spend twenty to thirty seconds recalling the Sugar Bowl story and feeling those feelings. I asked him to keep a log of anything he noticed during or after recalling the story.

In addition, we looked into the strengths demonstrated in his peak stories. He reported that he had recently gotten so little positive feedback that talking about his strengths made him remember that he had many valuable skills in his arsenal. As the half-day session progressed, his defensiveness dissolved. We discussed his professional goals. He found the conversation to be liberating. I asked him how he might apply his strengths to his goals. He was silent, but I could see something was happening for him, so I waited. He said he had never thought about making his wishes and goals materialize by applying his strengths to them. Afterwards, he brainstormed many options for making his goals happen.

Paul has continued to use the tools he learned through coaching to manage himself and maintain a positive attitude at work. He reports experiencing a greater sense of control and more energy at work as well. Paul's relationships are also now moving in the right direction, per the feedback received.

I (Sandra) met Judith Glaser when we were both coaches for a leadership development program designed for newly promoted partners in a professional services firm. From the outset, I knew that Judith's communication with us all and her way of coaching clients were exceptional. While already a best-selling author of six other business books, including 42 Rules for Creating We and The DNA of Leadership,[21] Judith interacted with her colleagues with a compelling combination of self-assurance, in-depth experience, and humility. I invited her to share a synopsis of the work described in her 2014 book, Conversational Intelligence: *How Great Leaders Build Trust and Get Extraordinary Results.*[22] In particular, I wanted her to share the element of her executive coaching focused on establishing trust.

In the following paragraphs, she will bring her highly successful approach to life for you with her TRUST Model. We think you will be motivated to learn much more about her work.

What We Mean by Conversational Intelligence
by Judith E. Glaser

When I was sixteen, I had a teacher named Harry Weinberg, who introduced me to Alfred Korzybski's work in a field that was called general semantics. Dr. Weinberg, who was a chemist by training, drew a picture on the board that opened my mind's curiosity to the implications of every word we speak. He said that we human beings first experience the world at a chemical level, and then everything else is an abstraction. Once we put words into the equation we start to make stuff up. It all comes from our own minds and experiences. Korzybski said "the word is not the thing," and after these two huge new insights I was unable to stop thinking about *conversations.* I envisioned conversation as the "golden thread" that holds one human being in relation to another.

Conversational Intelligence was born in my mind at that young age and grew into this extraordinarily rich framework for ongoing research that enables scientists and practitioners to join forces in expanding our wisdom and scientific knowledge of the nature of how humans connect, navigate, and grow. Feral children, for example, who wander way from their families and are adopted by animals—wolves, for example—do not develop the capacity to communicate symbolically, through words. When found, and brought back to society, they often cannot adjust; their brains have passed the developmental point to be able to use symbols (language) to communicate. Conversations are our capacity to connect, to symbolize, to abstract, and to carry our worldview with us as we engage and grow with others. What we have discovered in this astounding new field is that each person holds a world in their heads. We create our imprints of reality and at all three levels—neurochemical, relational, and transformational—we make sense of our inner world and our outer world, and we talk about these worlds throughout our whole lives.

We used to think that conversations were about exchanging information. They are much more than this. Conversations are the hardwired ability to connect, navigate, and grow with others. Conversations actually take place on three levels. Level I is *transactional*, where we are confirming what we know. Level II is *positional*, where we try to persuade others of our point of view. Conversations can also be *transformational*—Level III— where we are sharing and discovering what we don't know. Level III is a whole new set of dynamics where we are open to sharing, open to influence, open to changing our minds. When we are able to elevate into Level III, we are actually "writing new realities" with each other—we are transforming the future.

Most companies and people spend more of their time in Levels I or II, confirming what they already know or convincing others they are right. This is because our brain thrives on certainty—and even though we may be making stuff up, our brain's neurochemistry drives for certainty and closure. Leaders who are able to help their organizations move into and sustain higher amounts of Level III conversations crack the code on taking their organizations to the next level of greatness. And leaders who are able to "level set" conversations— moving in and out of the levels that are appropriate for the situation—become the most agile and effective leaders in their organizations.

The key behind great conversations is trust. When we distrust others, our brain closes down and we are unable to communicate effectively. We are driven by fear, and move into protective behaviors. Our brain produces high levels of cortisol, the fear hormone, and we are unable to move into Level III conversations. However, when we believe that others will not harm us, that we can trust them to be friends, not foes, we gain an astounding ability to open up and access our executive brain—our prefrontal cortex, which has the capacity to transform our thinking and positively impact the world. When we are operating out of Level III, we tap our Wisdom, Innovation, Strategic thinking, and Empathy: we become WISE. And when we elevate how our brain works, we develop Foresight and Insight and sustain Trust. These are the skills that advance us in the moment and also evolve our human DNA. Conversational Intelligence truly is how great leaders build trust and get extraordinary results.

Priming for Trust Using the TRUST Model

Conversational Intelligence asks us to be mindful of the quality of the conversational space we create with others. When we are fearful, we cannot connect with others in healthy ways. However, when we focus on priming the conversational space for trust, reality changes right in front of our eyes. The TRUST Model has five steps: Transparency, Relationship, Understanding, Sharing, and Testing.

Step Into Trust	Refocus on Actions to Build and Sustain Trust
Step 1: *Transparency* *Quelling Fear*	*Take the lead.* Quell the amygdala by talking about the threats and fears that are standing in the way of building trust. Be open and communicate with others to share and quell threats. This sends messages of trust that the amygdala understands and translates into "I trust you will not harm me." *Refocus* on quelling the Reptilian Brain (amygdala) by shaping the conversations to openly talk about the threats and fears that are standing in the way of building trust. Open, candid, and caring conversations send messages of trust.
Step 2: *Relationship* *Through Heart Coherence*	*Take the lead.* Extend the olive branch even to people you might see as foes. Connect and engage in building relationships. Extending trust sends messages of friendship that shift the energy toward appreciation. Heart appreciation shifts our attention and intention to seek connectivity, reducing the fear of power over energy, and building power with connectivity. *Refocus* on engaging the Heart Brain by shaping the conversation to extending trust and by sending messages of appreciation to others. When we refocus on heart appreciation we create higher levels of heart coherence, which enables us to activate the wisdom of the five brains.

Step Into Trust	Refocus on Actions to Build and Sustain Trust
Step 3: *Understanding* *Through Sharing* *and Understanding* *Needs and* *Emotions*	*Take the lead.* Be inclusive. Invite people into the inner circle. Talk openly about needs and aspirations. Reframe and relabel uncomfortable conversations as opportunities to get to know what's on each other's minds. Listening with this focus in mind and heart opens new channels of communication and quells the doubts about "where I fit in." This moves us from states of distrust of others' intentions to understanding and trusting each other. *Refocus* on engaging the Limbic Brain by shaping the conversations to invite others to be included openly in conversation about their needs and emotions. Stepping into each other's shoes and seeing the world from their eyes validates the other person's worldview.
Step 4: *Shared Success* *Through Opening* *Minds to Others* *and Creating* *Strategies for* *Mutual Success*	*Take the lead.* Have conversations that focus on mutual success. Lower your attachment to being right and shift the conversation from entrenchment to discovery. Look at what success means from each other's point of view and build benchmarks for measuring success; focus on co-creating what success looks like with others. *Refocus* on engaging the neocortex by shaping the conversations to enable you to put issues and conflicts on the table without fear of reappraisal and retribution. Weave deeper threads of trust in the relationship.
Step 5: *Testing* *Assumptions &* *Telling the Truth* *Through Truth,* *Empathy, and* *Judgment*	*Take the lead.* Test assumptions about reality and perceptions. Be candid and discover gaps. Focus on closing the gaps between what you expect and what you get from others. Step into each other's shoes, and see the world from the other person's perspective—the highest level of trust that we humans are able to experience together. Then truth can be discovered together—and one view of the world emerges. *Refocus* on engaging the prefrontal cortex—the executive brain—by shaping conversations that enable stepping into each other's shoes, and seeing the world from another's perspective.

Executive coaching focuses on enabling executives to connect, navigate with, and grow employees to be the best they can be. Leaders hire the best talent they can find, put them in the best roles for their skills, and set them loose to do the best work they can. Yet we each know story after story of unmet expectations and failure to deliver on promises. This is not because people want to make mistakes, or plan to under-deliver. It's because everyone maps reality differently—we each have our own way of mapping success, or mapping what great performance looks like, and even if we are using the same words, the meanings are different.

When leaders' expectations are not met, they often act out their frustration by yelling, re-educating, or, worse, fall victim to the Tell-Sell-Yell Syndrome or Addicted to Being Right. Their levels of sensitivity to others goes down, as their fear of looking bad in front of the organization goes up. The TRUST Model is a reliable way to reconnect with others—to start over, to make up, to be transparent about what is not working, to be open, to figure out how to remap success together. Coaching executives to understand how to use this model is a game-changer in organizations.

Executives find that they can face difficult conversations with less anxiety of hidden emotional frustration, and with greater compassion to work as a partner with their employees, teams, and even clients. An incredible bonus in using the TRUST Model is that these five steps trigger the trust networks in the brain, located in the prefrontal cortex. They are the steps to access higher levels of our hardwired Conversational Intelligence. By taking these steps, we activate and co-create the brain connections in our trust network, as well as in the others with whom we are engaging. By learning to step into each other's shoes and to

> see the world from another's perspective, we can attain the highest level of sustained trust, we can overcome difficult and challenging issues, and we can bring out the best in ourselves and others—the core of what makes leaders great, and the impact that every leader aspires to be known for.
>
> *Reprinted with permission from the author, Judith E. Glaser, author of Conversational Intelligence and CEO of Benchmark Communications, Inc.*

ENGAGEMENT AND FLOW: CSIKSZENTMIHALYI AND WHAT CONSTITUTES GOOD BUSINESS

We cite Mihalyi Csikszentmihalyi's work on time and spending it well in Chapter 6. Many of you are familiar with his concept of *flow*; perhaps you have experienced it while running, or being immersed in a crossword puzzle or a meaningful conversation with friends. To us, his research on flow is the foundation in understanding the positive impact of engagement at work.

In the following section, we briefly summarize the findings described in his book, *Good Business: Leadership, Flow and the Making of Meaning*,[23] and the implications for us as coaches in helping our clients create positive workplaces.

Csikszentmihalyi beautifully demonstrates in this book the culmination of a long career spent thinking about how life and work can be more satisfying and how each person's actions could potentially improve the situation in the world. Csikszentmihalyi and his research team conducted in-depth interviews with thirty-nine American corporate leaders, who had been nominated by CEOs and by professors at major business schools. Interviewees included Anita Roddick, founder of the Body Shop, Yvon Chouinard, founder of Patagonia, Alfred Zeien, former CEO of Gillette, and Jack Greenberg, then CEO of McDonald's. The book offers conclusions drawn from the compilation of their comments, and many quotes are cited to illustrate the main ideas.

What is good business? Csikszentmihalyi, writing shortly after the Enron scandal, states first what it is *not*: not being deceitful, not selling harmful products like tobacco, and not treating employees like cogs in a machine. Good business is, as Csikszentmihalyi asserts unreservedly, enterprise where employees experience flow and develop toward greater complexity (growth), and where the organization's end product or service contributes to (positive) human growth.

The CEOs and founders interviewed for the book had, in Csikszentmihalyi's view, demonstrated that they were visionary leaders who possessed a number of important traits: optimism; integrity; ambition (defined as the desire to be the best in their industry); perseverance; curiosity; empathy; gratitude; faith in an overall purpose in their lives, or even a sense of being "called" to do what they were doing; and caring for others. The visionary leader's view could be best summed up in a quote from Max De Pree, former CEO of Herman Miller: "The most important question is not, what are we doing but rather, who do we intend to become?" It is worth noting that many of these traits are cited by Daniel Goleman as those embodying Emotional Intelligence. Goleman asserts that when these and other EI skills are consistently practiced by managers and leaders, better working conditions *and* higher profits are the results. You may also note that a number of these traits are VIA strengths as well.

The visionary leaders Csikszentmihalyi describes in his book created organizations with conditions that maximized the opportunities for experiencing flow. Specifically, the organization was a well-functioning enterprise whose employees worked "without strain" on interesting tasks and projects, with some variety, and with a sense of feeling empowered to give input on their choices about the focus of their work. While perhaps not meeting Csikszentmihalyi's optimal conditions for flow (employees are all doing work they like to do and doing it skillfully), these companies did provide pleasant working conditions, were concerned about employee development, and had clearly communicated the organization's mission as a purpose beyond just making a profit. Csikszentmihalyi cites companies such as sports-apparel maker Patagonia and real estate firm Trammell Crow as exemplary in their charitable giving, their very public stance on sustainable development in Third World countries, and their outcry against sweatshops, child labor, and polluting by multinational companies.

He sums up the lessons that can be gleaned from the interviewees as: show respect for your employees, and find ways to help each one develop in their jobs and as people. To create the conditions for flow in your workplace:

1. Set clear goals, and communicate the organization's mission often and articulately.
2. Provide immediate feedback on employee performance whenever possible.
3. Match the challenges of each job to each employee's skills.

You may be asking yourself how an actual organization, particularly in an economic down-turn, can deal with the competition and at the same time create the climate at work that Csikszentmihalyi recommends. Certainly, he is urging organizational leaders to examine their business practices and exhorting them to transform what they are doing and how they are doing it. He offers readers a high standard to strive for, by presenting the stories of leaders who he believes embody these ideals. What Csikszentmihalyi highlights as "flow," other researchers, particularly Gallup, call "engagement."[24] Having the opportunity, at work, to do what one does best is tied to higher productivity and lower turnover, as well as greater profit, customer satisfaction, and workplace safety. So, how engaged, involved, or positively "stretched" people feel at work is not just interesting theoretically but has a bottom-line impact as well. A convergence of research results points to the importance of experiencing well-being, and even (ideally and inspirationally) flow, at work.

CHAPTER 9

Coaching through Transitions and Change

C oaching to facilitate smooth transitions from one life stage to another or following a significantly challenging event can be very valuable to our clients. We believe that the techniques discussed in this chapter will be helpful for both new and experienced coaches who view themselves as having a transitions coaching niche or are finding that more of their clients want to be coached around the challenges of change.

This chapter brings together several points of view around helping clients navigate difficult shifts in their lives. We have invited our colleague and College of Executive Coaching senior faculty member Randall P. White, PhD, to share his expertise in helping those in the workplace adapt to constant ambiguity around the rapid changes at work and in their personal lives. We also cite Fred Luskin's work on forgiveness as we discuss coaching to assist clients recovering from difficult personal losses or setbacks, or disruptions in their workplace.

CHANGE THEORY AS IT APPLIES TO ORGANIZATIONS

Before we turn to specific interventions for helping clients, we briefly review the research on change theory as it applies to organizations. There is a rich literature describing how organizations can manage change, as well as findings relevant to working with individuals and teams. We look first at the established business-school approach to educating those who lead, and their followers, about transition and change. A well-known text we find helpful is *Managing Change and Transition*, a volume in the Harvard Business Essentials series.[1]

In this book, the authors review four approaches that organizations (referring primarily to private-sector companies rather than not-for-profit entities or government institutions) undertake in their attempt to change and improve when faced with disappointing business metrics, a competitor's gaining market share, or other conditions like existing technologies becoming obsolete. Companies may try to *restructure*, for example by combining units of the business to streamline processes, buying another company for its technology or customers, or selling off parts of the business that are underperforming or have become redundant. Organizations may resort to *cost-cutting* to improve profitability, which can mean eliminating departments, shrinking the budgets of functions like human resources, and ultimately laying off employees. A third possible response is to *streamline processes*—how the company's procedures are handled—to enhance efficiency, increase customer satisfaction, or boost profitability. Lastly, organizations may attempt to change by *transforming their culture*, for example to improve employee relations, by enhancing engagement, or by focusing more attention on clients or customers.

THEORY E AND RESTRUCTURING, AND THEORY O AND TRANSFORMATIONAL CHANGE

Readers who have studied business or been involved in leadership development will recognize the two main theories underlying organizational approaches to change. Theory E and Theory O are the work of two Harvard Business School professors, Michael Beer and Nitin Noria. "The explicit goal of Theory E change," they write, "is to dramatically and rapidly increase shareholder value, as measured by improved cash flow and share price."[2] This type of change is mandated by the leadership and is therefore "top down." Often external strategy consultants are hired who opine on the company's future direction while internal human resource staff implement decisions to shrink the workforce and conserve cash.

In contrast, "the goal of Theory O is to develop an organizational culture that supports learning and a high performance employee base."[3] This approach is meant to increase engagement and involvement with employees, with the goal that individuals and teams perform more optimally and that the company's bottom line will reflect the impact of this higher productivity.

Each approach produces an effect. The research on downsizing (Theory E) indicates it can destroy morale and greatly diminish participation among those who remain. Thus, cost-cutting, in the form of downsizing, "right sizing" or restructuring, may not save the company.[4] Theory O, in principle, is fundamental to building positive organizations and positive leadership. We think of Gallup's 2015 report on engagement and the beneficial impact it can have on a company's well-being.[5] A key issue faces companies that earnestly wish to become positive workplaces. Theory O programs to enhance employee autonomy and engagement may take several years to produce significant results. In that amount of time a very troubled company could go bankrupt, before the benefits of enhancing employee engagement and customer focus can have the desired beneficial impact on profitability and sustainability. The theorists thus suggest that a combination of E and O approaches is probably the best approach for saving and improving a company in difficulty.

You may be asking yourself what this has to do with coaching. Many business and personal coaches work with clients who face sometimes daunting challenges as employees of struggling organizations. Clients may seek coaching for help in navigating tough times in their organization, making decisions about their career, or setting transitional goals. When we take the time to gain an understanding of what is happening at the organizational level in their companies, we are better informed and able to more deeply comprehend their circumstances. Developing our overall business acumen and specific knowledge of our client's company aids us when assisting people with tough problems around change at work.

THE FOUR STAGES OF ORGANIZATIONAL CHANGE

These same authors, Michael Beer and Nitin Noria, set out a theory regarding the four stages of change that individuals experience in response to upheaval in the workplace. They describe the "sense of loss and anxiety" that employees experience following a shift in workplace status, the loss of the meaning the person derived from a particular role, and the ending of the responsibility the person once held.[6]

The apprehension and distress accompanying this diminution of one's fortunes and status at work can be significant, even devastating, for some. Many of our coaching clients are anxious about the unknown and feel uncertain about the future outcomes of their organization's change. Clients may also feel uneasy with the risks they associate with behaving in ways that are new to them. Some may wonder whether they can muster the wherewithal to learn and deploy new skills.

The four stages of change are presented by Beer and Noria as a linear sequence akin to the grief process as elaborated by authors such as Kubler-Ross.[7] The first stage is shock, which may manifest as denial that the change is happening, or the person's becoming "immobilized" and shutting down, with a resulting decrease in productivity. The second stage, which the authors refer to as "defensive retreat," is characterized by anger, attempts to maintain old patterns, and remaining tied to ideas and methods from the past.[8] The third stage is the person's "acknowledgement" of having "lost something" of importance. There is mourning, which may bring up both "grief and liberation." During this stage, the person gains some psychological distance from what has happened and begins the process of reflecting on the possible future and its promises, as well as leaving behind what was. The fourth and final stage is "acceptance and adaptation," during which the person may perceive the benefits of the change and begin the process of moving forward.[9] As coaches, we find such a stages-of-change framework helpful, and we commend this book to you as a useful guide in understanding change in the workplace. We also heed the authors' caution that the stages of change are not truly linear and people sometimes find themselves stuck at mid-stage. Those who struggle with workplace changes may be particularly those, the authors note, who are "emotionally fragile" due to long-standing employment circumstances or because they are facing upheaval in their personal lives, like a relationship breakup.[10]

We note an interesting recommendation the authors make to those in charge of initiating and carrying out major change in their organizations. Instead of one major program rolled out all at once with a period of no interventions thereafter, they advocate a longer-term process of continuous change. This refers to staging change programs as a series of continuous smaller interventions over a longer period of time to help minimize disruption, to help prepare employees for the reality of uncertainty and risk, and to sustain a learning curve that produces beneficial effects for the company.

CHRIS ARGYRIS ON EXPLAINING POSSIBLE AVENUES OF CHANGE TO EXECUTIVE COACHING CLIENTS

When we do executive coaching with clients who must help lead and implement change, we know that our time with these clients may be brief. Even with coaching engagements of six months or longer, we know that we compete for our client's attention. Our conversations take place in the context of numerous responsibilities, pressures, organizational political intrigues, and personal obligations and problems.

We want to bring as much value as possible to our clients in a relatively short time. In this section, we describe how we share with our clients a specific theory of learning as it relates to change. We believe that this assists our executive coaching clients in discovering that they have options in how they respond to change and the depth of learning they choose to undertake as they grapple with organizational shifts. We hope to inspire clients around the possibility of embracing change as an opportunity for personal learning and even personal transformation.

Many readers have probably heard about the work of leadership development theorist Chris Argyris, best known for his elaboration of the concept of single-loop, double-loop, and triple-loop learning.[11] Single-loop learning involves a person improving their performance of an existing skill without questioning the context in which the skill was acquired, or the personal characteristics that kept the skill from developing, or the beliefs that sustained the skill in its current state.

For example, a line manager, we'll call him Tom, receives 360° feedback that makes it clear that his raters generally view him as talking too much in an overbearing manner, as if his opinion were the only one that mattered. In their comments, some raters describe Tom as a poor listener. Prompted by his boss, the line manager agrees to speak more succinctly, come to the point more quickly, and deliberately yield the floor to others sooner.

When Tom implements these incremental improvements for several weeks, his boss observes his new behaviors and praises him for changing. The heat is off, for the moment. However, Tom has not dug deep to explore the importance of and means for lasting change. The modifications in behavior are superficial, because there has been little reflection or learning on his part.

We realize that brief coaching engagements may focus on change based on single-loop learning. We aspire to facilitate greater and longer-lasting learning with our clients and encourage you, our readers, to do the same. We thus advocate for approaches involving double-loop learning. Double-loop learning involves a person examining the patterns underlying their thinking and behavior, or, as Argyris puts it, "the cognitive rules or reasoning they use to design and implement their actions." Through taking time to ponder what they are doing and being encouraged to learn to "reason productively," a person can begin to move away from reacting defensively or blaming others when asked why they engaged in a particular action.[12]

To encourage double-loop learning, Argyris recommends that an organization's leaders create a case study to "examine their own ineffective behavior." This "legitimizes talking about issues that people have never been able to address before."[13] In the case of Tom the line manager, we would first explain the benefits of his understanding the reasons behind the behaviors that had his raters appraising him negatively. We would acknowledge that he might feel inclined to blame them for misperceiving him or failing to see the value in his opinions. However, we would express the hope that Tom would be curious about learning deeply from this feedback as a way of becoming a more effective leader.

We then begin a process of thought partnering with Tom around exploring and really identifying his listening shortcomings, from his raters' point of view. We encourage Tom to identify whether he is missing key listening skills, or may possess them but not deploy them with the peers and subordinates who were his raters. We discover that Tom does in fact listen to his boss, whose opinions and instructions he considers important to his success. In contrast, Tom does not feel it worth his time to be attentive to the inputs of his peers or the people who report to him.

We facilitate Tom's probing further into his realization, and he discovers that he devalues the opinions of many of those who are not his superiors. We then can ask him about an alternative listening strategy: to distinguish listening attentively to the *content*, as distinct from listening to the *source* of the content, that is, the person he undervalues. We ask him to reflect on his thoughts and feelings when reading or hearing the opinions of his subordinates and peers.

Triple-loop learning, as explained by Argyris, involves the organization itself in the learning. The leadership takes on tough questions about its business decisions and the basis for these decisions. There is an attempt to understand how past actions of the organization influence events happening in the present, and how these could inform future actions.

HARGROVE'S APPROACH TO TRIPLE-LOOP LEARNING

We find Robert Hargrove's approach to triple-loop learning extremely valuable in helping executive coaching clients think through actions that resulted in unanticipated errors they later recognized, mistakes pointed out to them by others, or other difficult circumstances surrounding a challenge they have faced.

Hargrove describes the steps like this. "I guide my thinking about what is needed by asking myself the following questions: 1) Does the person need to switch a way of being or a role, perhaps becoming a leader instead of a manager? 2) Does the person have ways of thinking that are leading to an inability to solve the problem or to misfired actions? and 3) Does the person need a tip on how to do the same thing better?"[14]

LEARNING AGILITY AND ITS IMPACT ON A PERSON'S RESPONSE TO TRANSITIONS AND CHANGE

Much time and effort has been devoted to assessing and teaching *learning agility*.[15] Early research on this topic came from the work of behavioral scientists at the Center for Creative Leadership, who described the ability to learn as fundamental to managing challenges and change.[16] Instrumental in the development of the learning-agility model were the authors of the book, *The Lessons of Experience: How Successful Executives Develop on the Job*. These were Morgan McCall of the University of Southern California's Marshall School of Business and Michael Lombardo and Ann Morrison of the Center for Creative Leadership in San Diego.[17] These authors concluded that, essentially, the greatest leadership development came not from mentoring, formal training, MBA programs, or even coaching. Instead, it was challenging assignments and the resulting on-the-job experience that accelerated learning and an employee's career trajectory from manager to leader. In later research, those who were found to be learning agile benefitted the most from real-time lessons on the job while being responsible for *fix it* situations or completing international assignments that placed them in vastly different business environments and in cultures strange to them. Eichinger and Lombardo can be credited with definitively describing learning agility as a person's ability to learn from their experience and then to later apply that learning to perform well when in new conditions, for example after a promotion.[18]

These authors assert that individuals with high learning agility are able to glean the right lessons from experience. Eichinger and Lombardo also considered learning agility to be one important element of potential.[19] So, when we coaches talk about identifying the high-potentials or *hi-po's* in an organization, we are talking, in part, about the level of learning agility demonstrated by employees.

Key elements in learning agility have to do with adapting rapidly to novel situations with a sense of curiosity, a desire to grow, a willingness to take risks, and an appreciation of the wisdom of uncertainty. One of the most eloquent speakers on embracing the uncertainty that comes with change is our colleague, Randall White, PhD. Randy was involved in the Center for Creative Leadership from its early days, working closely with Eichinger and Lombardo. He has become an often consulted expert in leadership development programs for large multinational companies, as well as an internationally recognized coach. He and his colleague Philip Hodgson, a long-time professor at the famous Ashridge Business School in the United Kingdom, authored the book *Relax, It's Only Uncertainty.*[20]

We asked Randy White to share with you his key points as useful coaching tips. You may also be interested in becoming certified in the use of his 360° instrument for assessing capability around managing change, the Ambiguity Architect.

Harnessing the Opportunity of Ambiguity
Randall P. White, PhD

Uncertainty is uncomfortable for everyone. For some, however, uncertainty is also a catalyst. As an emotional response to an ambiguous situation, uncertainty is inevitable in our work, our careers, and our home lives. In our work of coaching global executives we see that the response to ambiguity (uncertainty) can derail an otherwise promising career. And we have detected a pattern that suggests that successful executives share an important skill in this regard: the ability to effectively engage uncertainty by heading toward it.

In over three decades of coaching, classroom work, and evaluation of data from thousands of subjects using our multi-rater assessment, the Ambiguity Architect,[21] we believe that being adept with uncertainty is one primary behavior of successful leaders. We are equally confident that it can be measured, developed, and improved, which is a large part of what our firm does while teaching leadership and coaching leaders for development.

The Ambiguity Architect™ hinges on ratings for eight Enabler scales and eight Restrainer scales. Enablers and Restrainers are tendencies we all have in varying degrees, and the rating a subject receives from the Ambiguity Architect is derived from the numerically weighted responses to sixty-four questions in the assessment.

For this discussion, we will focus on the Enablers, because they each validate the principles of positive psychology while articulating behaviors that are demonstrably linked not only to executive success but also to engagement and fulfillment in our work and day-to-day lives. Those who show high

continued...

tolerance for ambiguity can see a very negative workplace situation and, rather than complain, seek the positive energy or actions that are causing the conflict or chaos. They are not merely optimists. They are able to infer opportunities where others only see problems.

For executive coaching outcomes we suggest that being comfortable with the uncertainty of ambiguous situations— markets in a state of flux, post–financial crisis dynamics, rapidly changing technology—is an asset, because ambiguity in the marketplace is like reshuffling a deck of cards: you can benefit from being dealt a new hand. This presents an opportunity for the intrepid, the curious, the insightful, and the imaginative to introduce new ideas and methods, unbound by old perceptions and gatekeepers.

Henry Mintzberg, a thought leader in business strategy, was known for his emphasis on the importance of *emergent* strategy—unintentional patterns in organizations that are observed and adopted—as a complement or alternative to *deliberate* strategy. The nature of emergent strategies is such that an executive may not see the patterns if he is too focused on certainty. Mintzberg said, "Organizational effectiveness does not lie in that narrow minded concept called rationality. It lies in the blend of clearheaded logic and powerful intuition."[22]

THE EIGHT ENABLERS AND THEIR BENEFITS

1. *Being Motivated by Mysteries.* People who are mystery seekers appear to get their energy from the unknown or from the state of not knowing. They might even be happy when an attempt or experiment doesn't work out the first time. And sometimes they will test themselves even when they are fairly certain of

continued...

the correct solution, positing other options before locking in on one.

It is possible to be too certain. Often we make decisions too quickly, or we never make decisions, because we never feel satisfied with the information at hand. Mystery seekers are able to moderate that natural desire for the first idea and entertain others. They are the type to take an unfamiliar route home or explore a new path solely to see where it leads.

2. *Being Risk Tolerant.* Risk tolerance is linked to being motivated by mysteries. In the quest for decisions, trying multiple options (exploring the mystery) is often risky, because one component of risk is missing crucial deadlines. Risk tolerators are not impetuous, but they are adept at, first, understanding or calculating a risk, second, exploring options, and third, timing their final decisions to minimize the risk. Risk tolerance allows a person to make a decision even without all the information that would make it easier. We have seen that the most valuable behavior of risk tolerators is, as one client described it, "to fail fast and fail forward."

3. *Scanning Ahead.* We call people with this tendency Future Scanners, but it includes two tendencies: being a futurist and drilling deep. You will notice that the Ambiguity Architect's Enabler scales heavily value the process of questioning. Scanning ahead is where it is most vital. Future Scanners are interested in discovering the details that drive a business. They may ask questions like, "What would happen if this were to occur under different circumstances?" and "What are the implications of that action?" Future scanners are sensitive to

continued...

the faintest signals of what the future might be and are willing to exploit that to gain some advantage.

In a collaborative work environment or in leading a team, these future-scanning behaviors enhance inclusion and open the door for others to offer their own innovative suggestions. They create a Socratic learning environment that tends to flatten hierarchy and reward good thinking.

4. *Tackling Tough Issues.* Loving a challenge and being tenacious in surmounting it is one behavior we look for when assessing an executive's ability to work with states of ambiguity. These individuals don't have to be in a majority to pursue their ideas. "Confidence" doesn't describe them as well as "determination" does. We have worked with scores of top executives of global consumer brands who have demonstrated the power of tenacity with challenges in leading the development of sometimes sublime consumer innovations. With resolve as strong as Winston Churchill's, they never give up.

5. *Creating Excitement.* Our research suggests that senior executives average sixty hours or more per week on the job, often with extensive travel and most often with plenty of interpersonal interaction. This becomes as physically demanding as it is mentally exhausting. If you cannot be in a state of enthusiasm during all of this, burnout, derailment, and failure are likely.

Those who are excited about their work and also able to breed excitement in others around them are more likely to attract and inspire followers and protégés. They motivate others who want to explore the unknown in their search for innovative ideas and opportunities.

continued...

6. *Being Flexible.* This tendency is what we call our "universal compensator." With the other enablers celebrating tenacity, enthusiasm, focus, exploration—each of which can easily be overplayed to negative effect—the ability to flexibly adjust provides interpersonal leavening, so the executive is not seen as obsessive, self-absorbed, or maniacal. Instead, she is able to admit to being wrong and is able to convince others to follow and adjust to changing circumstances as they arise.

7. *Being a Simplifier.* The quote often attributed to Pascal is a clever description of the value of simplifying ideas: "I have made this longer than usual because I have not had time to make it shorter." To achieve this, as it is measured by the Ambiguity Architect, requires being an essence detector, a clarifier, and an interpreter. Sales professionals are taught to recite elevator pitches, and publishers ask authors for one-page book proposals. Marketable ideas are usually the ones that are easiest to understand.

8. *Being Focused.* Some call strategy a science of essentials. The Critical Few is the expression once used by executives at Corning Glass, referring to a short (four to five) list of engagements to which the whole organization must be attuned. The ability to maintain focus on strategic goals, according the context of a position, without being distracted carries some interpersonal risks. Others may feel slighted when what they perceive as a priority is ignored. But those who master this tend to earn their credit following the successful completion of the critical task.

continued...

THE RESTRAINERS THAT INHIBIT LEARNING

The eight Restrainers we have identified and measured with the Ambiguity Architect offer some behavioral insights of their own, but for our purposes here, they can thought of somewhat as the negative counterparts of the Enablers:

1. Having Trouble with Transitions
2. Not Motivated by Work
3. Fear of Conflict
4. Muddy Thinking
5. Complex Communication
6. Hooked on Detail
7. Narrow-band Thinking
8. Tethered to the Past

APPLYING FEEDBACK FROM THE AMBIGUITY ARCHITECT RESULTS

The Ambiguity Architect solicits assessment from peers, superiors, and subordinates to reveal scales for each Enabler and each Restrainer. As coaches, we compile the assessment data and draw feedback points for the person being coached. We try to convey this not in terms of pass or fail, but rather do more of this, less of that. And, because we believe that tolerance for ambiguity can be learned and developed, we might suggest specific actions or on-the-job experiments that allow our clients to model the behaviors they hope to make habitual.

There are two reasons to examine ourselves for these tendencies and develop our behavior to better manage ambiguity. Primarily, in our practice, the first reason is to adapt behavior that has been consistently revealed in high-performing and high-potential executives. In this sense we treat

continued...

adeptness with ambiguity as vital to senior leadership roles in which leaders must identify productive areas of uncertainty and confusion and lead their organizations into those areas to find competitive advantages.

The second reason is more important to our discussion in the context of positive psychology: to be more engaged, enlivened, and effective in our work and lives. Uncertainty is a challenge for everyone, and by its nature it is difficult to control. What can be controlled is our response to it and our ability to see ambiguous situations, looming uncertainty, and change as zones in which we can invigorate our thinking, make improvements to our lives, and experience breakthroughs and innovation. Sometimes when guidelines, expectations, and authority seem ambiguous it is a chance for each of us to establish our own rules and paths forward—or simply to invent a new future.

Coaching Applications for Harnessing the Opportunity of Ambiguity

I (Sandra) have been happily influenced by Randy's work and enjoy using principles from his book to inform my coaching. The following are three exercises I use with both personal and executive coaching clients. We think you may find them helpful.

Discovering Lessons from Past Experience

Today we can explore how to apply what you've learned from past experience to how you are approaching/going after your current goal. How does that sound to you?

Think of a past situation in which you successfully made a change that was important to you. This could be starting a new behavior that was healthy or more productive, or lessening the impact of a behavior you wanted to curtail or stop, or quitting altogether some habit or pattern that you decided you no longer wanted to engage in at all.

- Tell me about that time when you decided to behave differently.
- Briefly tell me the context around the situation.
- How did you decide to do this?
- How did you approach your goal?
- I'm thinking that you could have gone about this change in a number of different ways. Do you recall what your thinking was at that time? Why did you choose the approach that you did?
- What was the process like for you?
- What was the impact then? And now?

continued...

- What did you take away from/learn from that experience?
- As you say aloud what those lessons learned were, what themes or patterns do you notice, if any?
- What might be principles or rules of thumb that you see in what you did, if any?
- How could you apply those lessons learned as you think about reaching your current goal?

Helping a Client Develop Greater Tolerance for Ambiguous Situations and the Feeling of Uncertainty

Often, when people want to develop new well-being or other positive behaviors, they feel like they may be stepping into uncharted or new territory. The circumstances can feel ambiguous or unclear. People can wonder what will happen when they try new things. Let's take some time to explore what researchers call *ambiguity tolerance*. When working on a new goal, it can help to enhance your capacity to navigate situations which feel or may actually be quite new, unclear, and anxiety-provoking. We'll look at ways to activate other emotions and motivations to help offset what many people experience as the unpleasant emotion of uncertainty.

- When you think about your future vision of who/what you hope to become as a result of reaching this goal, what do you imagine? Tell me in detail what you imagine as your desired end result.
- What helps make this desired end result seem more real to you? It might be some role model you think of, some shared desire with another person who is important to you, or a past state where you felt more like the person you wish to become.

continued...

209

- What are your drivers/motivators for going after this goal?
- What can you do to strengthen these motivators? Some people ask support from others pursuing the same or a similar goal and might even communicate with them, in person or on social media sites.
- Imagine feeling curious about doing something new. Perhaps it's a new goal you have in mind, or maybe it's rekindling your interest in a pursuit that was important to you in the past.
- Describe the experience of being curious. Check now to see if the feeling of curiosity is pleasant. If so, we can explore what you can do to enhance this feeling of curiosity to help motivate you as you think about your current goal.
- If you feel there are obstacles in the way of reaching your goal, please say what they are.
- Then let's look at ways to overcome or work around each of these obstacles.
- Let's then look at ways you could reframe a setback, or even what you might call a failure, as an opportunity to learn something important for the future from that past situation.
- To help put these obstacles in perspective, it may help to ask yourself, "What are the five toughest things I've ever done?"
- Then ask, "What enabled me to do them?"

Helping the Client Develop Greater Overall Tolerance for Ambiguous Situations and the Feeling of Uncertainty

- Try something you would consider frivolous or silly with your family, partner, or other loved ones this weekend. See if you can behave in a more spontaneous way and notice how it feels.

continued…

- If possible, plan a short vacation to some place you've never been before.
- Visit a place (which could be a different part of your city) where another culture and language predominate. Allow yourself to experience not understanding what you are hearing and getting around as best you can without knowing the language. You may need to rely on gestures and other nonverbal cues to communicate.

FORGIVENESS AS A VALUABLE TRANSITION COACHING INTERVENTION

Why forgiveness? For some readers, forgiveness may sound like the softest side of the soft skill applications in positive psychology. Others may be thinking that forgiveness is not a topic for coaching but is better addressed by pastoral or rabbinic counseling, or by psychotherapy. We see forgiveness as a potentially helpful process to allow a client to move forward and feel freer to pursue goals and experience more positive emotions.

Seligman considers forgiveness to be of crucial importance in sustaining happiness. Forgiveness is a key component in one of the three temporal foci of positive psychology, those being past, present, and future. Our satisfaction with the past, as proposed by Seligman in *Authentic Happiness*, is determined by our capacity to feel gratitude for our blessings and to embrace and practice forgiveness. As we note in Chapter 3, forgiveness is one of the VIA strengths. To quote Seligman, "When people forgive, their basic motivations or action tendencies regarding the transgressor become more positive (benevolent, kind, or generous) and less negative (vengeful or avoidant)."[23]

Sonja Lyubomirsky also writes of the importance of forgiveness, in her book *The How of Happiness*.[24] She believes that forgiving others is one of the intentional actions an aggrieved person can take to move from being upset to being more at peace. She asserts that this process can help increase that person's happiness.

Forgiveness is of course a cornerstone of Christian theology; it also appears as a theme in writings by followers of Mohammed and in the work of Stephen Levine on death and dying.[25] The speeches of His Holiness the Dalai Lama urging compassion for those who wrong us also provide guidance and comfort for many in both East and West. Numerous spiritual traditions speak to the issue of showing mercy, compassion, and also forgiveness.

Studies show beneficial effects of forgiveness on the one who forgives. Researchers have shown the efficacy of even very simple interventions, such as *imagining* forgiving the transgressor, and these interventions may be done without any specific religious framework. The end result is decreased anger and bitterness and less chance of continued wear and tear on body systems from the surges of neurotransmitters and hormones associated with the fight-or-flight response, which is triggered by hateful thoughts about the transgressor.[26]

One of the largest empirical investigations of forgiveness was the Stanford Forgiveness Project, which was undertaken by Fred Luskin as his doctoral dissertation for Stanford University's Counseling Psychology program, for which I (Sandra) then served as faculty. Fred's self-help book *Forgive for Good* explains in straightforward terms what the simple interventions are and provides numerous anecdotes regarding participants in his research, some of whom experienced life events that may be relevant for many of our coaching clients.[27]

Refusing to forgive can result in people's remaining stuck in downward spirals of negative rumination, and diminished physical well-being, particularly in cardiovascular function. Indeed, anger and a related negative emotion, hostility, are key factors in heart disease, possibly more destructive in their influence than smoking.[28] Being stuck in "grievance stories," as Luskin calls them, along with relentless blaming, keeps people from getting on with their lives.

If a person is mired in a distressing past, it is much more difficult to be focused on the present moment, actualizing one's strengths and enjoying the love and care of others in the here and now. It is also difficult to pursue goals, both personally important ones and those at work. All of these factors have relevance for our coaching.

STEPS TO FORGIVENESS

Here is a summary of the steps in Fred's process for forgiveness. These processes are similar to programs used in other research studies.

1. Understanding What Forgiveness Is and What It Is Not

Forgiveness is the peace of mind that comes from allowing the negative rumination about the offender to occupy less thinking time (mind-share) and therefore less emotional space.

Forgiveness is for the one forgiving and not for the transgressor.

Forgiveness allows the one who forgives to take back personal power.

Forgiveness increases the sense of personal responsibility in the one who forgives.

Forgiveness helps the healing for the one who forgives.

Forgiveness is a learnable skill.

Forgiveness helps increase control over negative emotions for the one who forgives.

Forgiveness can help improve the physical and mental health of the one who forgives.

Forgiveness is the choice of the one who forgives.

Forgiveness is *not* condoning unkindness or unfairness.

Forgiveness is *not* excusing illegal or unethical behavior.

Forgiveness is *not* forgetting that something painful happened.

Forgiveness does not have to involve a religious or spiritual experience, although it may.

Forgiveness is *not* denying or minimizing the hurt of the one who was aggrieved.

Forgiveness does *not* require reconciliation with the offender, although some who forgive may choose to do this.

Forgiveness does *not* mean that the one who forgives cannot have feelings.

2. Recognizing the Grievance Story

A grievance story is the tale we repeatedly tell others about the person or group that has wronged us. We start formulating the story when we have strongly personalized a transgressor's actions, forgetting their history and the fact that many bad things happen to many people, including good people.

Recognition of the grievance story is a very difficult step. Luskin's book is a great help in explaining the concepts of taking things too personally and losing sight of the big picture. We also want to highlight the fact that people with a history of sexual and physical assault were excluded from Luskin's forgiveness research and received other, appropriate referrals. Therapy for the post-traumatic stress disorder that often follows such incidents must be initiated first, before any process of forgiveness is suggested in the context of coaching.

A key element of a grievance story is perpetual blame of the transgressor and the amount of mental space the story of the bad deeds occupies. The number of times that the story of blame is recited to others is another indicator that the grievance story is still operating in a person's life. The time devoted to blaming another (who has probably moved on) is often correlated with giving up personal power and control, trapping the person who has not forgiven in the past. A new story is necessary.

3. Creating the New Story

In this stage we realize that the distress began with our not getting something we wanted or finding ourselves in a situation we did not want. We recognize the "unenforceable rules," as Luskin calls them, that were applied in our thinking about the transgressor.

The book offers several examples of unenforceable rules (what some readers will recognize as the irrational beliefs from cognitive behavioral therapy), including *reasonable desires* that are nevertheless unenforceable for others whom we loved and trusted. For example, most people desire and expect that their partners or spouses will not cheat on them; but this is an unenforceable rule. Likewise, it is highly desirable that each child be cherished by two loving parents. The fact that it did not happen in the lives of many people makes it no less desirable; but it is an unenforceable rule.

Being stuck in an unenforceable rule makes it more difficult to take constructive action, such as filing for divorce and thus creating the conditions to initiate and sustain a loving relationship with another partner at some point in the future, or seeking new employment after a boss's unfair treatment. To move on from blame and inaction is the rationale for this step.

4. Setting the Stage for Forgiveness

In this stage we reflect on and do our best to understand what our feelings are concerning what happened and the transgressor's actions. Be clear about the action that wronged you. Share your experience with one or two trusted others. Luskin distinguishes this sharing from the ceaseless retelling of the grievance story to many people.

5. Forgiving the Transgressor

In this step you imagine you have forgiven the transgressor.

This does *not* mean that one has to actually reconcile with the offender. In the research, the benefits occurred when this act of forgiveness *was simply imagined*. The timing of this step is important.

As a coach, if you were to suggest this too soon, your client could feel misunderstood, put off, or upset. For some people, this step would not make sense at *any* time. Use your best judgment as a coach about timing as you explore with the client the nature of their current interaction with the transgressor—for example, still sharing custody with the ex-spouse who cheated, or still reporting to the difficult boss.

A second idea that some clients have is that forgiveness is always about *forgive and forget*. This is not implied in Luskin's work, nor do we believe that it is helpful. It may be necessary for a client to take legal or civil action against a transgressor or actively keep some distance from this person or group. Rather than forgetting, the intent is to help the client shift their focus from relentless recall of the transgression and the resulting distress to moving forward with their life, with lessons learned.

6. Shifting Attention

When negative thoughts about the transgressor come up, shift your attention to something more positive, count your blessings, or engage in an act of kindness. You can also try the Heart Focus exercise (see sidebar).[29,30,31]

Heart Focus

1. Assume a comfortable position you can maintain for ten to fifteen minutes.
2. Gently bring your attention to your breathing as it flows in and out. As you inhale, allow the air to gently push your belly out. As you exhale, consciously relax your belly so that it feels soft. Practice this focusing of your attention for about five minutes.
3. Now bring to your mind either a memory of an experience with another person when you felt a powerful feeling of love, or a scene in nature that filled you with beauty and

tranquility. Do not choose someone for this exercise whom you are trying to forgive.

4. When the image of that experience is clear in your mind, try to re-experience in the present moment the associated peaceful and loving feelings. Many people like to imagine that the good feelings are centered in their heart.

5. Hold those peaceful feelings for as long as you can. If you find that your attention wanders, return to step 2.

6. After ten to fifteen minutes, slowly open your eyes and resume your regular activities.

Reprinted with the permission of the author, Frederic Luskin.

HOW WE WORK WITH THESE IDEAS IN COACHING

Before you suggest to a client that she forgive someone who has caused personal hurt or damaged a career, try these interventions for yourself. When a client's life is affected by what she describes as an unforgivable transgression, we gently and respectfully bring up this research and its results. If the client expresses interest, I (Sandra) share the methods used in the Stanford study. I ask the client to decide for themselves whether it makes sense to proceed with the process of forgiving the person in question. If the client chooses to do so, we look at the results together.

The steps in this process are very personal and may best be done entirely in private. We encourage you to experience the impact for yourself, as we have done, before exploring the forgiveness process with a client.

Clients to whom we have recommended Luskin's book have found it comforting and highly useful in assisting them in getting on with their lives, especially when framed in the context of an action plan to move on with life and refocusing on a better future.

CHAPTER 10 When There's Too Much of a Good Thing

CAN THERE BE TOO MUCH POSITIVITY?

In a coaches' manual where we propose the use of applications of positive psychology research, we want to strike a balance and ask an important question: How much positivity is a good thing? Can someone be *too* positive in their relationships with others?

While a number of you may be familiar with John Gottman's research on marriage,[1] you may not have thought of his findings as highlighting positive versus negative exchanges between a husband and wife. This researcher and his colleagues at the University of Washington observed in real time the nonverbal behavior and communication between spouses in intact marriages. The videotaped recordings of the interactions were later coded, and Gottman followed the couples' progress for several years. In couples whose marriages had endured and who reported feeling satisfaction with their spouse and the relationship, there were five positive exchanges for every negative exchange. In those marriages that failed, there was only one positive exchange for each negative exchange.

Is there a ratio that describes being *too* positive when interacting with others at work? It turns out that Fredrickson proposed one. While her theories on ratios of positive to negative emotions have been challenged (as we noted in Chapter 2), we find useful the notion that people could demonstrate too many positives in their interactions with their co-workers. Fredrickson suggested that (in general) a ratio of eleven positive exchanges to one negative would describe a state of too much positivity.[2] With this preponderance of positives, we can imagine that the productive and creative interactions among members of a work team would break down because of a lack of questioning, debate, and challenging of one another. We have a picture of people avoiding discussion of any problem or difficult issue; inauthentic agreement; and forced smiles.

If we are unrelentingly positive, we can fail to be emotionally resonant when someone else is grieving or experiencing difficulty, perhaps telling them to "look for the silver lining" or to "get over it" because their negative emotions are disturbing to others. If we insist on a too high proportion of positivity, we may avoid conflict and allow problems to fester. We might lose the power of righteous anger, a potent force behind social change.

This overly positive state is not what we are aiming for in our work in applying the positive psychology research. We are looking for ways to raise the *proportion* of positivity when people are languishing. We are looking to help our clients create enduring states described as flourishing, where the proportion of positive emotions is higher relative to negative emotions. When a person is experiencing a preponderance of negative life events, we can coach them around the benefits of creating positive emotions that may help mitigate the adverse impact of illness. We can also coach them around gaining valuable learning from loss, setbacks, mistakes, and disappointments.

WHAT ABOUT OVERUSING OUR STRENGTHS?

If we can overuse positive emotions with one another in the workplace, can we likewise overuse our strengths?

It turns out that there is substantial literature indicating that we can indeed deploy a strength too much of the time.[3] In a chapter entitled "Every Strength a Weakness and Other Caveats," Morgan McCall makes the case for how strengths can become weaknesses.[4] These overused strengths can contribute to a previously successful leader's derailment, and they may get fired, demoted, or stall in their career progression.

Why We Assess for Possible Overuse of Strengths

As proponents of helping our coaching clients leverage their strengths, we also want to clearly state the importance of their managing their weaknesses. Much of our success in life comes from using our strengths—for example, the determination that enables people to complete difficult projects or to develop daily and weekly practices for well-being. However, challenges we face in moving into our future often involve attempting new things that are difficult and unfamiliar. We may continue using strengths that served us well in the past but are no longer appropriate for what is needed in the present.

In our work as personal and executive coaches, we have found it very helpful to have clients identify their strengths with assessments such as the VIA Survey[5] and the Gallup StrengthsFinder.[6] However, there is nothing in these assessments that prompts an individual to consider whether they might be using one of their strengths too much of the time.

For coaches in business settings, we can suggest the Leadership Versatility Index (LVI),[7] which measures the use and overuse of important leadership behaviors. We are fortunate to have our colleague Rob Kaiser sharing his work on the aspects of leadership versatility. In the following paragraphs, Rob discusses the benefits of this instrument.

USING THE LEADERSHIP VERSATILITY INDEX 360 TO GAIN A BALANCED VIEW—BY ROB KAISER, KAISER LEADERSHIP SOLUTIONS

The Leadership Versatility Index uses the 360° methodology of comparing ratings from superiors, peers, and subordinates with self-perceptions, but that's where the similarity to the typical 360° instrument ends.

One difference is that the LVI uses a unique rating scale that allows raters to indicate when managers do *too little* or *too much* of a particular behavior, as distinct from doing it the right amount (see Figure 1). This makes it possible to provide feedback regarding a strength's becoming a weakness through overuse. This aspect often goes undetected with the standard tools that use five-point rating scales and assume that more is better.

Figure 1. *The Too Little/Too Much Rating Scale*
On this scale the best score is zero, in the middle of the scale. The premise is that performance problems arise when managers do either too little or do too much of something.

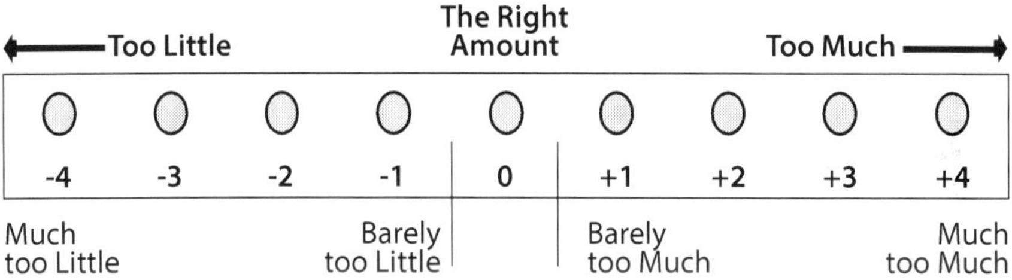

Warning. Some people misread this scale. Please do not mistake it for the usual type where higher scores are better.

Note. U.S. Patent No. 7,121,830. Copyright © 2013, Kaiser Leadership Solutions. All rights reserved. Reproduced with permission from the publisher.

Another feature distinguishing the LVI from other instruments is the model of leadership behavior on which it is based (see Table 1). Rather than a list of assorted and unrelated competencies, the LVI model consists of opposing but complementary behaviors, reflecting the tensions and trade-offs that make leadership a balancing act.

A leader's interpersonal style is represented by *forceful* versus *enabling* behaviors, and the leader's organizational focus is represented by *strategic* versus operational behaviors. Each pair of broad dimensions includes three pairs of sub-dimensions. For forceful or enabling style these are *taking charge* versus *empowering, declaring* versus *listening,* and *pushing* versus *supporting.* For strategic or *operational* focus they are *direction* versus *execution, growth* versus *efficiency,* and *innovation* versus *order.*

Table 1. *The LVI Model of Opposing but Complementary Leadership Behavior*

FORCEFUL   vs.   ENABLING
asserting personal and   *creating conditions for others*
position power   *to contribute*
Taking charge   **Empowering**
assuming responsibility   *giving people latitude to*
and control   *do a job*
Declaring   **Listening**
taking a position and   *including people and*
speaking up   *their input*
Pushing   **Supporting**
holding people to   *showing concern for people*
high standards

STRATEGIC   vs.   OPERATIONAL
positioning the organization   *focusing the organization*
to be competitive in   *to get things done*
the future   *in the near term*
Direction   **Execution**
setting the course and   *managing the details of*
painting the vision   *implementation*
Growth   **Efficiency**
reaching for more   *conserving resources*
Innovation   **Order**
encouraging change and   *using process discipline*
creativity

By combining the too little/too much rating scale with the model of opposing but complementary leadership behaviors, feedback from LVI results helps managers understand where they have struck an effective balance as well as where they are overusing some behaviors at the expense of others. The Versatility Score, an aggregate metric that represents the extent to which a leader uses all of these behaviors appropriately, as indicated by the proportion of ratings of "the right amount," is highly correlated with employee engagement, unit productivity, and overall effectiveness.

Because of its robust model of leader behavior, the LVI can be used in many different leadership development activities—such as executive coaching and high-potential development. Because of its conceptual relationships with the dynamics of managerial derailment, the LVI is also well suited for coaching managers through an upward transition like a promotion—just the sort of career change where derailment is most likely to occur.

Upward transitions are fraught with several concurrent challenges: an increase in scope of responsibility and the scale of resources the leader needs to access and deploy; greater complexity and ambiguity in the operating environment; and more stakeholders with greater power and competing political interests. Unfortunately, most transitioning managers receive little preparation for these challenges or support in grappling with them as they move into higher-level jobs. The result is often sink or swim.

We have designed a fairly simple yet robust method for facilitating an upward transition and minimizing the risk of derailment. The method involves clear communication of expectations, assessment, and feedback to course-correct, if needed, during an employee's critical transition.

PREPARATION FOR A NEW ROLE

The first step involves setting appropriate expectations, and requires providing the promoted manager with a realistic preview of the requirements in the new job. This can be done in conversation with the new boss and, if possible, the incumbent. A frank discussion of strategic priorities, key performance indicators, primary deliverables, resources, and obstacles helps to clarify the job and what needs to be done. It is helpful to take stock of these requirements in terms of the person's repertoire and experience:

- What skills and behaviors have been central to effectiveness in their prior roles and will also be needed in this role? (*Keep doing.*)
- What skills and behaviors may not have been required in prior roles but will be needed in the new role? (*Start doing.*)
- What skills and behaviors may have been critical in prior roles but are less relevant, or perhaps even detrimental, in this new role? (*Stop doing.*)[8]

Even with careful and thoughtful preparation, the transition period can be a turbulent time of stress and uncertainty for newly promoted managers. Most managers in transition experience strong feelings of anxiety as they struggle to comprehend their new responsibilities and make sense of a more complex operating environment. When under this kind of stress, people have fewer resources for self-monitoring and regulating their behavior. As a result, their counterproductive tendencies are likely to be expressed. Therefore, we also recommend preparing for the transition by conducting an assessment of the "dark side" of personality—the self-protective but often counterproductive dispositions that emerge when people are under stress.

The Hogan Development Survey (HDS) is a particularly effective tool because it was designed to measure the "dark side" traits that can interfere with sound judgment, disrupt relationships, and lead to derailment.[9] The purpose of the HDS assessment is for the person (and their coach) to identify derailing tendencies and create greater self-awareness about the kinds of situations that provoke them, along with identifying self-regulatory strategies for managing them. Knowing their triggers helps managers prevent their hot buttons from interfering with key relationships and disrupting important decisions as they navigate a major transition.

ONBOARDING INTO A NEW ROLE

During the first few weeks of the person's onboarding period, we recommend periodic meetings between the newly promoted manager and their boss as checkpoints for monitoring progress and keeping communication channels open. It is helpful to focus the conversation around key performance requirements as well as the skills and behaviors identified previously in terms of *start doing, keep doing,* and *stop doing.* It is not uncommon for managers to rely on a style or approach that worked before but that may not be best suited for the current role. Feedback and guidance from their new boss can help the manager make the necessary adjustments.

We recommend conducting a 360° feedback assessment with the LVI between three and six months into the new job. This may seem rather soon. We used to think it took nine to twelve months for co-workers to have sufficient opportunity to observe performance and to provide valid and useful feedback. However, the pace of change has accelerated in recent years. We have observed that many leaders have a shorter time period to establish themselves. If you wait nine months to a year to fix problems or adjust your behavior, you might be too late.

The LVI is particularly well suited to providing feedback during the onboarding period. First, the rating scale maps naturally onto the *start doing, keep doing, stop doing* framework by allowing coworkers to indicate what the manager does too little (start doing), the right amount (keep doing), and too much (stop doing). Second, the behavioral content of the LVI covers the key themes found to often be associated with derailment. The two major causes of derailment are when (1) managers rely too much on technical skills and fail to lead from a more strategic perspective, and (2) when managers have relationship problems, usually due to an abrasive and overbearing style.

The first issue is indicated by LVI ratings of overuse of operational behaviors and underuse of strategic behaviors. We also look for ratings of too much forceful behavior and too little enabling behavior. Finally, another factor commonly associated with derailment is a lack of self-awareness. One indication of this is self-ratings that differ significantly from coworker ratings.

Theoretically, the "dark side" traits on the HDS are conceptualized as overused strengths—for example, extreme excitable behavior looks like labile emotion; extreme dutiful behavior looks like excessive obedience. The LVI allows co-workers to indicate which behaviors are being used too much by the manager. The LVI and HDS together offer insights that are useful when a person is trying to adapt to the demands of a role with greater responsibility.

We want to coach our clients to be versatile—to display the right amount of their strengths for the situation at hand. We think of a person of high versatility as *a master of opposites*. For example, managers or leaders can be evaluated for versatility by looking at pairs of leadership attributes such as forceful versus enabling and calculating how close their ratings are to the right amount on both dimensions.

We advocate balancing our strengths-based coaching approaches with a realistic assessment of where and how an individual may simultaneously be overusing their strengths.

PRESENTING A BALANCED VIEW OF STRENGTHS TO CLIENTS

As organizational applications based on positive psychology have become more popular, we sometimes encounter skepticism on the part of potential executive coaching clients or their bosses or HR managers. Some business people wonder if positive psychology might be too good to be true. The coaching frameworks and techniques we present here are well supported by scientific research and successful practice. We want to present a thoughtful and balanced view to our clients and the stakeholders in their organizations, so we cite the research to support our recommendations for positive psychology applications for the workplace. We value the views expressed by Rob Kaiser as a respected, long-time contributor to the research in leadership development. We know that he is concerned that positive psychology theory not become an ideology or an oversimplification of the impressive research outcomes that have emerged as a result of highly respected professionals conducting gold standard research.

Kaiser edited a book, *The Perils of Accentuating the Positive*, with chapters from several thought leaders that highlight, as he puts it, "the rest you need to know about strengths based development."[10] His intention was not to dismiss the strengths approach. Rather, he set out to describe several critical considerations that he believes can get lost in an enthusiasm solely for the positive side. We agree that these are important for positive psychology–oriented coaches to understand and keep in mind.

One of his most important points is this. While the emphasis in strengths-based approaches is on building on a person's existing strengths, the nature of a specific strength and its alignment with performance requirements at work is crucial. Secondly, Kaiser reminds us that the distinction between strengths and weaknesses is not always clear-cut, and that strengths can become weaknesses when overused. We must not simply focus on strengths and ignore weaknesses. Finally, he asks us to remember that sometimes development requires that our clients learn to do what doesn't come naturally or easily to them. Therefore, we as coaches want to support our clients in remaining motivated while addressing their skill deficits.

Using Kaiser's book as a reference, we explore these issues in greater detail in the next few pages. We then offer some recommendations to keep in mind when doing strengths-based coaching in the workplace.

BUILDING ON THE RIGHT STRENGTHS

It might seem obvious what qualifies as a strength. However, it requires a deeper look to define a strength and how it relates to personal and organizational success. For example, Bob Eichinger and his colleagues at Korn/Ferry International, Guangrong Dai and King Yii Tang, considered different ways to define a strength.[11] They identified several types, including what one does best (a *personal best strength*); what one does better than other people (a *competitive strength*); what one does better than other people and few people are good at (a *distinctly competitive strength*); and what one does better than others, few people are good at, and is aligned with what organizations most need from their managers (a *distinctly competitive and aligned strength*).

The assumption guiding their work was that not all strengths are equally valuable. Some are more important than others to career success or competent performance in a particular role. For instance, personal best strengths are not as crucial as competitive strengths when it comes to career success insofar as competitive strengths are what distinguish a stronger candidate from the others vying for a job.

Further, the *distinctly competitive and aligned* strengths have been most strongly and consistently correlated with managerial and executive career success in Lominger research over the last two decades.[12] These are the strengths (though referred to as competencies in most of their writings) that separate the most effective and successful leaders and include building teams, motivating and inspiring, strategy agility, vision, planning, innovation, creativity, and dealing with ambiguity.

The researchers also conducted a study to determine how many managers have the various types of strengths.[13] They analyzed competency ratings collected between 2005 and 2007 for 1,857 North American managers and executives from a variety of industries. The initial finding concerned *competitive strengths*— things people did better than their peers. About a quarter (26 percent) of the sample had none—not a single competency rated in the 90th percentile or higher compared to norms. As a result, the authors noted, it would be a struggle for these managers to stand out compared to their peers.

The even more unsettling finding concerned the *competitive and aligned* strengths. Two-thirds of the sample (67 percent) didn't have any of them, meaning that the majority of managers and executives do not have strengths in the areas that distinguish the best leaders. The researchers thus concluded that an exclusive reliance on strengths is a weak career strategy for most managers. They recommended that the best approach for driving organizational effectiveness through leadership development is to help leaders become ongoing learners who can develop beyond their natural inclinations to acquire the skills that few have but that differentiate the most effective leaders.

THE RELATIONSHIP BETWEEN STRENGTHS AND AN ORGANIZATION'S STRATEGIC NEEDS

Jean Leslie and Anand Chandrasekar, researchers with the Center for Creative Leadership, looked at the relationship between strengths and organizational needs.[14] They analyzed the results of a survey that compared the skills and competencies that organizations say they need to be successful with the level of skill that their managers currently possess. Across three different cultures—the United States, Singapore, and India—they found a striking similarity in the competencies organizations need most (for instance, leading people, strategic planning, and managing change), and in the competencies in which managers are most skilled (for example, respecting individual differences, doing whatever it takes, and cultural adaptability).

But more importantly, in all three countries there were major gaps between the former and the latter—between what organizations need and the strengths their managers possess. Overall, half of the top ten *most needed* competencies across all three cultures were also among the *least developed* and deployed by managers: leading people, inspiring commitment, employee development, strategic planning, and managing change. The researchers concluded that encouraging managers to maximize their current strengths, to the neglect of improving less developed areas, runs the risk of widening the critical skill gap and leaving organizations without the capability they need to execute their strategies.

This research highlights two potential drawbacks to focusing on what managers are already good at. First, for managers whose standout strengths are in areas other than those most central to management jobs, these strengths may not actually help them advance in their careers. Second, a focus on what managers are naturally good at turns attention away from what organizations need from their managers to be competitive in the global economy.

STRENGTHS CAN BECOME WEAKNESSES: LINKS TO DERAILMENT

Kaiser notes that phrases like "too much of a good thing" and "more isn't better" have been around for a long time. The ancient Greeks used the phrase *areté hamartia* to describe when a great power became a tragic flaw. This concept was introduced to the language of leadership development, in the phrase "strengths can become weaknesses," in pioneering research on career derailment conducted by Morgan McCall and Mike Lombardo.[15] Their initial study involved in-depth interviews with co-workers who were in a position to observe the behavior of twenty successful executives and twenty derailed executives. The researchers noted a paradoxical pattern that characterized the derailed executives. Certain qualities described as assets, that helped executives get ahead, also operated as liabilities that got them fired. Several examples were provided: competiveness came to be perceived by others as abrasiveness; ambition became self-centeredness; loyalty became cronyism; and detail orientation became micromanagement. Lombardo and Eichinger's 2006 research also identified several strengths commonly associated with career success and documented how they are simultaneously associated with career trouble: being smart (arrogant), independent (cold, aloof), loyal (showing favoritism), results-oriented (overmanaging), personable (too soft on performance problems), and creative (a poor administrator).[16]

McCall concluded that *every* strength has the potential to be taken to counterproductive extremes, from diplomacy (being too nice and conflict-avoidant), to intelligence (talking over people's heads), and even to integrity (if being principled becomes being rigid and moralizing).[17] McCall found that this dynamic explains a surprising number of CEO derailments, some of which have made headlines in recent years.

The consensus view among experts is that about half of all senior leaders eventually derail.[18] The Center for Creative Leadership has studied derailment for three decades and has found that, in addition to the factor of overused strengths, derailment can often be traced back to a weakness of one kind or another.

CCL's research found the same five recurring themes at different organizational levels, for both men and women, across different industries, and across different cultures. The five "fatal flaws," as they have been termed, include relationship problems; inability to build a team; inability to adapt to change; inability to think strategically; and missed business targets. Signs of the fatal flaws are usually evident early in a person's career, but can be compensated for with other strengths and then left to fester. For instance, deep technical expertise can mask a person's difficulty in seeing the big picture in functional jobs. Or a sharp, but sometimes abrasive, star performer may be able to get by because of their brilliance.

As Bill Gentry and Craig Chappelow point out, the real tragedy of derailment is that in many cases it is preventable.[19] Preventing derailment requires that managers come to terms with their own weaknesses and learn how to manage and/or improve them before they become habitually ingrained and resistant to change later in a career, where their disruptive effects are amplified.

TAKING STRENGTHS TO COUNTERPRODUCTIVE EXTREMES

There is interesting research demonstrating that the more pronounced a leader's natural talent and the stronger their strengths, the greater the chance of their being taken to counterproductive extremes. In a sample of 110 upper-level managers in three organizations, Kaiser and Overfield compared leaders' areas of talent as identified by the StrengthsFinder to co-worker ratings on the LVI. There was a clear association between talent themes and overdoing related behaviors.[20]

For instance, leaders who had talent in such StrengthsFinder areas as Achiever, Activator, and Command were more often rated "too much" on LVI Forceful leadership. Leaders whose StrengthsFinder talents were Developer, Harmony, and Includer were more often rated "too much" on LVI Enabling leadership. Interestingly, leaders were even more likely to neglect complementary behaviors. For example, every manager with talent at Command was rated "too little" on LVI Enabling leadership. Every manager with talent at Includer was rated "too little" on LVI Forceful leadership. Overall, there was a 50-percent chance that leaders overdid behaviors related to their areas of natural talent and a 90-percent chance that they underutilized complementary behaviors.

Based on their quantitative research findings, Kaplan and Kaiser explained the dynamics that can turn a strength into a weakness.[21] First, most managers don't fully know or understand their strengths. Second, not knowing their strengths, managers are understandably likely to be overly reliant on them. They may apply their strengths to a greater extent than is required by the conditions and contextual factors, or apply them in situations where another approach might yield a better outcome.

In addition to undermining their strengths, overuse also leads managers to underuse complementary behaviors. The assertive, take-charge executive often relies on a forceful approach, to the neglect of more inclusive and enabling people-oriented behaviors (a complementary approach). This results in a lopsided leadership style that can diminish their effectiveness.

A FEW MORE COMMENTS ON ASSESSMENT OF STRENGTHS

The research on overused strengths suggests that if we simply coach our clients to maximize their strengths we run the risk of their inadvertently turning their strengths into weaknesses. We believe strongly that our clients at work do need to discover their strengths and identify ways to leverage them in their jobs over the course of a career. We likewise recommend focusing our coaching on how clients can calibrate and balance the use of their strengths. This can be aided by feedback from people they work with regarding strengths overuse or the underuse of more appropriate skills and approaches.

We are reminded that overusing strengths may be explained by a human tendency to think dichotomously, that is, by identifying strengths and weaknesses as either end of a continuum, with something like "low" at one end and "high" at the other. Kaplan and Kaiser point out that this common dichotomous construction does not leave a place for strengths deployed to excess or for the person to subsequently discover the consequences of doing so.[22] Their recommendation is to expand our mental model to three categories: *shortcomings* (skills and abilities that a person lacks or applies too little), *strengths* (skills and abilities that a person possesses and applies optimally), and *overused strengths* (skills and abilities that a person possesses but applies too intensely or indiscriminately).

This tripartite conception is important in conducting assessments to help leaders understand and calibrate how they use their strengths. Unfortunately, most behavioral assessments, including nearly all 360° feedback instruments, involve co-worker ratings on a five-point scale that assumes that higher scores are better. However, there are alternatives, like the LVI, that do account for strengths being overused. Likewise, Korn/Ferry's proprietary 360° assessment, Voices®, offers a query to raters to indicate whether a competency they are evaluating is being overused by the person they are rating.[23]

Finally, interviews or open-ended surveys can also be structured to elicit rich qualitative feedback about shortcomings, strengths, and overused strengths. One particularly useful way to frame the questions is to ask what a leader should *start doing, continue doing,* or *stop doing.* One advantage to open-ended questions is that the feedback is not restricted to just the behaviors represented by assessment survey items.

STRENGTHS IN LEARNING AND DEVELOPMENT

A final risk in playing only to strengths is that, when taken to the extreme, it can create leaders who lack the repertoire of skills needed to adapt to change. The only constant in today's workplace is change, and the accelerating pace of change requires people to constantly bend and flex in new directions. It is unwise to rely solely on strengths at such times because a strength can be a mixed blessing.

There is an emerging consensus that the key to thriving in the complex, fast-moving modern working environment is continuous learning and dealing with the unknown, untested, and untried.[24] Overreliance on strengths during times of chaotic change may have a short-term advantage—you can capitalize on deep smarts and well-honed skills, which increases the likelihood that you will do your job the right way. However, this strategy has a long-term disadvantage that may be easy to overlook: the opportunity cost in not experiencing the diversity of job activities needed to develop a seasoned and well-rounded leader for the future.[25]

HOW POSITIVE PSYCHOLOGY APPLICATIONS CAN HELP

We have spent considerable time discussing the perils of overusing strengths. We now return to the importance of positive psychology applications in our coaching. As coaches, we can apply the principles of positive psychology to help guide managers through the transitions needed to become adept at demonstrating the new skills required for different roles.

The core notion in Frederickson's broaden-and-build theory is that positive emotional states help our clients be more receptive to the kinds of learning experiences it takes to acquire new skills and to form new relationships. As coaches, we can coach our clients in ways that they can increase their experience of positive emotions and enhance their engagement at work while demonstrating competence in the skills related to their jobs. For managers seeking increasingly complex, higher-level roles, we know that the performance requirements will change with a promotion. When refining and honing a narrow set of talents into standout strengths comes at the expense of learning and adapting, managers risk not being able to keep up with the changes they need to make to advance.

As coaches, we can aid our clients in carefully assessing their strengths and identifying where these can be leveraged, while paying attention to not overdoing them. We can help our clients assess their competence in the key skills needed to perform well in their present jobs. We can then assist them in determining what skills will be outdated, irrelevant, or not useful at the next level of leadership to which they aspire.

We can help them find ways to recognize an understandable human tendency to want to hang on to skills that have made them successful in the past. We can help them develop a growth mindset that can underpin their learning as they build new competencies and acquire the new knowledge critical for succeeding in a new role. We can remind them how their identified strengths can still serve them, again while being alert to their overuse. We can help them flourish.

CHAPTER 11

Leveraging Positive Psychology in Culturally Competent Coaching

One of the most important qualities to possess in our rapidly changing and culturally diverse world is not IQ but cultural intelligence—the ability to function effectively in a range of cultural contexts. This includes national, ethnic, generational, and organizational cultures.[1] Research conducted in over thirty countries shows us that people who are high in cultural intelligence are better able to adapt and succeed in the complex life and work situations that characterize our globalized world.[2] Since positive psychology is the study of the strengths and virtues that enable individuals, communities, and organizations to thrive, a discussion of positive psychology would not be complete without exploring cultural intelligence.

Positive psychology began in the United States and was popularized by researchers who may have been raised in other cultures, but who spent significant time in the United States. Positive psychology has occasionally been criticized as having an American focus and a Western set of values. We are concerned that the cross-cultural application of US-based research may be inappropriate in some situations. Recommending positive psychology applications that were developed with Western culture in mind to clients from other cultures may be experienced as offensive.

As two Caucasian American coaches, we are aware that our experience is limited, even as we strive to apply what we have learned from others with differing backgrounds and from living abroad. We know that the language used to express theories and techniques in positive psychology may not readily be understood or appreciated by those whose cultural background is different from ours. Therefore, we believe that it is important to broaden our understanding of cultural nuances and translate this knowledge to positive psychology applications that are effective in different cultures.

We asked experts knowledgeable in cross-cultural research to contribute their wisdom of how best to be culturally sensitive and agile when applying positive psychology principles, research results, and methods. In this chapter you will hear from Antonella Delle Fave, a physician and researcher working in Italy who has spent her career conducting cross-cultural research. We also asked well-known coach practitioners such as Philippe Rosinski (from Belgium) and Zeina Ghossoub El-Aswad (from Lebanon) to share their perspectives with us.

There are three purposes to this chapter. The first is to understand that there are cultural differences that must be taken into account when studying positive psychology and when crafting positive psychology–based coaching approaches. We address this by discussing some of the research that finds cultural and global differences in the areas of values, well-being, and happiness, as well as intervention studies. The second purpose is to present approaches, concepts, and frameworks designed to measure and develop cultural awareness and cultural intelligence. We address this by examining concepts, models, and questions related to cultural orientation, cultural dimensions, and cultural intelligence. The third purpose is to emphasize that for the coach to be most effective, coaching interventions should be nuanced in accordance with the cultural orientation of the client and in the context of the client's goals and setting. Since there is not yet adequate research on the effectiveness of specific interventions tailored to individual cultural contexts, this topic will not be explored in depth from an outcome-research perspective. Rather, we propose that the cultural intelligence of the coach will better enable them to sensitively fine-tune coaching approaches with culture in mind, and we provide eight tips to help the coach operate in the most culturally attuned manner possible.

CROSS-CULTURAL SIMILARITIES AND DIFFERENCES RELEVANT TO POSITIVE PSYCHOLOGY

Tadmor and his colleagues conducted research that supports the view that valuing cultural differences leads to enhanced success.[3] They investigated the effects of biculturalism on the creativity and professional success of individuals living abroad. The researchers hypothesized that bicultural individuals—those who identify with both their home and host cultures—would have a higher capacity for combining multiple perspectives than those who identify only with their home culture. They completed three studies, which showed that biculturalism contributed to professional success, specifically rate of promotion, and that bicultural professionals also assimilated better in the host country.[4]

Is Positive Psychology Too Western-Focused?

The pioneering theory of positive psychology is undoubtedly ground-breaking. However, the constructs of the field, rooted in Western ideologies and assumptions, could benefit from additional examination before being applied to non-Western cultures. It is important for positive psychology to embrace the different approaches and the diverse nature of cultures' experiences of emotion and the general constructs they are built on.[5]

Positive psychology has been analyzed through this lens by Christopher and Hickinbottom, who assert that many of the Western assumptions which are at the foundation of positive psychology, such as individualism, happiness, and positive emotions, may not carry the same cultural significance in other cultures.[6] Much of the framework of positive psychology rests on Western ideologies of the "good life," which may not translate to other cultures' definitions of happiness.

The Western value of self-efficacy is a core construct in positive psychology. But self-efficacy is not valued equally in all cultures. In collectivistic cultures, interdependence and a sense of duty are valued over independence. As outlined by Hoshmand and Ho, one

Western view of obedience is that it is an obstacle preventing people from reaching their full potential, while in many East Asian cultures, obedience to one's elders exemplifies maturation and high-quality moral fiber.[7]

Snyder and Lopez emphasize that all cultures have different constructs and ideals. Lyubomirsky asserts that in addition to identifying the many differences between Eastern and Western cultures, the role of culture in self-efficacy, and the pursuit of happiness especially, require further examination.[8] Snyder and Lopez asked whether happiness is as central to other cultures as it is in the Western world.[9] In collectivistic cultures, it is customary to adhere to social expectations and be dutiful to one's elders rather than striving for individual happiness.[10]

In the same way that happiness may not be of utmost importance in all cultures, we also know that there is not a unanimous interpretation of emotions or esteemed individual qualities. In the VIA Survey, which we have talked about in previous chapters, there are six universal virtues that are supposedly revered by all cultures.[11] This claim has been challenged by Christopher and Hickinbottom, who assert that the VIA classification focuses on commonalities and disregards the differing interpretations of such values by other cultures.[12]

Several researchers have claimed that Eastern and Western views of happiness are vastly different. They say that Eastern cultures value accordance with social expectations over their individual happiness,[13,14,15] whereas Western cultures place greater value on personal achievement and success when it comes to happiness. If individual happiness is not a central value in Eastern cultures, the pursuit of happiness may not even be a motivation for individuals in those cultures.

Though happiness may not be the *most important* goal for some coaching clients in certain cultures, some research demonstrates that, regardless of their cultural background, individuals still benefit in terms of well-being by increasing happiness levels through positive psychology coaching interventions. In research performed by Otake, Shimai, Tanaka-Matsumi, Otsui, and Fredickson in 2006, the effect of happiness interventions on two Japanese samples showed increased well-being in the intervention group (who kept track of kind acts they performed each day) compared to the control group.[16] More recently, a study was conducted that included a Western sample for comparison and involved subjects performing acts of kindness (rather than just keeping track of them). Both US and Korean students reported being happier after completing the acts of kindness when they had the support of their peers. Boehm and colleagues found that foreign-born Asian Americans saw smaller increases in well-being from happiness-increasing interventions.[17] Even so, Asian Americans for the most part reported greater increases in well-being after other-focused activities compared to self-oriented activities.

Identifying Cultural Competence in the Coach
by Antonella Delle Fave

Despite the common assumption that our world is becoming globalized and increasingly homogeneous, culture-bound attitudes, behaviors, and habits still represent a major component of individuals' characterization. On the other hand, in most countries institutions and communities at various levels—schools, workplaces, organizations, healthcare services, and municipalities—are becoming increasingly multicultural.

The systematic exploration of cultural diversity is relatively recent in the social sciences. One of the most debated issues in this domain is the value dimension, which is an undeniable and crucial component of culture. As clearly stated by Tajfel

continued...

in a seminal work, a person's social identity is "that part of an individual's self-concept which derives from his knowledge of his membership in a social group (or groups), together with the value and emotional significance attached to that membership."[18] In multicultural contexts, individuals who are members of minority groups may develop a sense of connectedness and belonging toward two different types of communities: the circumscribed social network with which they share a native language, traditions, and values; and the broader society, with which they share citizenship, work and public roles, and civic rights and responsibilities.

Scientists have prominently focused on the social-psychological processes arising when a cultural minority comes into contact with a dominant culture, as happens in migration. This phenomenon is called acculturation, and it includes two dimensions: socio-cultural adjustment, consisting in the acquisition of social competences and behaviors typical of the host society; and psychological adaptation, which comprises the strategies individuals adopt to cope with the challenges of migration and their outcomes at the psychological level.[19] These strategies can be grouped into four major categories, or acculturation patterns. *Assimilation* occurs when the person's acquisition of values, habits, and behaviors derived from the dominant culture predominates over the preservation of the native ones. In *separation* individuals preserve their original cultural identity, and their strong identification with the minority community leads to the development of relatively isolated subcultures. *Marginalization* arises as a consequence of discrimination and stigmatization of minority members by the dominant culture. Finally, *integration* represents the most

continued...

complex, but also the most adaptive acculturation pattern. Integrated individuals develop a double cultural belongingness that allows them to build strong and harmonious relationships within both their local minority community and the broader society they live and work in. The acquisition of values and behaviors characterizing the dominant culture and the preservation of native traditions and habits allow the integrated individual to enhance their behavioral and psychological flexibility.

Only recently have researchers paid attention to the positive aspects of cross-cultural relations and multicultural communities.[20,21] At the individual level, this condition can foster the development of new competencies, goals, and meanings.[22] At the social level, cultural diversity can positively contribute to institutions, organizations, and societies by enhancing flexibility and creativity in problem solving.[23] At both levels, cultural pluralism fosters complexity and better adaptation to environmental challenges and changes. The social capital that derives from multicultural connections represents a key resource for the promotion of individual and community well-being.[24,25]

Moving from these premises, how can we draft the role of a competent coach, living in a multicultural environment and working with people who not only belong to different cultural backgrounds but are also adopting different acculturation strategies? Tseng and Streltzer have effectively identified the key components of a good relationship between a doctor and a patient who belong to two different cultures.[26] Some of these components are integrated in the list of six suggestions that are proposed for coaches here.

continued…

1. The first important aspect to implement is a critical awareness of one's own cultural values and beliefs, to keep them from intruding on the coaching work and undermining an intervention that should be as objective and goal-directed as possible.

2. The second asset of a culturally competent coach is cultural knowledge. A coach working in a multicultural context should be actively committed to acquiring information about the other culture's related beliefs, values, and social norms. Due to the broadness of this issue, cross-cultural supervision is highly recommended.

3. The third relevant aspect is the cultivation of cultural sensitivity, which implies the acknowledgement and respect of cultural diversity, as well as the identification of related strengths and beneficial implications for the coaching process and the coachee's goal pursuit.

4. The fourth component is cultural empathy. Cultural empathy implies openness to understand the coachee's emotions, their expression pattern, and their relationship with culture-grounded values and beliefs.

5. The fifth aspect is the readiness to structure the coaching process taking into account the acculturation pattern that the coachee has adopted in the interaction with the dominant culture. As described above, different acculturation patterns have very different outcomes in terms of social inclusion and sense of belongingness. The specific pattern adopted by the coachee and its implications for the coaching goals should be understood, accepted, and respected.

6. Finally, the coach should use culturally appropriate language, interaction style, and nonverbal communication,
continued...

to facilitate coachees' feelings of ease and relational comfort. Since the coaching process is grounded in language, special attention should be devoted to word choice, the coachee's comprehension level, and the cultural meanings and implications of the terms that are used during the sessions.

ETHNOCENTRIC VERSUS ETHNORELATIVE APPROACHES

As described above, the competent coach must value and address cultural differences. Even a well-meaning coach can fall into the trap of an ethnocentric view. Bennett describes ethnocentrism as the assumption that one's own culture is central to reality.[27] (See Table 1.)

Often this perspective has no negative intent, it is just naiveté or lack of awareness of cultural differences. Ethnocentrism shows up in three forms: ignoring differences, evaluating differences negatively, and downplaying the importance of differences. Coaches are likely to be most susceptible to that third category—underestimating the importance of cultural factors—because most coaches try to be accepting and nonjudgmental.

Table 1, adapted from Philippe Rosinski's *Coaching across Cultures*, emphasizes the pitfalls of ethnocentrism and highlights the hallmarks of an ethnorelative approach to multicultural interactions.

Table 1. Styles Of Dealing With Cultural Differences

ETHNOCENTRIC PITFALLS	ETHNORELATIVE APPROACHES
Ignore differences	**Recognize and accept differences**
• *Isolate from different cultures*	• *Acknowledge, appreciate,*
• *Deny differences*	*seek to understand differences*
Recognize differences but evaluate them negatively	**Adapt to differences**
• *Believe own culture is superior*	• *Move outside one's comfort zone to explore other cultures*
• *Conversely, could place others on a pedestal*	• *Empathetically understand others*
	Integrate differences
Recognize differences but minimize their importance	• *Able to see, analyze and evaluate situations from various cultural perspectives*
• *Deny uniqueness— "we are all the same"*	
	Leverage differences
	• *Make the most of differences*
	• *Seek the best of different cultures to help achieve desired goals*

Adapted from Milton Bennett (1993), "Toward Ethnorelativism: A Developmental Model of Intercultural Sensitivity"; and Phillippe Rosinski (1999), "Beyond Intercultural Sensitivity: Leveraging Cultural Differences." Reprinted with permission of the copyright holder.[28]

In the coaching world, Philippe Rosinski and Rodney Lowman have been proponents of developing cultural and global competency in coaching.[29,30] Rosinski has adopted Bennett's model with a special emphasis. We will refer to Rosinski and Bennett's thinking from *Coaching across Cultures* as we explore how to move up the developmental stages from ethnocentric pitfalls to ethnorelative strengths. In order from least to most sophisticated, the three ethnocentric pitfalls that could plague coaches are: ignoring differences; recognizing differences but evaluating them negatively; and recognizing differences but minimizing their importance.

If a coach or client is completely unaware of cultural differences, homework focusing on observing differences, such as uniqueness among cultures related to food, film, political and social systems, physical origin, and qualities of family relationships may be a good start.

Bennett has described three kinds of negative evaluation of differences: denigration, superiority, and reversal. Denigration means the individual sees other cultures as inferior, contributing to racism and negative stereotyping. Potentially helpful homework is to consider how people of a different country may contribute perspectives to handle complex global issues, or for a younger person to consider some of the contributions that elders have made to the world. Superiority goes beyond positive appreciation of one's culture and leads people to become overly nationalistic or zealous fundamentalists. Coaching homework may involve helping the individual dial back their need to impose their views on others. Reversal involves putting other cultures on a pedestal, above your own. Here we may help people develop a more balanced appreciation of their own background while still appreciating another culture.

When people recognize differences but minimize their importance, they have progressed far beyond the first two levels of ethnocentrism because they are not evaluating others negatively. However, there can be an overemphasis on similarity, and as such this perception is not constructive—differences are trivialized. In coaching situations, both coaches and the people they coach may project their values and normative expectations onto others. Coaching homework can include helping them see the value of other perspectives.

ETHNORELATIVE COACHING

Ethnorelative approaches avoid ethnocentric pitfalls and represent a more culturally and globally aware perspective. The culturally and globally aware coach recognizes that cultural differences are widespread and that they matter. A coach at this level of their development is curious to learn about such differences and use that knowledge to accept, appreciate, adapt, and respond appropriately in varied situations with diverse clients.

We may consider four stages of ethnorelative coaching approaches, from least developed to more masterful levels.[31]

1. *Recognizing and accepting differences.* At this level a coach recognizes and accepts differences such as different values, norms, and assumptions. For example, a coach may value directness in all situations, but when dealing with a client who has a value of indirectness when it comes to saying no may come not only to understand that it is a cultural style but also to truly respect their approach to the situation rather than privately condemning it.

2. *Adapting to differences.* Adaptation requires moving out of one's comfort zone, experiencing cultural differences and trying out new ways of thinking, being, and doing. After experiencing, and potentially relishing, the new cultural experience, the person can go back to what they are used to—their comfort zone—for recharging. I (Jeff) remember living in Cuernavaca, Mexico, in my twenties, in a local family's home, having meals three times a day with the huge family, speaking only Spanish, eating their favorite dishes, being immersed in the culture, adapting to different ways of eating, talking, and socializing, and then enjoying going back to my room to relax and recharge. This balance between immersion and recharge can create the conditions for the individual to joyfully experience and adapt to differences without becoming too overwhelmed. Coaches working in new cultures or countries often benefit

from researching cultural customs on the Internet and taking advantage of specialty publishers such as Intercultural Press.[32]

3. *Integrating differences.* Adaptation refers to a temporary shift in perspective; integration means being able to hold different perspectives in your mind at one time, allowing you to evaluate situations from multiple cultural perspectives. This ability allows the coach to ask perspective-broadening questions that explore alternative ways of viewing situations and challenges, beyond their culture of origin. The integration of differences is aided by well-developed empathy in the coach. We can see this as an advanced stage of coaching development and coaching presence. The coach has integrated cultural knowledge beyond his or her own, helping the coach see and inquire about the multiple ways of viewing and experiencing the same situation. Coaches who wish to reach the highest of Bennett's stages would be well served to intentionally immerse themselves in different situations with the intention of accepting, valuing, living, and enjoying the new culture.

4. *Leveraging differences.* Rosinski adds another level to Bennett's model and names a fourth level of ethnorelativism: leveraging differences. He defines this as a proactive process, where the coach looks for gems in one's own culture and mines treasures from other cultures too. The creative leveraging of cultural differences can set the stage for solutions more effective than relying on a single culture. Synergies may arise when appreciation and deployment of various cultural perspectives helps our globally diverse workforce adapt to new challenges.

CULTURAL ORIENTATION AND THE COMPETENT COACH

A competent positive psychology–oriented coach understands cultural orientations and cultural dimensions. A cultural orientation is an inclination to feel, think, or act in some way that is culturally influenced. A cultural dimension represents a spectrum on which cultural orientations can be placed. For example, in the United States people are usually direct in their communication: if they want to say no, they usually will. In some Asian cultures a more indirect style is valued, to avoid hurting a person's feelings. Cultural orientation is demonstrated at varying degrees of intensity by different people of the same culture and will vary in one person depending on the situation. A cultural orientation can then be measured as one's placement on a cultural dimension. For example, your client may tend to be direct 80 percent of the time and indirect 20 percent of the time. This client's cultural orientation could be said to be "direct" on the "indirect–direct" cultural dimension. Rosinski has outlined seventeen such cultural dimensions (Table 2).[33]

Table 2. Rosinski's Cultural Dimensions

CATEGORY	DIMENSION	DESCRIPTION
Sense of power and responsibility	Control/Harmony/ Humility	Control: People have power and responsibility to forge the life they want. Harmony: Strive for balance and harmony with nature. Humility: Accept inevitable natural limitations.
Time management approaches	Scarce/Plentiful	Scarce: Time is a scarce resource. Manage it carefully! Plentiful: Time is abundant. Relax!
	Monochronic/Polychronic	Monochronic: Concentrate on one activity and/or relationship at a time. Polychronic: Concentrate simultaneously on multiple tasks and/or relationships.
	Past/Present/Future	Past: Learn from the past. The present is essentially a continuation or a repetition of past occurrences. Present: Focus on the "here and now" and short-term benefits. Future: Have a bias toward long-term benefits. Promote a far-reaching vision.

CATEGORY	DIMENSION	DESCRIPTION
Definitions of identity and purpose	Being/Doing	Being: Stress living itself and the development of talents and relationships. Doing: Focus on accomplishments and visible achievements.
	Individualistic/ Collectivistic	Individualistic: Emphasize individual attributes and projects. Collectivistic: Emphasize affiliation with group.
Organizational arrangements	Hierarchy/Equality	Hierarchy: Society and organizations must be socially stratified to function properly. Equality: People are equals who often happen to play different roles.
	Universalist/Particularist	Universalist: All cases should be treated in the same universal manner. Adopt common processes for consistency and economies of scale. Particularist: Emphasize particular circumstances. Favor decentralization and tailored solutions.
	Stability/Change	Stability: Value a static and orderly environment. Encourage efficiency through systematic and disciplined work. Minimize change and ambiguity, perceived as disruptive. Change: Value a dynamic and flexible environment. Promote effectiveness through adaptability and innovation. Avoid routine, perceived as boring.
	Competitive/Collaborative	Competitive: Promote success and progress through competitive stimulation. Collaborative: Promote success and progress through mutual support, sharing of best practices, and solidarity.
Notions of territory and boundaries	Protective/Sharing	Protective: Protect yourself by keeping personal life and feelings private (mental boundaries) and by minimizing intrusions into your physical space (physical boundaries). Sharing: Build closer relationships by sharing your psychological and physical domains.
Communication patterns *continued on next page*	High Context/Low Context	High Context: Rely on implicit communication. Appreciate the meaning of gestures, posture, voice, and context. Low Context: Rely on explicit communication. Favor clear and detailed instructions.

CATEGORY	DIMENSION	DESCRIPTION
Communication patterns	Direct/Indirect	Direct: In a conflict or with a tough message to deliver, get your point across clearly, at the risk of offending or hurting. Indirect: In a conflict or with a tough message to deliver, favor maintaining a cordial relationship, at the risk of misunderstanding.
	Affective/Neutral	Affective: Display emotions and warmth when communicating. Establishing and maintaining personal and social connections is key. Neutral: Stress conciseness, precision, and detachment when communicating.
	Formal/Informal	Formal: Observe strict protocols and rituals. Informal: Favor familiarity and spontaneity.
Modes of thinking	Deductive/Inductive	Deductive: Emphasize concepts, theories, and general principles. Then, through logical reasoning, derive practical applications and solutions. Inductive: Start with experiences, concrete situations, and cases. Then, using intuition, formulate general models and theories.
	Analytical/Systemic	Analytical: Separate a whole into its constituent elements. Dissect a problem into smaller chunks. Systemic: Assemble the parts into a cohesive whole. Explore connections between elements and focus on the whole system.

Rosinski, P. (2003) Reprinted with permission of the copyright holder.

Once the cultural dimensions and orientations of the coach, the client or the organization are identified, the coach can assess cultural tendencies, explore cultural choices that are possible, recognize cultural differences, bridge the cultural gaps when needed, assist with describing and envisioning an ideal culture for the situation, and leverage cultural diversity for synergies. This cultural profile of the individual or organization does not necessarily determine one's actions. Personality preferences such as extroversion or introversion, thinking or feeling, will also have a critical role in determining behavior.

One's cultural profile does not limit one's choices or potential. Cultural orientations have potential advantages, or disadvantages, depending on the challenge at hand. The culturally competent coach is much better equipped to help individuals, teams, and organizations excel in our culturally and globally diverse world.

When we examine an individual's cultural orientation, we can ask:

- What does this person prefer in terms of each cultural orientation related to the context of coaching?
- What are their abilities and strengths in this orientation that are relevant to their goals?
- What is their behavioral flexibility in various cultural or global situations, that will be helpful for their goals?
- How does this person's orientation, combined with their personality, translate into how they approach the challenges presented by their emerging life or career chapter and their goals?

CULTURAL INTELLIGENCE

The definition of positive psychology usually includes the study of the strengths that enable individuals to thrive. Hence the importance of cultural intelligence. Cultural intelligence is the ability to function effectively across a variety of cultural contexts such as ethnic, generational, and organizational cultures. Cultural intelligence researchers are fascinated by the question: "Why can some individuals and organizations move in and out of varied cultures easily and effectively while others can't?"

Twenty years ago the importance of emotional intelligence (EI) became widely recognized as critical for interpersonal and career performance, and we use EI assessments and EI-building techniques often in our positive psychology coaching approaches. However, the enhanced social intelligence that our clients usually develop though coaching does not automatically or necessarily translate into improved handling of situations when cultural or global differences are involved.

For example, a heart-to-heart, highly direct and open conversation about a conflict, with lots of eye contact (leveraging high interpersonal relations and empathy, two emotional intelligence competencies), may lead to a positive outcome in one culture and just the opposite in another culture.

One of the major pioneers in the research of cultural intelligence is Soon Ang at Nanyang Technological University in Singapore. In the late 1990s, Ang discovered that the brightest IT professionals from around the world, who were working to solve the feared Y2K meltdown, could not work well together. They were technically competent, but were not able to collaborate effectively when it came to the execution of planned solutions. Emotional intelligence–building approaches were attempted, with disappointing results. Emotional and intellectual intelligence did help these scientists solve problems when working with others in their own cultures, but those strengths did not translate into success when working with colleagues from different cultures. Ang began working with a colleague, Christopher Earley, to articulate a different conceptualization of a workplace capability, which became known as cultural intelligence and was detailed in the 2003 book, *Cultural Intelligence: Individual Interactions across Cultures*.[34] In 2004, the *Harvard Business Review* described cultural intelligence as an essential capability for business success. Competence in cultural intelligence is necessary for positive psychology coaches and their clients who want to thrive in a complex world.

Recently a number of cultural intelligence assessments have entered the market.[35] These assessments provide a numerical rating of one's cultural intelligence, sometimes called CQ (cultural quotient), and usually measure some combination of how interested you are in functioning effectively in culturally diverse settings, your knowledge about how cultures are different or similar, how you make sense of your culturally diverse experiences, and your ability to adapt your behavior effectively in different cultural or global situations.

A Quick Scan of Your Cultural Intelligence

As you reflect on your interactions with people that are culturally and globally different than you:

1. What is your *motivation* level to learn and understand more about your differences and similarities?
2. What is your *knowledge and understanding level* of cultural and global differences?
3. What is your *ability to plan and strategize* how best to interact with others in diverse situations?
4. What is your *success level in terms of your actions and behavior* in dealing with culturally and globally diverse encounters with others?

In general, presuming that you have relatively accurate self-assessment, higher motivation, knowledge, ability to strategize, and successful behavior in multi-cultural situations suggest higher cultural intelligence.

Getting into action:
- Which of the four areas above are you strongest in?
- Which of the areas above do you want to fine-tune?
- What are some potential situations you will be in where you can evaluate how well you are doing in these areas?

RESEARCH ON THE BENEFITS OF CULTURAL INTELLIGENCE

Cultural intelligence is being able to think and respond in a more flexible manner depending on the situation. Considerable research supports the assertion that cultural intelligence is critical to thrive, both on a personal level and for business success, in a culturally diverse world. Here are some examples.

Cultural intelligence has been found to be more critical to cross-cultural success than an individual's age, experience, gender, location or IQ.[36] Cultural intelligence is a stronger predictor of effective decision making in cross-cultural situations than relying on intuition. Individuals with higher cultural intelligence are better able to anticipate and manage risks than those with lower cultural intelligence when complex multicultural factors are at play.[37] Individuals with higher cultural intelligence are more effective negotiators in cross-cultural negotiation situations. Due to ambiguities that often occur in intercultural communication, individuals with higher cultural intelligence show greater persistence and success in investing the effort to achieve positive outcomes for both parties.[38] Leaders who are higher in cultural intelligence are better able to develop trust with diverse groups of people, helping the leader be more effective at influencing, developing, and leading groups and projects around the world.[39] Increasing one's cultural intelligence has been shown to increase one's personal satisfaction and level of enjoyment in multi-cultural interactions with people and organizations.[40] Ninety-two percent of a group of companies that intentionally used a cultural intelligence focus with regard to training, hiring, and strategizing saw increased revenues within eighteen months, and each company named cultural intelligence as a significant factor that contributed to increased profits.[41]

Philippe Rosinski, author of *Coaching Across Cultures* and *Global Coaching*, has identified eight coaching tips for the positive psychology–informed, culturally competent coach,[42] which also fit well with the suggestions that Dr. Delle Fave gave us at the beginning of the chapter.

Tips for Coaching across Cultures and Positively Leveraging Cultural Differences
by Philippe Rosinski

1. Consider culture as a dynamic process rather than static. Our cultural behaviors, norms, values, and assumptions are not cast in stone. Move beyond current limitations by learning from other cultures.

2. Think *and* rather than *or* to promote inclusion and reduce exclusion and polarization.

3. Become aware of your attitude *vis-à-vis* cultural differences: beware of ethnocentric pitfalls and instead cultivate an openness and curiosity about alternative worldviews.

4. Going beyond respect, tolerance, or adaptation, strive to *leverage* cultural differences: promote the appreciation of diversity, and proactively look for gems in different cultures.

5. Acquire a vocabulary to describe salient cultural characteristics, considering that "the core difficulty in cross-cultural interaction is a failure to recognize relevant cultural differences".

6. Become aware of your own cultural orientations and abilities in various areas of importance such as sense of power and responsibility, time management, identity and purpose, organizational arrangements, notions of territory, communication patterns, and modes of thinking, by using the Cultural Orientations Framework assessment. Find out how your orientations affect your behaviors.

7. Discover your underused orientations. These may well constitute new avenues to unleash your versatility and creativity, and to effectively bridge cultural gaps when dealing with different people.

8. Remember that your actions speak louder than your words. Set an example of embracing alternative cultural perspectives in your own life and coaching practice. Your congruence and authenticity will stimulate others to favor inclusion and enable harmony.

An Example of Handling Multi-Cultural Issues in Coaching

by Zeina Ghossoub El-Aswad, Ph.D., PCC

In this section, an experienced coach shares with us an interesting coaching experience that demonstrates the nuances of coaching when complex cultural issues are involved.

Two years ago I had just finished coaching an obese thirty-nine-year-old woman. We had gone through a year of wellness coaching, diet and weight loss, exercise, and change of lifestyle. In doing so we had to dig deep into personal, emotional, cultural, physical, and sometimes social problems and barriers. Even though we were of the same nationality, we were of different religions, in which views of women and their roles and responsibilities are different.

I mention this story not because of the wonderful success but because it led me into an even more challenging situation. After a year of begging her older brother, she convinced him to "talk to me." Her brother was the CEO of a company located in Saudi Arabia, and forty-five at the time. He was Lebanese. He had lived most of his life in Saudi Arabia, and by his own words is more familiar with the culture of the Kingdom of Saudi Arabia than that of Lebanon. I was in Lebanon, and the differences between the two countries are as vast as the deserts between them. That was the background for a two-year relationship that ultimately transcended cultural, gender, religious, and physical barriers.

I met this young executive in late 2011. He walked into my center with his sister, and our first conversation was of niceties

continued…

and general topics. He claimed he was there at the behest of his sister, and wanted to see "who this coach his sister has been talking about is."

Let me set the background image for you before I proceed with describing the case from a coaching perspective. This is a young CEO who has around 500 employees under his command. He is a male living in Saudi Arabia. The culture and political make-up of Saudi Arabia is that of a monarchy that encourages male superiority and paternalism while minimizing the sociopolitical and economic position and role of females. I live in a country where things are much more liberal—women have a major role, and voting rights—and I am from a different religion. The gap between where we were at the beginning of the coaching relationship and where we ended up is enormous. And that gap was bridged step by step, meeting by meeting, word by word with these three underlying themes: trust, quest for understanding, and respect.

After the first meeting, where he was just visiting with his sister, it took a few days, but he called me to set up our first coaching session. Again, he refused to acknowledge my services as a coach. He stated that he wanted to talk, explore, and discuss his intrigue in my work. He loved the concepts I was talking about and wanted to hear more about them. That was his entry point to the world of coaching. After a few "talking sessions" and "learning," as my client put it, rapport was built. Before I continue with the coaching sessions and the process, let me pause and focus a bit on how a positive coach–client relationship developed.

In approaching the client, key issues had to be dealt with: trust, respect, and belief in the coach and the process.

continued...

First I helped him understand that this was a nonjudgmental encounter. He needed to know the difference between counseling and coaching. Whereas people may get offended for a perceived need to be "counseled," he took to the concept of coaching as a way to help maximize his own potential and abilities. I used the example of elite male athletes, Michael Jordan was an example, and how, no matter how great he was, he had to have the right coach in Phil Jackson to win a championship. That analogy helped him better understand the process and value of coaching.

The next step was to have him believe that a woman could do this job. Again, he is a man who takes care of his sisters, has a wife and children, and is responsible for all the women in his life. In his business he deals mostly with men. Initially, to sidestep the gender difference, I focused his attention on the issues and tasks by "talking shop." I spent most of my sessions listening as he spoke, uninterrupted, about himself and his accomplishments and his perceived goals. I just took notes. The way my office is set up, my chair puts me at a higher level than my clients—so I lowered it, and sat lower than him. But over the course of our sessions, that chair went back to where it originally was. By shifting the focus to him, and discussing his goals and his views, and appearing as if I was being taught and lectured, he eased into his CEO status and male comfort zone.

After a few sessions, his body language suggested relaxation. He was loose, sitting comfortably, accustomed to my "high chair." At this time I switched gears and started talking as a coach by offering solid examples and approaches based on the information he had provided. I spoke his language, used his

continued…

examples, and identified his goals, which he had stated clearly. Needless to say, I caught his attention, and the material and context took over the sessions gradually, as cultural, gender, and socioreligious barriers held less sway. I call this approach the "music-mixer approach." One fades out while the other is introduced. I apply this approach no matter the scenario—I ease my clients into a comfortable zone they create, and make them feel as if they are in their own gym, where they have practiced for years.

A contract was signed, goals were identified, and the journey began. After the initial sessions, I coached by telephone, since he had returned to Saudi Arabia. Every now and then he would come back and we would do some face-to-face coaching. The journey was enjoyable for both of us. I got to learn so much about him and the way he thinks and leads. He was also suffering from major burnout, extra weight, and high blood pressure. So we started off with wellness coaching and four goals: to lose ten pounds, lower his blood pressure (enough to get off medications), get more sleep, and enjoy life a bit more. Those goals were 80 percent achieved in the time set.

He liked the coaching so much that we renewed our contract for another three months, but this time the focus was more on self-development matters. Many assessment tools were used in this phase, and it was always very difficult to take the results as totally reliable because they were not culturally sensitive. He is very fluent in English, and the assessments such as MBTI and Emotional Intelligence EQi2.0 were administered in English. However, especially due to cultural issues, I always had to take the results provisionally and further investigate

continued...

them with my client. This phase of self-development did not take just three months but extended to nine months of truly pure understanding of himself, his abilities, strengths, personality, emotions, and his communication with others on professional and personal levels.

The models I used varied, but in every round of coaching I based my sessions on the simple guidelines of the GOOD Model, developed by Dr. Jeffery Auerbach of the College of Executive Coaching. The model is straightforward and suited this man. It helps the client in creating a plan with the coach, moving with momentum, commitment, and accountability. The G stands for *goals,* O for *opportunities,* another O for *obstacles,* and D for *do.* Further, to continue building trust, and improving his feeling of control and command of the session and approach, I employed this strategy: I clarified the long-term goals and short-term goals for each session. He felt he was in complete control, and that served him to "own the session" and be very comfortable and drop his guard, so to speak.

In addition, the sessions emphasized his strengths while gently illustrating either negative thought processes or ways to enhance existing positive ones. This created opportunities for him that he could clearly see, and he was driven to eliminate the challenges that lay ahead by finding solutions, either when we were coaching or between sessions. The time factor was very important to him because of his work overload and his wanting to be able to take control of his life as he likes to do—hence the deliverables. Each session would last anywhere between one and two hours. Typically, the sessions would recap the previous ones, go over homework

continued...

that was given, and then continue from where we last finished. After a year of coaching, we ended our coaching engagement. He still contacts me from time to time with a reflection or thought. I am proud to say that this was a successful partnership and that it ended extremely well. It had to transcend initial social, cultural, religious, physical, and gender barriers, and more importantly it was successful in helping the client achieve wellness and executive goals through a variety of coaching techniques and models that were dynamic, adaptive, and focused.

SUMMARY

Coaches are in a unique position to trigger the exploration within their clients of this critically important variable—how culturally aware, appreciative, and flexible our clients are in multicultural and global situations. Coaches can't do this unless they themselves have developed these cultural competence skills. As coaches, we are trained to help clients expand their awareness, increase their empathy, develop greater flexibility, and thrive in team-building, influence, and interpersonal relationships. Knowing how to do this in an ever-changing, culturally and globally complex world is a life-long learning curve that positive psychology–trained coaches are well suited to explore, facilitate, and develop.

CHAPTER 12
Negative Emotions in the Context of Positive Psychology

In a coaches' manual concerned with positive psychology applications, we believe it is important to speak to the role that negative emotions play in our coaching. As we refer back to Pawelski's piece on the meaning of *the positive* (Chapter 1), he notes, "Maya Tamir and James Gross ... define positive emotions as those that are adaptive for well-being. Pleasant emotions, they argue, 'could be either positive or negative, depending on their implications for well-being.'"[1]

As coaches, let us say where we stand on negative emotions in our work. First, we recognize that we must carefully assess a prospective client's situation to determine whether coaching is the most appropriate approach or psychotherapy is rather the best course of action. Psychotherapy is the appropriate intervention if the person is experiencing a persistent preponderance of negative thoughts and emotions arising from a serious setback or loss, unprocessed trauma, severe interpersonal conflicts with family, friends or co-workers, or other upsetting life circumstance. Psychotherapy is also indicated when a person has a significant history of anxiety or depression and their symptoms are recurring. Of course, we always ask whether a prospective client has been feeling suicidal, and if so, we make referrals immediately to psychotherapists we know and trust.

Second, having determined that coaching is the best approach, how do we then address negativity in the context of positive psychology coaching? We heed Pawelski's careful analysis of what is meant by *the positive*. We are informed by the notion proposed by Tamir and Gross that the experience of negative or positive emotions is tied to their implications for well-being. We believe that, as coaches, we should be concerned that our clients know about ways to adaptively respond to negative thoughts and emotions. We believe that this can aid in their flourishing. What this means is that we want to ensure that our clients know about actions they can take to manage negative thoughts and emotions if this has become an issue in our coaching.

Third, we also believe that we should encourage our clients to understand the importance of being able to navigate all of their emotions and have tools for learning from the negative experiences that they choose to share with us in the coaching.

WHAT THE RESEARCH SAYS ABOUT MANAGING NEGATIVE EMOTIONS

Both Seligman[2] and Lyubomirsky[3] cite the work of the late Susan Nolen-Hoeksema, who was a tenured professor of psychology at Stanford before she went to Yale. Nolen-Hoeksema's research explored how a person's emotional regulation strategies affect the likelihood of developing mood disorders.[4] In a popular self-help book[5] as well as in her peer-reviewed research, Nolen-Hoeksema described ways to manage negative rumination (overthinking, as she termed it) as one means of alleviating depressive symptoms. Lybomirsky and Nolen-Hoeksema collaborated in compiling the evidence indicating that overthinking is a troubling *habit* of thinking and advocated that it be managed in order for a person to be happier.[6]

We recognize that managing such overthinking is important in the treatment of depression. When our coaching clients experience a transient period of overthinking, we believe it is useful to make them aware of resources such as Nolen-Hoeksema's self-help book. From this resource, clients can learn about action steps for mitigating their negative rumination as one way of managing negative emotions.

DISPUTATION

Researchers in positive psychology including Seligman[7] and Fredrickson[8] recommend the cognitive therapy technique of disputation, which can help a person struggling with overly pessimistic thoughts. Disputation works by objectively examining the logic of self-statements and critically evaluating the unpleasant predictions that are associated with negative emotional states. Aaron Beck, MD, one of the founders of cognitive behavior therapy, helped bring this five-step technique to psychotherapists working with depressed and anxious patients.[9] The late Albert Ellis, founder of Rational Emotive Therapy, also proposed a three-step process for challenging irrational beliefs that are correlated with negative emotions.[10]

In *Positivity*, Fredrickson suggests the following as a disputation approach to managing a downward spiral of negative thinking and emotion: "Dispute negative thinking... the way a good lawyer would, by examining the facts.... What set it off? What negative thoughts and beliefs got triggered? What did those thoughts and beliefs in turn make me feel? And how do those thoughts and beliefs compare to reality? What are the facts of my situation? When I take in those facts—truly take them in—how do I feel?"[11]

ADVERSITY, BELIEFS AND CONSEQUENCES

In line with Beck's formulation, Seligman, in his book *Learned Optimism*, describes the process of arguing with the beliefs that emerge following an unpleasant event and lays out the steps of Adversity, Beliefs, Consequences, Disputation (the consideration of the situation in a fact-based manner), and finally Outcome (what is the resulting feeling state).[12] He also describes the steps as put forward by Ellis: Adversity, Beliefs, and Consequences.[13] As coaches, we suggest that these research-based techniques for managing upsetting thoughts have a place in coaching. We can think of times when our clients are experiencing setbacks at work or difficulties in their personal lives that may come up in the course of our coaching conversations or be the focus of the coaching engagement. In these situations, we observe them particularly weighed down by upsetting thoughts they recognize as excessive and particularly troubling. Rather than ignore these thoughts, we encourage them to reflect on their current circumstances and look for triggers (like recalling past events) that are prompting these thoughts in the present. We can suggest to clients a number of ways to manage this particularly negative state, including disputation or managing overthinking.

DISTRACTION, MEDIATION AND PROBLEM-SOLVING

When appropriate, we also recommend that our clients momentarily distract themselves from their negative states by finding respite in two or three specific activities that they enjoy. These can be returning to a hobby such as creating crafts, sewing or knitting, doing crossword puzzles, or playing music. We especially emphasize the positive effects of exercise and of walking in nature, which can be useful distractions from negative states as well as positive experiences in their own right. We can remind them of the value of gaining perspective on negative periods in their lives by asking how important in the overall scheme of things the unpleasant events will seem a year or more from now.

We can suggest that they undertake a meditation practice, mentioning specifically Fredrickson's Loving Kindness Meditation, and direct them to her website.[14] We can suggest that training in mindfulness meditation can also be helpful and recommend the research-based approaches taught by Jon Kabat-Zinn.[15]

We can actively engage them in issue-identification and problem-solving discussions in our coaching conversations. We can ask them to look for the root cause of the issue that is disturbing them and to think aloud with us regarding possible solutions they imagine might help resolve the problem. We assess with them the reasonableness and relevance of each solution and coach them in coming to a conclusion about what they think would be best to do. We then assist them in assessing their readiness for actually implementing the solution and aid them in determining what social support or other resources they need to take effective action.

We also remind our clients (as we noted in Chapter 2) that research conducted by Fredrickson and Levenson provides evidence that experiencing positive emotions may help attenuate the adverse impact of negative emotions on physiological functioning.[16]

LEARNING AND GROWING

Why is it important for our coaching clients to be able to embrace all of their emotions and to learn from negative events? We find compelling the argument expressed by one of our colleagues, Richard (Dick) Kilburg, who puts it this way (we are paraphrasing here). "Humans learn better from negative emotions than positive ones. It is important to learn about things that are dangerous and evolutionary. Emotion informs us; it is another form of data. What we're doing as coaches is to become masters of emotions—to understand our own and the impulses triggered by them—to be able to express our own emotions and to mirror back emotions to the client so we can be most effective."[17]

As positive psychology matures as a domain in general psychology, several trends have been emerging. One that we find of particular importance to coaching is how to enlist our clients in the discovery of what they can learn from the negative events that occur in their lives. This means helping them embrace the idea that all emotions, including negative ones, are part of life, are instructive, and can be navigated. What is even more important to us as coaches is to provide the thought partnering for clients to make sense and meaning from the negativity they experience and the events they label as difficult.

Our colleague, David Peterson, PhD, Director of Executive Coaching and Leadership at Google and a senior faculty member at the College of Executive Coaching, argues cogently for clients to develop through the negative experiences of discomfort and disruption. He offers this advice that we can use in our coaching.

Stretch Yourself
by David Peterson

CEOs around the world believe that the business world is becoming more complex, dynamic, and unpredictable. As a result, what has made them successful in the past is unlikely to lead to future success. Paradoxically, the more intent leaders are on optimizing performance to be successful in one environment, the greater the risk that they will fail as conditions change.

If our world is indeed more complex, ambiguous, and unpredictable, the way to succeed in the long run is to learn how to deal effectively with novel, diverse, and adverse situations. And the best way to do *that* is to aggressively seek experiences you've never faced before, with an attitude of experimentation and curiosity, so that you develop greater agility at handling ambiguous, complex challenges.

Stretch yourself to the edge of your comfort zone by tackling important problems that others avoid, with a mindset of exploring to see what you can discover. Another way to broaden your experience is to regularly expose yourself to people with very different views and learn to see things from their perspective. They key is seeking a *little* discomfort and disruption to your routine every day, so you expand your capacity to deal with it effectively. And then, after you try something new, develop a regular habit of reflection—even just one minute a day—to ask what you are learning and what you can do differently to keep dancing on the edge of your comfort zone.[18]

We note a trend in the recent publication of such books as *The Upside of Your Dark Side: Why Being Your Whole Self, Not Just Your Good Self, Drives Success and Fulfillment,* by Robert Biswas-Diener and his colleague Todd Kashdan.[19] These authors assert that every emotion is useful, and that in every emotional state humans experience there is some kind of adaptive advantage.

When such events are overwhelming, then the client is best served by psychotherapy, pastoral or rabbinic counseling, or some other form of intervention beyond what coaching can provide. However, particularly when a client is trying to make sense of negative past events in order to make better decisions in the present, our coaching conversations can be a valuable part of their development. We can pose questions like:

- When you think about that past situation and then observe what is happening now, what similarities do you notice?

- What do these observations tell you may be happening again?

- What lessons can you take from your past experience of ___ that can help you understand what is happening now?

- Thinking back on how you responded then to this situation, what would do differently, and why?

- How can you proceed now with a greater understanding of your role in what happened then, so that you can take effective action tomorrow?

- What is your key takeaway from this situation?
- What new-found wisdom can serve you now as you do ___?
- What strengths can you bring to this situation to help you navigate this difficult set of circumstances?
- What key learnings about yourself make it possible to cope well in this unsettling set of circumstances?

We also note a trend in the emerging discussion in positive psychology circles of *post-traumatic growth*. Seligman addresses this topic in *Flourish*.[20] In general, *reappraisal* is an important element in the post-traumatic growth process, as is learning from the experience. By reappraisal researchers mean exploring and redefining what the client can usefully glean from a tough experience. The difficult event can likewise be reframed as one that yields insights useful to the person in the future, even as they recover from the debilitating impact of the negative experience.

As coaches, we may be asked to be part of such conversations for clients who are reengaging with their work and personal lives after recovery from a life-threatening illness or traumatic event. If we assess their current situation carefully, we may conclude that coaching is indeed indicated as a way for them to move forward in working toward important goals.

Appendix

Getting Clear On The Positive In Positive Psychology
James O. Pawelski

A look at early documents in positive psychology reveals a variety of definitions of "positive". Most are to be found in a seminal article written by Seligman & Csikszentmihalyi in American Psychologist, in an issue entirely dedicated to positive psychology. The authors argue that mainstream psychology focuses on what goes wrong in people's lives, whereas positive psychology looks at what goes right. They emphasize that the work of mainstream psychology is important, but that it needs to be balanced by an examination of what is best in life, of what makes life most worth living. Differing from mainstream psychology in terms of its orientation, positive psychology, as they understand it, is a complement to—and not a replacement for—psychology as usual.

In addition to defining positive psychology as a complement to mainstream psychology, Seligman & Csikszentmihalyi also connect positive psychology to the rich philosophical tradition of the investigation and cultivation of the "good life." Both the definition of positive psychology as a complement to mainstream psychology and the definition of positive psychology as an approach to the good life have been taken up and repeated by researchers and practitioners around the world and have become part of the DNA of positive psychology. A closer look at these two definitions shows that they lead to two very different conceptions of the field. Understood as a complement to mainstream psychology, positive psychology seems to be about the best things in life; understood as an approach to the good life, however, it seems to be about creating the best life we can. These two conceptions are no doubt related (the best things in life are certainly important ingredients for creating the best life we can), but they are far from identical. A look at the debate about how to define positive emotions illustrates the point. Barbara Fredrickson on the one hand, defines positive emotions as those that have a "pleasant subjective feel". Maya Tamir and James Gross on the other hand, define positive emotions as those that are adaptive for well-being. Pleasant emotions, they argue, "could be either positive or negative, depending on their implications for well-being". Most people would no doubt classify positive emotions as some of the best things in life; however, if our goal is to create the best life we can, there are at least certain cases where unpleasant emotions may be more useful than pleasant ones.

Positive psychology defined as a complement to mainstream psychology seems to be a psychology of intrinsic goods ("the best things in life," including things like pleasant emotions); but positive psychology defined as an empirical investigation of the good life seems to be a psychology of instrumental goods (the things that lead to maximal well-being, including, at times, things like unpleasant emotions).

It is easy for practitioners to make the tacit assumption that all of positive psychology research is at the intersection of the intrinsically good and the instrumentally good. In this case, any intrinsic goods studied by researchers would be valid means for achieving the instrumental good of human flourishing. The debate about positive emotions explored above illustrates how dangerously incorrect this assumption can be. There may well be times where intrinsic goods (like pleasant emotions) are not instrumentally good. In these cases, asking clients to focus on intrinsic goods anyway may diminish their overall well-being and could actually cause them harm.

In its role as a complement to mainstream psychology, positive psychology is right to point out the dangers of overusing deficit-oriented approaches, since these may not take sufficient account of what is intrinsically good in life. Positive psychology, however, must be careful not to fall into the reciprocal danger of overusing strengths-based approaches, since these may not properly consider instrumental goods. If the overall goal is human flourishing, the means for achieving it will have to be some optimal balance between the instrumental use and mitigation of the negative and the enhancement of the intrinsically positive.

References

Fredrickson, B. L. (1998). What good are positive emotions? Review of General Psychology, 2, 300-319.

Tamir, M., & Gross, J. (2011). Beyond pleasure and pain? Emotion regulation and positive psychology. In K. Sheldon, T. Kashdan, & M. Steger (Eds.), Designing positive psychology (pp. 89-100). Oxford: Oxford University Press.

Plato. (1892). The republic. In The dialogues of Plato (Vol. I, pp. 589-879). (B. Jowett, Trans.). New York: Random House. (Original work written circa 380 B.C.E.).

Seligman, M. E. P., & Csikszentmihalyi, M. (2000). Positive psychology: An introduction. American Psychologist, 55, 5-14.

Auerbach Well-Being Coaching Client Questionnaire

Please take a reasonable amount of time (you define that!) to answer the following questions. There are no wrong answers. Some of the questions capture information about where you are today. Other questions will make you curious about what you want from coaching, from your career and from your life in general. Although the focus of our work together is your executive role, I ask some general and personal questions as a way of creating a more complete understanding of you. You are free to answer the questions as briefly or as in-depth as you wish. Your answers are generally confidential, similar to our coaching conversations, unless a rare situation arises where they warrant a release of information as required by law or ethical standards, such as a danger to self or others. Your responses will help us set a strong foundation for the coaching relationship.

Name: _____

Mailing Address: _____

Home Telephone: _____

Work Telephone: _____

Mobile Telephone: _____

Fax Number: _____

E-Mail Address: _____

Occupation/Job Title and Organization Name: _____

_____

Self-Verified 4 Letter MBTI Type: _____

List your Top 5 Character Strengths from the VIA Survey of Character Strengths

1. _____

2. _____

3. _____

4. _____

5. _____

Coaching:

1. What do you want to be sure to get from the coaching relationship?

2. How do you want me to be as your coach?

3. What do you want to work on in coaching?

4. What two steps could you take immediately that would help you move forward?

5. What can I say to you when you are stuck that will help you move forward?

6. What changes might you need to make to help your coaching be successful?

Career:
1. What is most positive about your career?

2. What changes do you want to make related to career?

3. What are your key career goals?

4. What do you need to change to help your career move forward?

Social Well-being: having strong and positive relationships
5. What is most positive about your relationships and social life?

6. What changes do you want to make related to your relationships and social life?

7. What are your key goals related to your relationships and social life?

8. What do you need to change to help your relationships and social life move forward?

Financial Well-being: maintaining sufficient, balanced finances

9. What is most positive about your financial situation?

10. What changes do you want to make related to your financial situation?

11. What are your key goals related to your financial situation?

12. What do you need to change to help your financial situation move forward?

Community Well-being: feeling engaged in one's community

13. What is most positive about your community situation?

14. What changes do you want to make related to your community situation?

15. What are your key goals related to your community situation?

16. What do you need to change to help your community situation move forward?

Physical and Psychological Well-being: living a healthy life

Please share any concerns or information you want to about:

Energy level:_____

Sleep: _____

Stress: _____

Depression/Anxiety: _____

Life Satisfaction: _____

Life Balance:_____

Exercise: _____

Weight: _____

Illness Issues: _____

Recovery Issues: _____

17. What is most positive about your health situation?

18. What concerns do you have about your health?

19. What changes do you want to make related to your health situation?

20. What are your key goals related to your health situation?

21. What do you need to change to help your health or a more healthy lifestyle move forward?

Personal

1. What special interests do you have?

2. What special knowledge do you have?

3. What do you believe in strongly?

4. Tell me about a time when you were operating in a peak performance phase, when things were going really well or you were very pleased with what you were doing or accomplishing. Don't be humble please. What was going on? Who was involved? What feelings did you have?

5. What do you do when things get stressful?

6. What activities have special meaning for you?

7. What vision do you have for your life?

8. Please tell me what you would like to about your family and personal life:

9. Please tell me about significant events in your life that you would like to share:

Donald O. Clifton: Positive Psychology Icon

Don Clifton was an active member of the Society of Psychologists in Management (SPIM). He served on the board of directors while I was president in the late 1990s and subsequently served as president himself. At that time, Don was president, CEO and chairman of the board of Gallup International. Serendipitously, this was also the time when the first of ten Gallup International Positive Psychology Summits was held. For this benchmark event, about sixty-five behavioral scientists, including myself, were invited to the Gallup Operations Headquarters in Lincoln, Nebraska, for a conference to study what was then known empirically about the "wellsprings of happiness."

My acceptance of Don's personal verbal invitation was followed by an e-mail confirmation, accompanied by a lengthy questionnaire about my involvement in positive psychology. This background information from each of the participants became part of the conference proceedings and marked the meticulous thoroughness of Don Clifton in everything he did. Fortunately for me, while a visiting scholar at the Cooper Institute in Dallas, Texas, I had developed an interdisciplinary university class titled Lifestyle Enhancement which incorporated many of the tenets of what was to soon be described as positive psychology. Also, as an organizational psychologist, the "sunny side" of leadership, attitude, and motivation were important perspectives of studying individuals, groups, and organizations.

This first summit was one of the benchmarks for the rapidly expanding empirical studies of positive psychology. The major TV and print media covered it. For example, it was the subject of a two-hour Good Morning America program on ABC. For me, it was also an introduction to the Gallup organization as an example of positive psychology in action. This was as invigorating as the summit itself. Don Clifton had been studying "what is right about people" for decades and this accumulated knowledge was applied in building a crown jewel of a family consulting business. As recognized by the American Psychological Association, Don was the Father of Strengths-Based Psychology and the Grandfather of Positive Psychology.

During our conversations at the summit, Don agreed to edit a special issue of the SPIM journal on positive psychology. Working with Don on this endeavor, as well as focusing SPIM conference programming on application of positive psychology to leadership, was a basis for a strong personal friendship that I highly value to this day. Don also agreed for Gallup to publish the SPIM journal for several years, and along with Al Parchem of RHR, to underwrite its costs.

Why write this brief description of my friendship with Don Clifton and how I knew him? For one, Don's friendship and collegial mentoring was evident in all of his interactions with everyone. I have the distinction of having participated in all ten of the Gallup Summits, several times as a presenter, and was able to witness the growth of positive psychology and Don's stellar life and legacy. He certainly had a major impact on my life and career. Also, "Sam" Foster asked me to do this, and positive psychology's posture of the heart is answering the call, as Don modeled so well, with a smile and an enthusiastic YES.

Paul J. Lloyd, PhD
Professor Emeritus
Southeast Missouri State University

Notes

CHAPTER 1: THE INTEGRATION OF POSITIVE PSYCHOLOGY AND COACHING

1. Auerbach, J. E. (2001). *Personal and executive coaching: The complete guide for mental health professionals.* Ventura, CA: Executive College Press.

2. *Ibid.*

3. Gallwey, T. W. (1997). *The inner game of tennis.* New York, NY: Random House.

4. Grant, A. M. (2003). The impact of life coaching on goal attainment, metacognition and mental health. *Social Behavior and Personality, 31(3),* 253–264.

5. Seligman, M. (2011). *Flourish.* New York, NY: Free Press.

6. Seligman, M. E. P. (2002). *Authentic happiness.* New York, NY: Free Press.

7. Fredrickson, B. L. (2009). *Positivity.* New York, NY: Crown.

8. Fredrickson, B. L. (1998). What good are positive emotions? *Review of General Psychology, 2,* 300–319.

9. Tamir, M., & Gross, J. (2011). Beyond pleasure and pain? Emotion regulation and positive psychology. In K. Sheldon, T. Kashdan, & M. Steger (Eds.), *Designing positive psychology* (pp. 89–100). Oxford, England: Oxford University Press.

10. Gold standard research involves selecting subjects who are equivalent in some key dimension at the outset of the study, randomly assigning them to a treatment group(s) compared with a non-treatment condition, and identifying outcome measures that include behavioral indicators in addition to self-reports of progress and change.

11. Seligman, M.E.P., and Schulman, P. (1986). Explanatory style as a predictor of productivity and quitting among life insurance agents. *Journal of Personality and Social Psychology, 50,* 832–838.

12. Fowler, R. D., Seligman, M. E. P., & Koocher, G. P. (1998). The APA 1998 Annual Report. *American Psychologist, 54(8),* 537–568.

13. *Ibid.*

14. Kobasa, S., Maddi, S., Kahn, S. (1982). Hardiness and health: A prospective study. *Journal of Personality and Social Psychology, 42(1),* 68–177.

15. Kobasa, S. C., Maddi, S. R., & Puccetti, M. C. (1982). Personality and exercise as buffers in the stress-illness relationship. *Journal of Behavioral Medicine, 5(4),* 391–404.

16. Solomon, G., & Temoshok, L. (1987). A psychoneuroimmunologic perspective on AIDS research: Questions, preliminary findings, and suggestions. *Journal of Applied Social Psychology, 17,* 286–308.

17. Auerbach, J., Oleson, T., and Solomon, G. (1992). A behavioral medicine intervention as an adjunctive treatment for HIV-related illness. *Psychology and Health, 6(4),* 325–334.

18. Rossi, E. (1991). The twenty minute break: *Reduce stress, maximize performance, improve health and emotional well-being using the new science of ultradian rhythms.* Los Angeles, CA: Tarcher.

CHAPTER 2: THE INTEGRATION OF POSITIVE PSYCHOLOGY AND COACHING

1. Fredrickson, B. L. (2001). The role of positive emotions in positive psychology: The broaden-and-build theory of positive emotions. *American Psychologist, 56(3)*, 218–226.

2. Frijda, N. H., Kuipers, P., & Schure, E. (1989). Relations among emotion, appraisal, and emotional action readiness. *Journal of Personality and Social Psychology, 57*, 212–228.

3. Easterbrook, J. A. (1959). The effect of emotion on cue utilization and the organization of behavior. *Psychological Review, 66*, 183–201.

4. Fredrickson, B. L., & Levenson, R. W. (1998). Positive emotions speed recovery from the cardiovascular sequelae of negative emotions. *Cognition and Emotion, 12*, 191–220.

5. Fredrickson, B. L. (2001). The role of positive emotions in positive psychology: The broaden-and-build theory of positive emotions. *American Psychologist, 56(3)*, 218–226.

6. Fredrickson, B. L. (2009). *Positivity*. New York, NY: Crown.

7. Fredrickson, B. L. (2013). *Love 2.0*. New York, NY: Hudson Street Press.

8. Fredrickson, B. L. (2001). The role of positive emotions in positive psychology: The broaden-and-build theory of positive emotions. *American Psychologist, 56(3)*, 218–226 (p. 221).

9. Fredrickson, B. L. (1998). What good are positive emotions? *Review of General Psychiatry, 2*, 300–319.

10. Isen, A. M., Rosenzweig, A. S., & Young, M. J. (1991). The influence of positive affect on clinical problem solving. *Medical Decision Making, 11*, 221–227.

11. Fredrickson, B. L. (2013). *Love 2.0*. New York, NY: Hudson Street Press (p. 17).

12. http://positivityresonance.com/meditations.html.

13. Cacioppo, J. T., Gardner, W. L., & Berntson, G. G. (1999). The affect system has parallel and integrative processing components: Form follows function. *Journal of Personality and Social Psychology, 76*, 839–855.

14. Isen, A. M., & Daubman, K. A. (1984). The influence of affect on categorization. *Journal of Personality and Social Psychology, 47*, 1206–1217.

15. Isen, A. M. (1990). The influence of positive and negative affect on cognitive organization: Some implications for development. In N. Stein, B. Leventhal, & T. Trabasso (Eds.), *Psychological and biological approaches to emotion* (pp. 75–94). Hillsdale, NJ: Erlbaum (p. 89).

16. Isen, A. M., Rosenzweig, A. S., & Young, M. J. (1991). The influence of positive affect on clinical problem solving. *Medical Decision Making, 11*, 221–227.

17. Derryberry, D., & Tucker, D. M. (1994). Motivating the focus of attention. In P. M. Neidenthal & S. Kitayama (Eds.), *The heart's eye: Emotional influences in perception and attention* (pp. 167–196). San Diego, CA: Academic Press.

18. Folkman, S., & Moskowitz, J. T. (2000). Stress, positive emotion, and coping. *Current Directions in Psychological Science, 9(4)*, 115–118.

19. Cohn, M. A., Fredrickson, B. L., Brown, S. L., Mikels, J. A., & Conway, A.M. (2009). Happiness unpacked: Positive emotions increase life satisfaction by building resilience. *Emotion, 9(3)*, 361–368. doi:10.1037/a0015952.

20. Cohen, S., Doyle, W. J., Turner, R. B., Alper, C. M., & Skoner, D. P. (2001). Emotional style and susceptibility to the common cold. *Psychosomatic Medicine, 63*, 652–657.

21. Cropanazo, R., & Wright, T. A. (1999). A 5-year study of change in the relationship between well-being and job performance. *Consulting Psychology Journal: Practice and Research, 51*, 252–265.

22. Van Katwyk, P. T., Fox, S., Spector, P. E., & Kelloway, E. K. (2000). Using the Job-Related Affective Well-being Scale (JAWS) to investigate affective responses to work stressors. *Journal of Occupational Health Psychology, 52,* 219–230.

23. Judge, T. A., Thoresen, C. J., Pucik, V., & Welbourne, T. M. (1999). Managerial coping with organizational change: A dispositional perspective. *Journal of Applied Psychology, 84,* 107–122.

24. Fredrickson, B. L., & Levenson, R. W. (1998). Positive emotions speed recovery from the cardiovascular sequelae of negative emotions. *Cognition and Emotion, 12,* 191–220. Frijda, N. H. (1986). *The emotions.* Cambridge, England: Cambridge University Press.

25. Seligman, M. E. P. (2002). *Authentic happiness: Using the new positive psychology to realize your potential for lasting fulfillment.* New York, NY: Free Press.

26. Fredrickson, B. L., & Levenson, R. W. (1998). Positive emotions speed recovery from the cardiovascular sequelae of negative emotions. *Cognition and Emotion, 12,* 191–220.

27. *Ibid.*

28. Fredrickson, B. L. (2000). Why positive emotions matter: Lessons from the broaden-and-build model. The *Psychologist-Manager Journal, 4,* 131–142.

29. www.positivityratio.com/single.php.

30. Meichenbaum, D. (1989). *Stress inoculation training.* London, England: Plenum.

31. Diener, E., Sandvik, E., & Pavot, W. (1991). Happiness is the frequency, not the intensity, of positive versus negative affect. In F. Strack, M. Argyle, & N. Schwarz (Eds.), *Subjective well-being: An interdisciplinary perspective* (pp. 119–139). New York, NY: Pergamon.

32. Brown, N. J. L., Sokol, A. D., & Friedman, H. L. (2013). The complex dynamics of wishful thinking: The critical positivity ratio. *American Psychologist, 68(9),* 801–813.

33. Fredrickson, B. L., & Losada, M. F. (2005). Positive affect and the complex dynamics of human flourishing. *American Psychologist, 60(7),* 678–686.

34. Losada, M. F., & Heapy, E. (2004). The role of positivity and connectivity in the performance of business teams. *American Behavioral Scientist, 47(6),* 740–765.

35. Fredrickson, B. L. (2013). Updated thinking on positivity ratios. *American Psychologist, 68(9),* 814–822.

36. Brown, N. J. L., Sokol, A. D., & Friedman, H. L. (2013). The complex dynamics of wishful thinking: The critical positivity ratio. *American Psychologist, 68(9),* 801–813 (p. 801).

37. Fredrickson, B. L. (2013). Updated thinking on positivity ratios. *American Psychologist, 68(9),* 814–822 (p. 820).

38. Fredrickson, B. L. (2013). Updated thinking on positivity ratios. *American Psychologist, 68(9),* 814-822 (p. 814). doi: 10.1037/a0033584.

39. Boehm, J. K., & Lyubomirsky, S. (2008). Does happiness promote career success? *Journal of Career Assessment, 16(1),* 101–116 (p. 101).

40. Lyubomirsky, S. (2007). *The how of happiness: A scientific approach to getting the life that you want.* New York, NY: Penguin.

41. Lyubomirsky, S. (2013). *Myths of happiness: What should make you happy but doesn't, and what shouldn't make you happy but does.* New York, NY: Penguin.

42. *Ibid.*

43. *Ibid.*

44.   Diener, E., Suh, E. M., Lucas, R. E., & Smith, H. L. (1999). Subjective well-being: Three decades of progress. *Psychological Bulletin, 125,* 276–302. Suh, E. M., Diener, E., & Fujita, F. (1996). Events and subjective well-being: Only recent events matter. *Journal of Personality and Social Psychology, 70,* 1091–1102.

45.   Lyubomirsky, S., & Lepper, H. (1999). A measure of subjective happiness: Preliminary reliability and construct validation. *Social Indicators Research, 46,* 137–155.

46.   David Lykken of the University of Minnesota was an early investigator of the role genetics played in happiness (defined as "having a sunny, easy-going personality," "dealing well with stress," and "feeling low levels of depression and anxiety"). He studied 4,000 sets of twins born in Minnesota from 1936 to 1955. He and his colleague, Auke Tellegen, evaluated the happiness metrics in identical twins versus fraternal twins. Based on their analyses, they concluded that 50 percent of the variance relating to happiness and overall satisfaction with life was explained by genetic factors. Lykken, D., & Tellegen, A. (1996). Happiness is a stochastic phenomenon. *Psychological Science, 7,* 186–189. Lykken's website is at www.psych.umn.edu/psylabs/happness/hapindex.htm.

47.   Frederick, S., & Loewenstein, G. (1999). Hedonic adaption. In D. Kahneman, E. Diener, & Schwartz, N. (Eds), *Well-being: The foundations of hedonic psychology* (pp. 302–329). New York, NY: Russell Sage.

48.   Lyubomirsky, S. (2001). Why are some people happier than others? *American Psychologist, 56(3),* 239–249.

49.   Lyubomirsky, S., & Dickerhoof, R. (2010). A construal approach to increasing happiness. In J. Tangney & J. E. Maddux (Eds.), *Social psychological foundations of clinical psychology* (pp. 229–244). New York, NY: Guilford Press.

50.   Lyubomirsky, S. (2007). *The how of happiness: A scientific approach to getting the life that you want.* New York, NY: Penguin (p. 67).

51.   Lyubomirsky, S., Dickerhoof, R., Boehm, J. K., & Sheldon, K. M. (2011). Becoming happier takes both a will and a proper way: An experimental longitudinal intervention to boost well-being. *Emotion, 11,* 391–402.

52.   Layous, K., & Lyubomirsky, S. (2014). The how, why, what, when, and who of happiness: Mechanisms underlying the success of positive interventions. In J. Gruber & J. Moscowitz (Eds.), *Positive emotion: Integrating the light sides and dark sides* (pp. 473–495). New York, NY: Oxford University Press.

53.   Nelson, S. K., & Lyubomirsky, S. (2012). Finding happiness: Tailoring positive activities for optimal well-being benefits. In M. Tugade, M. Shiota, & L. Kirby (Eds.), Handbook of positive emotions. New York, NY: Guildford.

54.   Jacobs, K., & Lyubomirsky, S. (2013). The rewards of happiness. In S. Boniwell & S. David (Eds.), *Oxford handbook of happiness* (pp. 119–133). Oxford, England: Oxford University Press.

55.   Lyubomirsky, S., Sheldon, K. M., & Schkade, D. (2005). Pursuing happiness: The architecture of sustainable change. *Review of General Psychology, 9,* 111–131.

56.   Lyubomirsky, S. (2007). *The how of happiness: A scientific approach to getting the life that you want.* New York, NY: Penguin (pp. 92–95).

57.   *Ibid.*

58.   Lyubomirsky, S., Tkach, C., & Yelverton, J. (2004). Pursuing sustained happiness through random acts of kindness and counting one's blessings: Tests of two six-week interventions. (Unpublished data.) Department of Psychology, University of California, Riverside.

59.   Layous, K., Nelson, K., Oberle, E., Schonert-Reich, K. A., & Lyubomirsky, S. (2012). Kindness counts: Prompting prosocial behavior in preadolescents boosts peer acceptance and well-being. *PLOS 1, 7(12),* e51380.

60.   Sheldon, K. M., Boehm, J. K., & Lyubomirsky, S. (2012). Variety is the spice of happiness: The hedonic adaptation prevention (HAP) model. In I. Boniwell & S. David (Eds.), *Oxford handbook of happiness* (pp. 901–914). Oxford, England: Oxford University Press.

61. Seligman, M. E. P., Steen, T. A., Park, N., & Peterson, C. (2005). Positive psychology progress: Empirical validation of interventions. *American Psychologist, 60*, 410–421.

62. Boehm, J. K., Lyubomirsky, S., & Sheldon, K. M. (2011). A longitudinal experimental study comparing the effectiveness of happiness-enhancing strategies in Anglo Americans and Asian Americans. *Cognition & Emotion, 25*, 1152–1167.

63. Chancellor, J., Layous, K., & Lyubomirsky, S. (in press). Recalling positive events at work makes employees feel happier, move more, but interact less: A 6-week randomized controlled intervention at a Japanese workplace. *Journal of Happiness Studies.*

64. Goleman, D., Boyatzis, R., & McKee, A. (2002). *Primal leadership.* Boston, MA: Harvard Business School Press.

65. Kouzes, J. M., & Posner, B. Z. (1995). *The leadership challenge: How to keep getting extraordinary things done in organizations.* San Francisco, CA: Jossey-Bass.

66. Chowdhury, S. (2002). *Management 21C.* Glasgow, Scotland: Bell & Bain.

67. Lyubomirsky, S., & Lepper, H. (1999). A measure of subjective happiness: Preliminary reliability and construct validation. *Social Indicators Research, 46*, 137–155.

68. Chancellor, J., Layous, K., & Lyubomirsky, S. (in press). Recalling positive events at work makes employees feel happier, move more, but interact less: A 6-week randomized controlled intervention at a Japanese workplace. *Journal of Happiness Studies.*

69. Based on Emmons, R. A., & McCullough, M. E. (2003). Counting blessings versus burdens: An experimental investigation of gratitude and subjective well-being in daily life. *Journal of Personality and Social Psychology, 84*, 377–389.

70. Layous, K., & Lyubomirsky, S. (2014). The how, why, what, when, and who of happiness: Mechanisms underlying the success of positive interventions. In J. Gruber & J. Moscowitz (Eds.), *Positive emotion: Integrating the light sides and dark sides* (pp. 473–495). New York, NY: Oxford University Press.

71. Seligman, M.E.P. (2011). *Flourish.* New York, NY: Free Press.

72. *Ibid.*

73. Layous, K., & Lyubomirsky, S. (2014). The how, why, what, when, and who of happiness: Mechanisms underlying the success of positive interventions. In J. Gruber & J. Moscowitz (Eds.), *Positive emotion: Integrating the light sides and dark sides* (pp. 473–495). New York, NY: Oxford University Press.

74. King, L. A. (2001). The health benefits of writing about life goals. *Personality and Social Psychology Bulletin, 27*, 798–807. Sheldon, K. M., & Lyubormirsky, S. (2006). How to increase and sustain positive emotions: The effects of expressing gratitude and visualizing best possible selves. *Journal of Positive Psychology, 1*, 73–82.

75. Layous, K., Nelson, S. K., & Lyubomirsky, S. (2013). What is the optimal way to deliver a positive activity intervention? The case of writing about one's best possible selves. *Journal of Happiness Studies, 14*, 635–654.

76. Chancellor, J., Layous, K., & Lyubomirsky, S. (in press). Recalling positive events at work makes employees feel happier, move more, but interact less: A 6-week randomized controlled intervention at a Japanese workplace. *Journal of Happiness Studies.*

77. Lyubomirsky, S., & Lepper, H. (1999). A measure of subjective happiness: Preliminary reliability and construct validation. *Social Indicators Research, 46*, 137–155.

CHAPTER 3: CHARACTER STRENGTHS, VIRTUES AND TALENTS

1. Greenberg, C. L., & Avigdor, B. A. (2009). *What happy mothers know: How new findings in positive psychology can lead to a healthy and happy work/life balance.* Hoboken, NJ: John Wiley & Sons.

2. Reynolds, M. (2004) *Outsmart your brain! How to make success feel easy.* Phoenix, AZ: Covisioning.

3. Linley, P. A., Nielsen, K. M., Gillett, R., & Biswas-Diener, R. (2010). Using signature strengths in pursuit of goals: Effects on goal progress, need satisfaction, and well-being, and implications for coaching psychologists. *International Coaching Psychology Review, 5(1),* 6–15.

4. Seligman, M. E. P., Steen, T. A., Park, N., & Peterson, C. (2005). Positive psychology progress: Empirical validation of interventions. *American Psychologist, 60(5),* 410–421.

5. Rath, T., & Conchie, B. (2008). *Strengths based leadership: Great Leaders, teams, and why people follow.* New York, NY: Gallup Press.

6. Judge, T., & Hurst, C. (2007). Capitalizing on one's advantages: Role of core self-evaluations. *Journal of Applied Psychology, 92(5),* 1212–1227.

7. Peterson, C., & Seligman, M. E. P. (2004). Character strengths and virtues: A handbook and classification. Washington, DC: American Psychological Association. www.viacharacter.org.

8. *Ibid.*

9. Baumeister, R. F., & Tierney, J. (2011). *Willpower: Rediscovering the greatest human strength.* New York, NY: Penguin.

10. Emmons, R. A. (2013). *Gratitude works!* San Francisco, CA: Jossey-Bass.

11. Seligman, M. E. P., Ernst, R. M., Gillham, J., Reivich, K., & Linkins, M. (2009). Positive education: Positive psychology and classroom interventions. *Oxford Review of Education, 35(3),* 293–311.

12. *Ibid.*

13. Seligman, M. E. P., Steen, T. A., Park, N., & Peterson, C. (2005). Positive psychology progress: Empirical validation of interventions. *American Psychologist, 60(5),* 410–421.

14. *Ibid.*

15. *Ibid.*

16. *Ibid.*

17. Govindji, R., & Linley, P. A. (2007). Strengths use, self-concordance and well-being: Implications for strengths coaching and coaching psychologists. *International Coaching Psychology Review, 2(2),* 143–153.

18. *Ibid.*

19. *Ibid.*

20. Linley, P. A., Nielsen, K. M., Gillett, R., & Biswas-Diener, R. (2010). Using signature strengths in pursuit of goals: Effects on goal progress, need satisfaction, and well-being, and implications for coaching psychologists. *International Coaching Psychology Review, 5(1),* 6–15.

21. Proctor, C., Tsukayama, E., Wood, A. M., Maltby, J., Eades, J. F., & Linley, P. A. (2011). Strengths gym: The impact of a character strengths-based intervention on the life satisfaction and well-being of adolescents. *Journal of Positive Psychology, 6(5),* 377–388.

22. Peterson, C. (2006). *A primer in positive psychology.* Oxford, England: Oxford University Press.

23. Gander, F., Proyer, R. T., Ruch, W., & Wyss, T. (2012). The good character at work: an initial study on the contribution of character strengths in identifying healthy and unhealthy work-related behavior and experience patterns. *International Archives of Occupational and Environmental Health, 85(8)*, 895–904.

24. Lehnert, A. B. (2009). *The influence of strengths-based development on leadership practices among undergraduate college students.* (Doctoral dissertation). Retrieved from ProQuest Dissertations and Theses.

25. Linley, A., Willars, J., & Biswas-Diener, R. (2010). *The strengths book: Be confident, be successful, and enjoy better relationships by realizing the best of you.* Coventry, England: CAPP Press.

26. *Ibid.*

27. Bass, B. M., & Avolio, B. J. (1993). Transformational leadership: A response to critiques. In M. M. Chemers & R. Ayman (eds.), *Leadership theory and research: Perspectives and directions* (pp. 49–80). San Diego, CA: Academic Press.

28. Mackie, D. (2014). The effectiveness of strength-based executive coaching in enhancing full range leadership development; A controlled study. *Consulting Psychology Journal: Practice and Research, 66(2)*, 118–137.

29. Peterson, C., Ruch, W., Beermann, U., Park, N., & Seligman, M. E. (2007). Strengths of character, orientations to happiness, and life satisfaction. *Journal of Positive Psychology, 2(3)*, 149–156.

30. Peterson, C., & Seligman, M. E. P. (2004). *Character strengths and virtues: A handbook and classification.* Washington, DC: American Psychological Association. www.viacharacter.org.

31. Nadler, R. S. (2011). *Leading with emotional intelligence: Hands-on strategies for building confident and collaborative star performers.* New York, NY: McGraw-Hill.

32. Zenger, J., Sandholtz, K., & Folkman, J. (2004). *Leadership under the microscope.* Oren, UT: Extraordinary Performance Group.

33. *Ibid.*

34. The VIA-IS is available for free online (www.viastrengths.org); for a fee, more detailed reports are available.

35. *Ibid.*

36. Biswas-Diener, R. (2010). *Practicing positive psychology coaching: Assessment, activities, and strategies for success.* Hoboken, NJ: John Wiley & Sons.

37. Schubring, B. (2013). Why StrengthsFinder. http://www.leadershipvisionconsulting.com/why-strengthsfinder/.

38. Rath, T. (2007). *Strengths Finder 2.0.* New York, NY: Gallup Press.

39. *Ibid.* The Strengthsfinder 2.0 assessment is copyrighted. This content is used with permission; however, Gallup retains all rights of republication.

40. Seligman, M. E. P., Steen, T. A., Park, N., & Peterson, C. (2005). Positive psychology progress: Empirical validation of interventions. *American Psychologist, 60(5)*, 410–421.

CHAPTER 4: COACHING FOR WELL-BEING

1. Fave, A., Wissing, M., Vella-Brodrick, D., & Freire T. (2012). In A. Waterman (Ed.), *The best within us: Positive psychology perspectives on eudaimonic functioning.* Washington, DC: American Psychological Association.

2. Lyubomirsky, S., King, L., & Diener, E. (2005). The benefits of frequent positive affect: Does happiness lead to success? *Psychological Bulletin, 131(6)*, 803–855.

3. Diener, E., & Chan, M. Y. (2011). Happy people live longer: Subjective well-being contributes to health and longevity. *Applied Psychology: Health and Well-Being, 3(1)*, 1–43.

4. Chida, Y., & Steptoe, A. (2008). Positive psychological well-being and mortality: A quantitative review of prospective observational studies. *Psychosomatic Medicine, 70(7)*, 741–756.

5. Brief, A. P., & Motowidlo, S. J. (1986). Prosocial organizational behaviors. *Academy of Management Review, 11(4)*, 710–725.

6. Oishi, S. (2012). *The psychological wealth of nations: Do happy people make a happy society?* Malden, MA: Wiley-Blackwell.

7. Diener, E., Nickerson, C., Lucas, R. E., & Sandvik, E. (2002). Dispositional affect and job outcomes. *Social Indicators Research, 59*, 229–259.

8. Aknin, L. B., Sandstrom, G. M., Dunn, E. W., & Norton, M. I. (2011). It's the recipient that counts: Spending money on strong social ties leads to greater happiness than spending on weak social ties. *PLoS ONE, 6(2)*, e17018. doi:10.1371/journal.pone.0017018.

9. Priller, E., & Schupp, J. (2011). Social and economic characteristics of financial blood donors in Germany. *DIW Economic Bulletin, 6*, 23–30.

10. Shin, N., Vaughn, B. E., Akers, V., Kim, M., Stevens, S., Krzysik, L., & Korth, B. (2011). Are happy children socially successful? Testing a central premise of positive psychology in a sample of preschool children. *Journal of Positive Psychology, 6*, 355–367. doi:10.1080/17439760.2011.584549.

11. Boehm, J. K., & Lyubomirsky, S. (2008). Does happiness lead to career success? *Journal of Career Assessment, 16*, 101–116. doi:10.1177/1069072707308140.

12. Peterson, C. (2006). *A primer in positive psychology.* Oxford, England: Oxford University Press.

13. Diener, E., Oishi, S., & Lucas, R. E. (2015). National accounts of subjective well-being. *American Psychologist, 70(3)*, 234–242.

14. "High levels of flourishing are also associated with economic benefits due to less absenteeism and under-performance in schools and work places, lower healthcare costs and less need for expenditure on the effects of social disintegration."

15. *Ibid.*

16. Rath, T. & Harter, J. (2010). *Wellbeing: The Five Essential Elements.* New York, NY: Deckle Edge.

17. *Ibid.*

18. Diener, E., Wirtz, D., et al. (2009). New well-being measures: Short scales to assess flourishing and positive and negative feelings. *Social Indicators Research, 97(2)*, 143–156.

19. Huppert, F., & So, T. (2009). *What percentage of people in Europe are flourishing and what characterizes them?* Well-Being Institute, University of Cambridge.

20. *Ibid.*

21. Diener, E., Emmons, R. A., Larsen, R. J., & Griffin, S. (1985). The Satisfaction with Life Scale. *Journal of Personality Assessment, 49(1)*, 71.

22. Larson, R., & Csikszentmihalyi, M. (1983). The experience sampling method. *New Directions for Methodology of Social and Behavioral Science, 15*, 41–56.

23. Kahneman, D., Krueger, A., Schkade, D., Schwarz, N., & Stone, A. (2004). A survey method for characterizing daily life experience: The day reconstruction method. *Science, 306(5702)*, 1776–1780.

24. Auerbach, J. (2014). *The Well-Being Coaching Workbook.* Pismo Beach, CA: Executive College Press.

25. Walmpold, B. E. (2001). *The great psychotherapy debate: Models, methods and findings.* Maweah, NJ: Lawrence Erlbaum.

26. http://coachfederation.org/credential/landing.cfm?ItemNumber=2206.

27. The correlations between happiness and all other subscales can be found in the 2011 EQI User's Handbook, Appendix A, Table A.19 (https://ei.mhs.com/EQi20FAQ.aspx). The College of Executive Coaching (www.executivecoachcollege. com) is the approved provider for the EQI2.0 Certification, which specializes in coaching applications for emotional intelligence.

28. *Ibid.*

29. Kolb, D. A., & Boyatzis, R. E. (1970). Goal-setting and self-directed behavior change. *Human Relations, 23(5),* 439–457.

30. Butterworth, S. Linden, A., McClay, W., & Leo, M. C. (2006). Effect of motivational interviewing-based health coaching on employees' physical and mental health status. *Journal of Occupational Health Psychology, 11(4),* 358–365. doi:10.1037/1076-8998.11.4.358.

31. Linden, A., Butterworth, S. W., & Prochaska, J. O. (2010). Motivational interviewing-based health coaching as a chronic care intervention. *Journal of Evaluation in Clinical Practice, 16(1),* 166–174.

32. Prochaska, J. O., & DiClemente, C. C. (1986). Toward a comprehensive model of change. *Applied Clinical Psychology, 13,* 3–27.

33. Kolb, D. A., & Boyatzis, R. E. (1970). Goal-setting and self-directed behavior change. *Human Relations, 23(5),* 439–457.

34. Seligman, M. (2011). *Flourish: A Visionary new understanding of happiness and well-being.* New York, NY: Free Press.

35. Sheldon, K. M., Kasser, T., Smith, K., & Share, T. (2002). Personal goals and psychological growth: Testing an intervention to enhance goal-attainment and personality integration. *Journal of Personality, 70,* 5–31.

36. Green, S., Oades, L., & Grant, A. M. (2006). Cognitive-behavioural, solution-focused life coaching: Enhancing goal striving, well-being and hope. *Journal of Positive Psychology, 1(3),* 142–149.

CHAPTER 5: COACHING FOR ACCOMPLISHMENT

1. Seligman, M. E. P. (2011). *Flourish: A visionary new understanding of happiness and well being.* New York, NY: Free Press (pp. 18–20).

2. White, R. P. (2009). Strengths-based development in perspective. In R. B. Kaiser (Ed.), *The perils of accentuating the positive* (pp. 161–170). Tulsa, OK: Hogan Press.

3. Lombardo, M. M., & Eichinger, R. W. (2006). *The leadership machine.* Minneapolis, MN: Lominger (p. 5).

4. *Collins Concise Dictionary.* (2000). Glasgow, Scotland: Harper Collins.

5. See definitions of skilled, unskilled, and overused skill in Lombardo, M. M., & Eichinger, R. W. (2009). *For your improvement: A guide for development and coaching* (5th ed.). Minneapolis, MN: Lominger.

6. I (Sandra) was working for Korn/Ferry's leadership practice when it acquired Lominger in 2006 and had the good fortune to become trained and experienced in many of its assessment tools and development guides.

7. McCauley, C. D., Mosley, R.S., & Van Velcro, E. (Eds.) (1998). *The Center for Creative Leadership handbook of leadership development.* San Francisco, CA: Jossey-Bass.

8.   Lombardo, M. M., & Eichinger, R. W. (2009). *For your improvement: A guide for development and coaching* (5th ed.). Minneapolis, MN: Lominger.

9.   Eichinger, R. W. , Lombardo, M. M., & Ulrich, D. (2006). *100 things you need to know: Best people practices for managers and HR*. Minneapolis, MN: Lominger.

10. Timmreck, C. W., & Bracken, D. W. (1997). Multisource feedback: A study of its use in decision making. *Employment Relations Today, 24(1)*, 21–27.

11. Tornow, W. W., London, M., & CCL Associates. (1998). *Maximizing the value of 360-degree feedback*. San Francisco, CA: Jossey-Bass.   Johnson, J. W., & Ferstl, K. L. (1999). The effects of interrater and self-other agreement on performance improvement following upward feedback. *Personnel Psychology, 48*, 1–34.

12. Leslie, J. B. (2009, June). *The leadership gap: What you need, and don't have, when it comes to leadership talent*. Greensboro, NC: Center for Creative Leadership.   Leslie, J. B., & Chandrasekar, A. (2009). Managerial strengths and organizational needs: A crucial leadership gap. In R. B. Kaiser (Ed.), *The perils of accentuating the positive* (pp. 27–38). Oklahoma City: Hogan.

13. Eichinger, R. W., Dai, G., & Tang, K. (2009). It depends upon what you mean by a strength. In R. B. Kaiser (Ed.), *The perils of accentuating the positive* (pp. 15–25), Oklahoma City, OK: Hogan.

14. Lombardo, M. M., & Eichinger, R. W. (2006). *The leadership machine*. Minneapolis, MN: Lominger.

15. *Ibid.*

16. Lombardo, M.M., & Eichinger, R.W. (2003). *Leadership architect norms and validity report*. Minneapolis, MN: Lominger, Inc.

17. Lombardo, M. M., & Eichinger, R. W. (2006). *The leadership machine*. Minneapolis, MN: Lominger.

18. Charan, R., Drotter, S., & Noel, J. (2001). *The leadership pipeline*. San Francisco, CA: Jossey-Bass.

19. Freedman, A.M. (1998). Pathways and crossroads to institutional leadership. *Consulting Psychology Journal: Practice and Research, 50(3)*, 131–151.

20. Name changed to protect anonymity.

21. StrengthsFinder, www.gallupstrengthscenter.com

22. Lombardo, M. M., & Eichinger, R. W. (2009). *For your improvement: A guide for development and coaching* (5th ed.). Minneapolis, MN: Lominger.

23. There are a number of 360° instruments available, such as CCL's Benchmarks, CEB SHL's Multi-rater Feedback System, and DDI's Leadership Mirror. Certification training is required to purchase them. This is also true for Lominger's Voices® 360. Since Korn/Ferry's acquisition of Personnel Decisions International (PDI), the Leadership Architect competency framework was updated in 2013 to reflect PDI's research. A new version of *For Your Improvement* is also available, as well as new global competencies. See Lominger's website for the latest norms for Voices® and to review the other Lominger tools we have mentioned in this chapter.

24. Morgan McCall and others at CCL are credited with creating this formula for development. Lombardo and Eichinger then conducted a survey deploying it and published their results in Lombardo, M. M., & Eichinger, R. W. (1996). *The career architect development planner* (1st ed.) Minneapolis, MN: Lominger.

CHAPTER 6: TIME AND HOW WE SPEND IT:

1. Seligman, M. E. P., & Csikszentmihalyi, M., Eds. (2000). *American Psychologist, 55(1)* [special issue].

2. Csikszentmihalyi, M. (2003). *Good business: Leadership, flow, and the making of meaning.* London, England: Hodder & Stoughton.

3. Hektner, J. M., Schmidt, J. A., & Csikszentmihalyi, M. (2007). *Experience Sampling Method: Measuring the quality of everyday life.* Thousand Oaks, CA: Sage.

4. Csikszentmihalyi, M., & Larson, R. (1986). *Being adolescent: Conflict and growth in the teenage years.* New York, NY: Basic Books.

CHAPTER 7: APPLYING THE LATEST RESEARCH ON GOAL SETTING AND MINDSET

1. Seligman, M. E. P. (2011). *Flourish: A visionary new understanding of happiness and well-being.* New York, NY: Free Press.

2. Halvorson, H. G. (2010). *Succeed.* New York, NY: Hudson Street Press.

3. Locke, E., & Latham, G. (2002). Building a practically useful theory of goal setting and task motivation. *American Psychologist, 57,* 705–717. Latham, G., & Locke, E. (2007). New developments in and directions for goal-setting research. *European Psychologist, 12,* 290–300. Trope, Y., & Liberman, N. (2003). Temporal construal. *Psychological Review, 110,* 403–421.

4. Grant, H., & Dweck, C. S. (2003). Clarifying achievement goals and their impact. *Journal of Personality and Social Psychology, 85(3),* 541–553. Elliott, A. J., Shell, M. M., Henry, K., & Maier, M. (2005). Achievement goals, performance contingencies, and performance attainment: An experimental test. *Journal of Educational Psychology, 97,* 630–640.

5. Halvorson, H. G. (2010). *Succeed.* New York, NY: Hudson Street Press (p. 66).

6. Higgins, E. T., Friedman, R. S., Harlow, R. E., Idson, L. C., Ayduk, O. N., & Taylor, A. (2001). Achievement orientations from subjective histories of success: Promotion pride versus prevention pride. *European Journal of Social Psychology, 31,* 3–23. Crowe, E., & Higgins, E. T. (1997). Regulatory focus and strategic inclinations: Promotion and prevention in decision making. *Organizational Behavior and Human Decision Processes, 69,* 117–132. Lockwood, P., Jordan, C. H., & Kunda, Z. (2002). Motivation by positive or negative role models: Regulatory focus determines who will best inspire us. *Journal of Personality and Social Psychology, 83,* 854–864.

7. Halvorson, H. G. (2010). *Succeed.* New York, NY: Hudson Street Press (p. 81).

8. *Ibid.*

9. *Ibid.*

10. Ehrenreich, B. (2010). Bright-sided: *How the relentless promotion of positive thinking has undermined America.* New York, NY: Metropolitan Books.

11. Halvorson, H. G., & Higgins, E. T. (2013, March). Do you play to win—or not to lose? *Harvard Business Review.*

12. *Ibid.*

13. *Ibid.*

14. Dweck, C. S. (2007). *Mindset: The new psychology of success.* New York, NY: Ballantine Books.

15. Stanford University's Carol Dweck on the "Growth Mindset and Education." *OneDublin.org,* June 19, 2012.

16. http://mindsetonline.com/changeyourmindset/natureofchange/.

17. Alderson, M. (2004). *Blockbuster plots: Pure & simple*. Los Gatos, CA: Illusion Press. Alderson, M. (2011). *The plot whisperer*. Avon, MA: Adams Media. plotwhisperer.blogspot.com.

CHAPTER 8: APPLYING POSITIVE PSYCHOLOGY FOR PRODUCTIVITY AND WELL-BEING AT WORK

1. Diener, E., Nickerson, C., Lucas, R. E., & Sandvik, E. (2002). Dispositional affect and job outcomes. *Social Indicators Research, 59*, 229–259.

2. Harter, J. K., Schmidt, F. L., & Keyes, C. L.(2002). Well-being in the workplace and its relationship to business outcomes: A review of the Gallup studies. In C. L. Keyes & J. Haidt (Eds.), *Flourishing: The positive person and the good life* (pp. 205-224). Washington, DC: American Psychological Association.

3. Rath, T. (2006). *Vital friends: The people you can't afford to live without*. New York, NY: Gallup Press.

4. Rath, T., & Harter, J. K. (2010). *Wellbeing: The Five Essential Elements*. New York, NY: Gallup Press.

5. Boehm, J. K., & Lyubomirsky, S. (2008). Does happiness promote career success? *Journal of Career Assessment, 16(1)*, 101–116. doi:10.1177/1069072707308140.

6. *Ibid.*

7. *Ibid.*

8. Rath, T., & Harter, J. K. (2010). *Wellbeing: The Five Essential Elements*. New York, NY: Gallup Press.

9. Gallup (2015). *State of the American workplace*. Princeton, NJ: Gallup.

10. Linley, A. (2008). *Average to A+. Realising strengths in yourself and others*. Coventry, England: CAPP Press. Linley, A. Willars, J., & Biswas-Deiner, R. (2010). *The strengths book: Be confident, be successful, and enjoy better relationships by realizing the best of you*. Coventry, England: CAPP Press.

11. Linley, A., Harrington, S., & Garcea, N. (2013). *The Oxford handbook of positive psychology and work*. New York, NY: Oxford University Press.

12. *Ibid.*

13. *Ibid.*

14. Lewis, S. (2011). *Positive psychology at work*. Chichester, England: Wiley-Blackwell (p. xxiii).

15. *Ibid.*

16. *Ibid.*

17. Hammond, S. A. (1996). *The thin book of appreciative inquiry*. Plano, TX: Thin Book Publishers (p. 7).

18. Cooperrider, D. L., & Whitney, D. (2005). *Appreciative Inquiry: A positive revolution in change*. San Francisco, CA: Berrett-Koehler (p. 61).

19. Brun, P. H., & Cooperrider, D. L. (2015). *Leading from a strengths-based perspective: Toward the fully human organization*. New York, NY: Crown (p. 350). Laszlo, C., Saillant, R., Cooperrider, D. L., & Brown, J. S. (2014). *Flourishing enterprise: The new spirit of business*. Stanford, CA: Stanford University Press.

20. Cooperrider, D. L., & Whitney, D. (2005). *Appreciative Inquiry: A positive revolution in change*. San Francisco, CA: Berrett-Koehler.

21. Glaser, J. E. (Ed.) (2009). *42 rules for creating we.* Cupertino, CA: Superstar Press. Glaser, J. E. (2006). *The DNA of leadership: Leverage your instincts to communicate, differentiate, innovate.* Avon, MA: Platinum Press.

22. Glaser, J. E. (2014). *Conversational Intelligence: How great leaders build trust and get extraordinary results.* Brookline, MA: Bibliomotion.

23. Csikszentmihalyi, M. (2004). *Good business: Leadership, flow, and the making of meaning.* New York, NY: Penguin.

24. Harter, J. K., & Schmidt, F. L. (2003). Employee engagement, satisfaction, and business-unit-level outcomes: A meta-analysis. *Gallup Research Journal.*

CHAPTER 9: COACHING THROUGH TRANSITIONS AND CHANGE

1. *Managing Change and Transition.* Harvard Business Essentials series. Boston, MA: Harvard Business School Press.

2. *Ibid.*

3. *Ibid.*

4. *Ibid.*

5. State of the American Workplace (2015). Princeton, NJ: The Gallup Organization.

6. *Managing Change and Transition.* Harvard Business Essentials series. Boston, MA: Harvard Business School Press (p. 85).

7. Kubler-Ross, E. (1970) *On death and dying.* New York, NY: Simon & Schuster.

8. *Managing Change and Transition.* Harvard Business Essentials series. Boston, MA: Harvard Business School Press (p. 86).

9. *Ibid.*

10. *Ibid.*

11. Argyris, C. (1999). *On Organizational Learning.* (2nd ed.). Malden, MA: Blackwell Business.

12. Argyris, C. (2004). *Teaching smart people how to learn.* Harvard Business Review on Developing Leaders. Boston, MA: Harvard Business School Publishing.

13. *Ibid.*

14. Hargrove, R.A. (2000). *Masterful coaching fieldbook: Grow your business, multiply your profits, win the talent war!* San Francisco, CA: Jossey-Bass Pfeiffer.

15. McCauley, C.D., Moxley, R.S., & Van Velsor, E. (1998). *The Center for Creative Leadership handbook of leadership.* San Francisco, CA: Jossey-Bass.

16. McCall, M., Lombardo, M.M., & Morrison, A.M. (1988). *The lessons of experience: How successful executives develop on the job.* Lexington, MA: Lexington Books.

17. Lombardo, M.M. & Eichinger, R.W. (2000). High potentials as high learners. *Human Resource Management, 39,* 321-330.

18. Hodgson, P, & White, R. P. (2001). *Relax, it's only uncertainty.* London, England: Financial Times/Prentice Hall.

19. White, R. P., & Hodgson, R. P. (2005). *Ambiguity Architect.* Greensboro, NC: Executive Development Group, LLC.

20. Mintzberg, M. (1973). *The nature of managerial work.* New York, NY: Harper and Row. Seligman, M.E.P. (2002). *Authentic happiness.* New York, NY: Free Press (p. 157).

21. Lyubomirsky, S. (2007). *The how of happiness.* New York, NY: Penguin Books.

22. Levine, S. (1982). *Who dies? An investigation of conscious living and conscious dying.* New York, NY: Doubleday.

23. Harris, A., Thoresen, C.E., Luskin, F., Benisovich, S., Standard, S., Bruning, J., & Evans, S. (2001, August). Effects of a forgiveness intervention on physical and psychosocial health. Paper presented at the annual meeting of the American Psychological Association, San Francisco.

24. Coyle. C.T., & Enright, R.D. (1997). Forgiveness intervention with post-abortion men. *Journal of Consulting and Clinical Psychology, 65,* 1042-1046.

25. Van Oyen, C., Ludwig, T., & Vander Laan, K. (2001). Granting forgiveness or harboring grudges: Implications for emotion, physiology, and health. *Psychological Science, 12,* 117-123.

26. Luskin, F. (2002). *Forgive for good.* New York, NY: Harper Collins.

27. Miller, T. Q., Smith, T. W., Turner, C. W., Guijarro, M. L., & Hallett, A. J. (1996). A meta-analytic view of research on hostility and physical health. *Psychological Bulletin, 119(2),* 322-348.

28. Developed by the Institute for Heart Math in Boulder Creek, California, this technique is but one of many "cardiac coherence" practices taught by the institute to small businesses and corporations as well as to individuals in the helping professions.

29. Childre, D.L. (1998). *Freeze-Frame.* Boulder Creek, CA: Planetary Publications (a HeartMath publication).

30. Tiller, W., McCraty, R., & Atkinson, M. (1996). Toward cardiac coherence: A new non-invasive measure of autonomic system order. *Alternative Therapies, 2(1),* 52-65.

CHAPTER 10: WHEN THERE'S TOO MUCH OF A GOOD THING

1. Gottman, J. M. (1994). *What predicts divorce? The relationship between marital processes and marital outcomes.* Hillsdale, NJ: Erlbaum.

2. Fredrickson, B.L. & Losada, M. (2005). Positive affect and the complex dynamics of human flourishing. *American Psychologist, 60,* 678–686 .

3. Le, H., Oh, I.-S., Robbins, S. B., Ilies, R., Holland, E., & Westrick, P. (2010). Too much of a good thing? The curvilinear relationships between personality traits and job performance. *Journal of Applied Psychology, 95,* 1-21.

4. McCall, M. W., Jr. (2009). Every strength a weakness and other caveats. In R. B. Kaiser (Ed.), *The perils of accentuating the positive.* Tulsa, OK: Hogan Press.

5. The VIA Survey is available for free online, and for a fee, more detailed reports are available www.viastrengths.org.

6. Rath, T (2007). *StrengthsFinder 2.0.* New York, NY: Gallup Press.

7. Kaiser, R. B., Overfield, D. V., & Kaplan, R. E. (2010). *Leadership Versatility Index version 3.0 Facilitator's Guide.* Greensboro, NC: Kaplan DeVries.

8. Peter Drucker is credited with coining the use of "keep doing," "stop doing," and "start doing." Drucker, P. (1967). *The effective executive.* New York, NY: Harper & Row.

9. Hogan, R., & Hogan, J. (2009). *Hogan Development Survey manual* (2nd ed.). Tulsa, OK: Hogan Assessment Systems. Kaiser, R. B. (Ed.) (2009). *The perils of accentuating the positive.* Tulsa, OK: Hogan Press.

10. Eichinger, R. W., Dai, G., & Tang, K. Y. (2009). It depends upon what you mean by a strength. In R. B. Kaiser (Ed.) *The perils of accentuating the positive* (pp. 13-25). Tulsa, OK: Hogan Press.

11. *Ibid.*

12. *Ibid.*

13. *Ibid.*

14. Leslie, J. B., & Chandrasekar, A. (2009). Managerial strengths and organizational needs: A crucial leadership gap. In R. B. Kaiser (Ed.) *The perils of accentuating the positive* (pp. 27-38). Tulsa, OK: Hogan Press.

15. McCall, M. W., Jr., & Lombardo, M. M. (1983). *Off the track: Why and how successful executives get derailed.* Greensboro, NC: Center for Creative Leadership.

16. Lombardo, M.M., & Eichinger, R.W. (2006). *The leadership machine* (3ʳᵈ ed.). Minneapolis, MN: Lominger Limited, Inc.

17. McCall, M. W., Jr. (2009). Every strength a weakness and other caveats. In R. B. Kaiser (Ed.), *The perils of accentuating the positive.* Tulsa, OK: Hogan Press.

18. Hogan, J., Hogan, R., & Kaiser, R. B. (2010). Management derailment. In S. Zedeck (Ed.) *American Psychological Association Handbook of Industrial and Organizational Psychology, Vol. 3* (pp. 555-575). Washington, DC: American Psychological Association.

19. Gentry, W. A. & Chappelow, C. T. (2009). Managerial derailment: Weaknesses that can be fixed. In R. B. Kaiser (Ed.) *The perils of accentuating the positive* (pp. 97-113). Tulsa, OK: Hogan Press.

20. Kaiser, R. B., & Overfield, D. V. (2011). Strengths, strengths overused, and lopsided leadership. *Consulting Psychology Journal: Practice and Research, 63,* 89-109.

21. Kaplan, R.E., & Kaiser, R.B. (2009). Stop overdoing your strengths. *Harvard Business Review, 87(2),* 100-103.

22. Kaplan, R. E. & Kaiser, R. B. (2006). *The versatile leader: Make the most of your strengths—without overdoing it.* San Francisco, CA: Pfeiffer.

23. Voices®. Lombardo, M. M., & Eichinger, R. W. (2005). Minneapolis, MN: Lominger.

24. Lombardo, M. M., & Eichinger, R. W. (2000). High potentials as high learners. *Human Resource Management, 39,* 321-330.

25. *Ibid.*

CHAPTER 11: LEVERAGING POSITIVE PSYCHOLOGY IN CULTURALLY COMPETENT COACHING

1. Livermore, D. (2011). *The cultural intelligence difference: Master the one skill you can't do without in today's global economy.* New York, NY: Amacom.

2. Ang, S., & Van Dyne, L. (2008). Conceptualization of cultural intelligence. In *Handbook of cultural intelligence: Theory measurement and applications.* Armonk, NY: M. E. Sharpe.

3. Tadmor, C. T., Galinsky, A. D., & Maddux, W. W. (2012). Getting the most out of living abroad: Biculturalism and integrative complexity as key drivers of creative and professional success. *Journal of Personality and Special Psychology, 103(3),* 520–542.

4. *Ibid.*

5. Kubokawa, A., & Ottaway, A. (2009). Positive psychology and cultural sensitivity: A review of the literature. *Graduate Journal of Counseling Psychology, 1(2),* 130–138.

6. Christopher, J. C., & Higginbottom, S. (2008). Positive psychology, ethnocentrism, and the disguised ideology of individualism. *Theory & Psychology, 18(5),* 563–589.

7. Hoshmand, L. T., & Ho, D. Y. F. (1995). Moral dimensions of selfhood: Chinese traditions and cultural change. *World Psychology, 1*, 47–69.

8. Snyder, C. R., & Lopez, S. J. (2007). *Positive psychology: The scientific and practical explorations of human strengths.* Thousand Oaks, CA: Sage.

9. *Ibid.*

10. Ahuvia, A. (2001). Well-being in cultures of choice: A cross-cultural perspective. *American Psychologist, 56(1)*, 77–78.

11. Peterson, C., & Seligman, M. E. P. (2004). *Character strengths and virtues: A handbook and classification.* Washington, DC: American Psychological Association/Oxford University Press.

12. Christopher, J. C., & Higginbottom, S. (2008). Positive psychology, ethnocentrism, and the disguised ideology of individualism. *Theory & Psychology, 18(5)*, 563–589.

13. Layous, K., & Lyubomirsky, S. (2014). The how, who, what, when, and why of happiness: Mechanisms underlying the success of positive activity interventions. In J. Gruber & J. Moskowitz (Eds.), *Positive emotion: Integrating the light and dark sides* (pp. 473–495). Oxford, England: Oxford University Press.

14. Diener, E., & Suh, E. (1999). National differences in subjective well-being. In D. Kahneman, E. Diener, & N. Schwarz (Eds.), *Well-being: The foundation of hedonic psychology* (pp. 434–452). New York, NY: Russell Sage Foundation.

15. Ucihda, Y., Norasakkunkit, V., & Kitayama, S. (2004). Cultural constructions of happiness: Theory and empirical evidence. *Journal of Happiness Studies, 5*, 223–239.

16. Otake, K., Shimai, S., Tanaka-Matsumi, J., Otsui, K., & Fredrickson, B. L. (2006). Happy people become happier through kindness: Accounting kindness intervention. *Journal of Happiness Studies, 7*, 361–375.

17. Boehm, J. K., Lyubomirsky, S., & Sheldon, K. M. (2011). A longitudinal experimental study comparing the effectiveness of happiness-enhancing strategies in Anglo Americans and Asian Americans. *Cognition & Emotion, 25*, 1263–1272.

18. Tajfel, H. (1978). *Differentiation between social groups.* London, England: Academic Press (p. 63).

19. Berry, J. W. (1997). Immigration, acculturation, and adaptation. *Applied Psychology, 46*, 5–34.

20. Berry, J. W. (2001). A psychology of immigration. *Journal of Social Issues, 57*, 615–631.

21. Youssef-Morgan, C. M., & Hardy, J. (2014). A positive approach to multiculturalism and diversity management in the workplace. In J. T. Pedrotti & L. Edwards (Eds.), *Perspectives on the intersection of multiculturalism and positive psychology* (pp. 219–233). Dordrecht, Netherlands: Springer.

22. Delle Fave, A., & Bassi, M. (2009). Sharing optimal experiences and promoting good community life in a multicultural society. *Journal of Positive Psychology, 4*, 280–289.

23. Chen, Y., Leung, K., & Chen, C. (2009). Bringing national culture to the table: Making a difference with cross-cultural differences and perspectives. *Academy of Management Annals, 3*, 217–249.

24. Helliwell, J. F., Huang, H., & Wang, S. (2014). Social capital and well-being in times of crisis. *Journal of Happiness Studies, 15*, 145–162.

25. Leung, A., Kier, C., Fung T., Fung L., & Sproule, R. (2011). Searching for happiness: The importance of social capital. *Journal of Happiness Studies, 12*, 443–462.

26. Tseng, W. S., & Streltzer, J. (2008). *Cultural competence in health care.* New York, NY: Springer.

27. Bennett, M. (1993). *Toward ethnorelativism: A developmental model of intercultural sensitivity.* Rosinski, P. (1999). *Beyond intercultural sensitivity: Leveraging cultural differences.*

28.   *Ibid.*

29.   Rosinski, P. (2003). *Coaching across cultures: New tools for leveraging national, corporate and professional differences.* Boston, MA: Nicholas Brealey. Reprinted with permission.

30.   Lowman, R. L. (Ed.) (2013). *Internationalizing multiculturalism: Expanding professional competencies for a globalized world.* Washington, DC: American Psychological Association.

31.   Livermore, D. (2011). *The cultural intelligence difference: Master the one skill you can't do without in today's global economy.* New York, NY: Amacom.

32.   Intercultural Press, http://nicholasbrealey.com/boston/subjects/interculturalpress.html. "For more than twenty-five years, Intercultural Press has been a trusted source of information on how to work well with and within other cultures."

33.   Rosinski, P. (2003). *Coaching across cultures: New tools for leveraging national, corporate and professional differences.* Boston, MA: Nicholas Brealey. Reprinted with permission.

34.   Earley, C., & Ang, S. (2003). *Cultural intelligence: Individual interactions across cultures.* Stanford, CA: Stanford University Press.

35.   Livermore, D. (2011). *The cultural intelligence difference: Master the one skill you can't do without in today's global economy.* Armonk, NY: M.E. Sharpe.

36.   Ang, S., & Van Dyne, L. (2008). Handbook of cultural intelligence: Theory measurement and applications. Armonk, NY: M. E. Sharpe.

37.   Ang, S., Van Dyne, L., Koh, C., Ng, K. Y., Templer, K. J., Tay, C., & Chandrasekar, N. A. (2007). Cultural intelligence: Its measurement and effects on cultural judgment and decision making, cultural adaptation, and task performance. *Management and Organization Review, 3,* 335–371.

38.   Imai, L., & Gelfand, M. J. (2010). The culturally intelligent negotiator: The impact of cultural intelligence (CQ) on negotiation sequences and outcomes. *Organizational Behavior and Human Decision Processes, 112,* 83–98.

39.   Ang, S., Van Dyne, L., & Tan, M. L. (2011). Cultural intelligence. In Robert Sternberg and Scott Barry Kaufman (Eds.), *Cambridge handbook of intelligence.* Cambridge, England: Cambridge University Press.

40.   Livermore, D. (2011). *The cultural intelligence difference: Master the one skill you can't do without in today's global economy.* New York, NY: Amacom.

41.   *Ibid.*

42.   Rosinski, P. (2011). Global coaching for organizational development. *International Journal of Coaching in Organizations,* 8(2), 30, 44–66.

CHAPTER 12: NEGATIVE EMOTIONS IN THE CONTEXT OF POSITIVE PSYCHOLOGY

1.   Tamir, M., & Gross, J. (2011) Beyond pleasure and pain? Emotion regulation and positive psychology. In K. sheldon, T. Kashdan, & M. Steger (Eds.). *Designing positive psychology* (pp. 89-100). Oxford, England: Oxford University Press.

2.   Seligman, M.E.P. (2011). *Flourish: A visionary new understanding of happiness and well-being.* New York, NY: Free Press.

3.   Lybomirsky, S. (2007). *The how of happiness.* New York, NY: Penguin.

4.   Nolen-Hoeksema, S. (2000). The role of rumination in depressive disorders and mixed anxiety/depressive symptoms. *Journal of Abnormal Psychology, 109 (3),* 504–511.   doi:10.1037/0021-843X.109.3.504.   Nolen-Hoeksema, S.

(2012). Emotion regulation and psychopathology: The role of gender. *Annual Review of Clinical Psychology, 8,* 161–187. doi:10.1146/annurev-clinpsy-032511-143109. Nolen-Hoeksema, S. (2003). *Women who think too much.* New York, NY: Henry Holt.

5.   Lyubomirsky, S., Caldwell, N. D., & Nolen-Hoeksema, S. (1998). Effects of ruminative and distracting responses to depressed mood on the retrieval of autobiographical memories. *Journal of Personality and Social Psychology, 75,* 166–177.

6.   Nolen-Hoeksema, S., Wisco, B. E., & Lyubomirsky, S. (2008). Rethinking rumination. *Perspectives on Psychological Science, 3,* 400–424.

7.   Seligman, M. E. P. (1998). *Learned optimism.* New York, NY: Pocket Books.

8.   Fredrickson, B. L. (2009). *Positivity.* New York, NY: Crown.

9.   Beck, A. T., & Dozois, D. J. A. (2011). Cognitive therapy: Current status and future directions. *Annual Review of Medicine, 62(2).* www.beckinstitute.org/aaron-beck

10.   Ellis, A. (1979). *Reason and emotion in psychotherapy.* New York, NY: Stuart. Ellis, A., Gordon, J., Neenan, M., & Palmer, S. (1997). *Stress counseling: A rational emotive behavioural approach.* London, England: Cassell.

11.   Fredrickson, B. L. (2009). *Positivity.* New York, NY: Crown (p. 161).

12.   Seligman, M. E. P. (1998). *Learned optimism.* New York, NY: Pocket Books. (pp. 210–216).

13.   *Ibid.*

14.   http://www.positivityresonance.com/meditations.html.

15.   Kabat-Zinn, J. (2012). *Mindfulness for beginners: Reclaiming the present moment—and your life.* Boulder, CO: Sounds True.

16.   Fredrickson, B. L., & Levenson, R. W. (1998). Positive emotions speed recovery from the cardiovascular sequelae of negative emotions. *Cognition and Emotion, 12,* 191–220.

17.   Kilburg, R. R. (2015, February 5). *Managing negative emotions in executive coaching engagements.* Presentation at the Society of Consulting Psychologists Midwinter Conference, San Diego, CA. His seminal book on executive coaching is: Kilburg, R. R. (2000). *Executive coaching: Developing managerial wisdom in a world of chaos.* Washington, DC: American Psychological Association.

18.   Peterson, D. B., & Hicks, M. D. (1995). *Development first.* Minneapolis, MN: Personnel Decisions International. Peterson, D. B., & Hicks, M. D. (1996). *Leader as coach.* Minneapolis, MN: Personnel Decisions International.

19.   Kashdan, T., & Biswas-Diener, R. (2014). *The upside of your dark side: Why being your whole self, and not just your good self, drives success and fulfillment.* New York, NY: Hudson Street Press.

20.   Seligman, M. E. P. (2011). *Flourish: A visionary new understanding of happiness and well-being.* New York, NY: Free Press (pp. 159–162).

Acknowledgments

Sandra:

Heartfelt gratitude goes to Jeff Auerbach, the "father" of this book. Jeff initiated this project and devoted his resources, time, and countless hours. Much as he was inspired to establish the College of Executive Coaching, he has created this manual for coaches to offer positive psychology applications underpinned by empirical research.

Without the good cheer of my life partner, Rolf, I would not have completed this project. He kept me positively focused on my goal every day. A huge thanks to my co-instructor for the Positive Psychology telecourse, Jonathan Aronoff, whose extensive well-being coaching experience enlivens our course and this book. Much gratitude also to Todd Kettner, my first co-instructor, for his development of great material for CEC students.

Rob Kaiser contributed significantly to our understanding of the perils as well as the importance of accentuating positive emotions. Rob's compelling descriptions of the research on strengths overused and derailment, as well as his long-time collaboration with Robert Hogan on personality assessment, are found in Chapter 10. I thank you heartily, Rob!

My deep appreciation goes to Antonella Delle Fave, whom I consider a role model for her graciousness, scholar's acumen, and cogent writing style. I thank Heidi Grant Halvorson for making her assessment and her fascinating research accessible to our readers. I am fortunate to be working with Judith Glaser and I am enormously grateful for her contribution on Conversational Intelligence. Many thanks to Fred Luskin for sharing his forgiveness project as a valuable coaching resource. James Pawelski brings a philosopher's perspective to what it means to flourish. I am indebted to James for his "Meaning of the Positive" piece. Many thanks to Geraldine Haley for describing the benefits of strengths artfully used by employees of Standard Chartered Bank.

I am incredibly grateful to Paul Lloyd for his remembrance of Don Clifton. Paul and I have written and lectured on positive psychology topics for our American Psychological Association colleagues, particularly in Division 13 (Consulting Psychology). I want to express my deep appreciation and high regard for Ann M. O'Roark, who has provided wise counsel for many years. I am extremely grateful to Stephanie Evans for all her support and for inviting me to launch the Positive Psychology lecture series at the Stanford University School of Medicine Department of Psychiatry.

I have been positively influenced by friends and colleagues in Division 13, especially Randy White and Sandy Shullman. Many thanks go to Stewart Cooper, Arthur Freedman, Vicki VandaVeer, Ed Nottingham, Kerry Cronan, and particularly to David Brewer, who is an exemplar of optimism and resilience.

The ground-breaking work of Michael Lombardo and Robert (Bob) Eichinger is featured prominently in the book. I am grateful to Bob for his advice on several occasions.

My deepest thanks to Sonja Lyubomirsky for her time and insights as we endeavored to bring her important work to coaching. We are also inspired by the profound impact of the research of Marty Seligman, Barbara Fredrickson, Mihaly Csikszentmihalyi, and the late Chris Peterson.

Jeff:

I would like to thank the many people who made this book possible and who contributed to making it a better book. This book would never have developed without the inspiration, knowledge, experience, and stellar drive for excellence of my co-author, Sandra Foster. Her commitment to scholarly excellence and practical application is world-class, and it has been a privilege to do this project together.

I would like to express tremendous gratitude to Kaleigh Carignan, who worked tirelessly to improve seemingly endless drafts with her attention to detail, editorial skill, and untiring work ethic. I would also like to express my deep appreciation to Micah Auerbach for his gifted wordsmithing of countless individual sentences to develop precise, accurate meaning.

Finding our editor, Roy Sablosky, was a much-needed breakthrough. Roy's ability to quickly, professionally, artfully analyze the development of the book, improving its flow and readability, and his detailed editing of the whole volume allowed us to meet our publishing deadline and to create a volume we are deeply proud of. I am thankful to the late John Bergez, the editor of my first book, for recommending Roy to me. Kirsten Janene-Nelson also contributed many suggestions to the first draft of the book.

Christine Diaz gave continual, thorough, and loyal support on countless projects that freed me up to focus on this book. Her dedication over the years has been tremendously important and helpful. I have the deepest gratitude to Jeanne Auerbach, who gave many excellent editorial suggestions, making the book much better, and has provided invaluable support at all levels for over twenty-three years, without which I would not have been able to accomplish this and many other projects. Ava Auerbach has made my daily experience more positive by delighting me with her many virtues, such as her sense of humor, her artistic style, her attention to interpersonal relationships, and her growth as an excellent writer.

Tremendous kudos go to my graphic designer extraordinaire, Frank Boross, for designing the book layout and cover. Frank is one in a million—excellent to work with, a perfectionistic in his attention to detail, fast, and committed to creating the best product possible.

This book would not have been possible without the support and contributions from many of my colleagues at College of Executive Coaching, which I have led for the past sixteen years. Special thanks go to Patricia Rachel Schwartz, Lynn Jones, Relly Nadler, Jonathan Aronoff, Erin Passons, David Peterson, Philippe Rosinski, Zeina Ghossoub El-Aswad, and Randall P. White for their contributions to our chapters, which we have featured in boxes throughout the text. I was also incredibly pleased that world-renowned psychologists Roy Baumeister and Robert Emmons contributed special sections, which we featured in our chapter on strengths.

I'm deeply appreciative of the wise counsel of my long-term College of Executive Coaching colleague, Ana Maria Irueste, and for the inspiration of co-faculty member and best-selling author, Cathy Greenberg. I have been supported by and learned from other key faculty at the College of Executive Coaching, as well as colleagues in the positive psychology field, and the International Coach Federation, Maynard Brusman, Sylva Leduc, Andrea Molberg, Rodney Lowman, Damian Goldvarg, Magda Mook, George Rogers, Todd Hamilton, Marcia Reynolds, David Mathew Prior, Meryl Moritz, Sonja Lyubomirsky, Anthony Grant, and Bobbie Sue Wolk.

CONTRIBUTORS

Jonathan R. Aronoff, PhD, is a licensed clinical psychologist, certified psychoanalyst, certified personal and executive coach, certified coach mentor, and certified fitness trainer. As faculty of the College of Executive Coaching, he co-teaches the Positive Psychology course with Dr. Sandra Foster. In his full-time coaching practice Dr. Aronoff implements positive psychology principles with individuals, couples, small businesses, and athletic teams, leveraging character strengths to enhance well-being and wellness. He is a frequent speaker and presenter on the book he is currently editing, *The Lost Generation of Boys.* He uses positive psychology principles to coach adolescent and adult males to become "presidential" so they can flourish in the five primary areas of well-being. Dr. Aronoff obtained his MS in experimental psychology at Ohio University and his PhD in clinical psychology at Brigham Young University.

Roy F. Baumeister, PhD, is one of the world's most prolific and influential psychologists. He has published well over 500 scientific articles and over 30 books. In 2013 he received the highest award given by the Association for Psychological Science, the William James Fellow Award, in recognition of his lifetime achievements. He is currently Eppes Eminent Scholar and professor of psychology at Florida State University, plus holding distinguished visiting professorships at King Abdulaziz University (Saudi Arabia) and the VU Free University of Amsterdam (Netherlands). His 2011 book *Willpower: Rediscovering the Greatest Human Strength* (with John Tierney) was a New York Times bestseller. He has appeared on television shows, such as NBC's Dateline and ABC's 20/20, Discover, PBS, National Public Radio, and countless local news shows. His work has been covered or quoted in the New York Times, Washington Post, Wall Street Journal, Los Angeles Times, the Economist, Newsweek, Time, Psychology Today, Self, Men's Health, Business Week, and many other outlets.

Antonella Delle Fave, MD, specializing in clinical psychology, is professor of psychology at the Medical School, Università degli Studi di Milano, Italy. Her studies concern daily experience, flow, and the process of psychological selection, based on the resource investment in activities subjectively perceived as meaningful and relevant. The cross-cultural studies conducted by her research group have produced the largest international data bank available on these topics. She developed international intervention projects in the domains of health and education, and supervised cooperation programs to promote resource implementation in disability and social maladjustment. Together with partners from thirteen countries she recently developed the Eudaimonic and Hedonic Happiness Investigation, aimed at identifying well-being components across cultures. She contributed to the development of positive psychology, as a founding member and president of the European Network of Positive Psychology and the International Positive Psychology Association. Author of scientific articles and books, she is currently editor-in-chief of the Journal of Happiness Studies.

Judith E. Glaser, MS, is founder and CEO of Benchmark Communications, Inc., and chairman of the Creating WE Institute, with over twenty-five years of business experience working with CEOs and their teams. Her transformational approaches using neuroscience and anthropology enable leaders to raise their Conversational Intelligence, profitability, and growth while building healthy, thriving organizations. Judith is the author of seven books and four best-sellers, including *Conversational Intelligence: How Great Leaders Build Trust and Get Extraordinary Results*. Since 2007 she has been listed in the top ten consultants globally in the Excellence Top 100 Consultants. She has appeared on the CBS Morning News, NBC's Today Show, ABC World News, and Fox News. She is frequently quoted in the New York Times and the Wall Street Journal and is a featured blogger for Harvard Business Review, Psychology Today, the Huffington

Post, and Entrepreneur. Judith is a founding member of the Harvard Coaching Institute.

Zeina Ghossoub El-Aswad, MS, is a credentialed and certified professional coach, group coach, executive coach, and wellness coach and employs different techniques ranging from emotional intelligence to other coaching principles. She has been coaching for over seven years. She is also a clinical dietitian and the founder and director of VieSaine, a wellness and healthcare center in Beirut, Lebanon. Zeina also practices wellness coaching in the United States, where she is based in Houston, Texas. Zeina is the highest-credentialed coach in Lebanon and the Middle East. She has created a unique concept in wellness and health that targets individuals, families, corporations, and businesses alike. She is very well known throughout the region and is frequently sought after for topics ranging from wellness to executive coaching. She has taught and lectured about coaching in the Middle East and the United States with the College of Executive Coaching. Zeina has co-authored several best-selling books. She has lectured on coaching, wellness and dietetics throughout the region. She has weekly television and radio shows and is an editor and contributor to several local and international magazines.

Heidi Grant Halvorson, PhD, is a social psychologist who researches, writes, and speaks on the science of motivation. She is the associate director of the Motivation Science Center at the Columbia Business School, senior consultant for the Neuroleadership Institute, and author of the best-selling books *Succeed: How We Can All Reach Our Goals, Nine Things Successful People Do Differently, Focus: Use Different Ways of Seeing the World for Success and Influence* (with E. Tory Higgins), and *The 8 Motivational Challenges.* Heidi is also a contributor to the Harvard Business Review, 99u, Fast Company, WSJ.com, Forbes, the Huffington Post, and Psychology Today. In addition to her work as author and co-editor of the highly regarded academic book *The Psychology of Goals* (Guilford, 2009), she has authored papers in her field's most prestigious journals, including the Journal of Personality and Social Psychology, Journal of Experimental Social Psychology, Personality and Social Psychology Bulletin, European Journal of Social Psychology, and Judgment and Decision Making. She has received numerous grants from the National Science Foundation for her research on goals and achievement.

Geraldine Haley is global head of executive talent and succession at Standard Chartered Bank, with responsibility for the resourcing, development, and succession of the top 100 leaders of the bank. She has over twenty years' experience in international human resources, with a career that has spanned both specialist and generalist roles. As a Chartered Psychologist and Master NLP Practitioner, she enjoys coaching and facilitating teams herself. Her work is based on the core belief that leaders can learn and adapt, particularly if they are self-aware and can play to their strengths, and that organizational success is about high-performing and collaborative teams.

Lynn K. Jones, DSW, is an International Coach Federation Professional Certified Coach, certified social work manager, consultant and trainer based in Santa Barbara. Her clients are leaders in non-profit organizations, public sector organizations and private corporations, as well as small business entrepreneurs. Dr. Jones has a Masters in Social Work and a Doctorate in Social Welfare from Yeshiva University in New York, along with 30 years of executive leadership experience. She specializes in Appreciative Inquiry and other strengths based coaching and team building approaches and was trained by the founder of Appreciative Inquiry, David Cooperrider. In addition, her expertise in Organizational Culture has proved to be highly valuable to her leadership clients, which have included: Patagonia, Haas Automation, Driscolls, Montecito Bank and Trust,

City of Santa Barbara, Santa Barbara Police Department, Haas Automation, Agriculture Commissioner's Office, Antioch University. Dr. Jones is a visiting faculty member for the USC School of Social Work Virtual Academic Center.

Rob Kaiser, MS, is an advisor, author, and authority on the subject of leadership. He is the president of Kaiser Leadership Solutions, a provider of assessment tools that have set a new standard for innovation and impact, such as the patented Leadership Versatility Index. He has coached executives and their teams in major global companies and advised CEOs and HR leaders on transforming their leadership culture. Rob is a prolific writer whose work on leadership assessment, selection, and development has been widely published. His books include *Executive Selection, Filling the Leadership Pipeline, The Perils of Accentuating the Positive,* and, with Bob Kaplan, *The Versatile Leader* and *Fear Your Strengths.* Rob is also an acclaimed public speaker who is regularly invited to deliver his unique, engaging, and provocative presentations to professional audiences around the world. He has an MS in organizational psychology from Illinois State University.

Frederic Luskin, PhD, directs the Stanford University Forgiveness Project. He is a senior consultant in wellness at the Stanford Health Center and a professor of clinical psychology at the Institute of Transpersonal Psychology. He is the author of the best-selling books *Forgive for Good* and *Forgive for Love,* as well as *Stress Free for Good.* His work has been featured on worldwide media and has been utilized to help struggling people throughout the world.

Relly Nadler, PsyD, is a licensed psychologist, Master Certified Coach (MCC), author, and CEO and president of True North Leadership, Inc., an executive and organizational development firm. Dr. Nadler has coached CEOs, presidents, and their staffs and developed and delivered innovative leadership programs for such organizations as Anheuser-Busch, BMW, EDS, Vanguard Healthcare, Baxter Healthcare, DreamWorks Animation, Comerica Bank, American Honda, the US Navy, and General Motors Defense. He is recognized around the world for his expertise in creating Emotional Intelligence tools and applications for top performance. He is the author of five best-selling books on leadership and team performance. The latest is *Leading with Emotional Intelligence: Hands-On Strategies for Building Confident and Collaborative Star Performers*. Dr. Nadler co-hosts a weekly radio show, Leadership Development News, where he interviews experts in leadership, coaching, peak performance, positive psychology, and neuroscience.

Erin Passons, MBA, is the president and founder of Passons Consulting. She has spent her career helping business leaders, managers, and employees improve their performance and effectiveness, and is an expert in coaching and facilitating workshops using StrengthsFinder. As a former consultant for Gallup, Erin has certified over 300 coaches in the strengths-based approach. During her tenure at Gallup, Erin worked with Fortune 500 companies to provide training and coaching in the areas of strengths-based performance, job alignment, career development, and management effectiveness. Today she leads her own consulting practice, helping people do what they do best, at work and in life. Erin is also the founder of StrengthsNetwork San Diego, an association for StrengthsFinder professionals and followers in the Southern California region. Erin received her MBA with an emphasis in organizational behavior from Georgetown University in Washington, DC.

James O. Pawelski, PhD, is director of education and senior scholar in positive psychology and adjunct associate professor of religious studies at the University of Pennsylvania. He is the author of *The Dynamic Individualism of William James*, editor of the philosophy section of the *Oxford Handbook of Happiness*, and co-editor of *The Eudaimonic Turn: Well-Being in Literary Studies*. In addition, he is the founding director of the University of Pennsylvania's Master of Applied Positive Psychology program and one of its principal faculty. A sought-after international keynote speaker and workshop presenter who regularly makes presentations in Spanish as well as English, he is the founding executive director of the International Positive Psychology Association. His current research interests include connections between positive psychology and the various disciplines in the humanities, the philosophical underpinnings of positive psychology, and the development, application, and assessment of interventions in positive psychology.

David Peterson, PhD, earned his PhD in counseling and industrial/organizational psychology at the University of Minnesota. He is a fellow of the American Psychological Association, the Society of Consulting Psychology, the Society for Industrial and Organizational Psychology, and the Harvard Institute of Coaching. David joined Google in 2011 as director of executive coaching and leadership. He coaches senior leaders, manages Google's network of external and internal coaches, and supports a variety of leadership, learning, and executive development initiatives at Google. Before joining Google, David served as leader of world-wide coaching services for PDI Ninth House. In addition to coaching top leaders in organizations, he provided consultation and thought leadership on how to design and manage organizational coaching programs, how to develop high-potential leaders and critical talent, and how to accelerate learning and leadership development at all levels.

David has published dozens of articles and chapters on coaching, is co-author of *Development FIRST: Strategies for Self-Development and Leader as Coach*, and co-editor of the *Handbook of the Psychology of Coaching and Mentoring*. A recent history of coaching listed him as one of the primary influencers in the field, both for his early influence on the emergence of executive coaching and for continuing to shape the field as someone "on the cutting edge of the profession, doing and saying surprising and thought-provoking things."

Philippe Rosinski, MS, is a world authority in executive coaching, team coaching, and global leadership development. He is the author of the seminal bestseller *Coaching Across Cultures*. He is widely regarded as the pioneer of intercultural coaching, having first systematically integrated the cultural perspective into coaching. He has trained hundreds of professional coaches and leaders across the world, helping them make the most of cultural differences. He is also the author of the Cultural Orientations Framework assessment tool and the first European to be designated Master Certified Coach by the International Coach Federation. Philippe earned a Master of Science from Stanford University. He is principal of Rosinski & Company and a professor in Tokyo (Kenichi Ohmae Graduate School of Business) and Prague (University of Economics). His latest book, *Global Coaching*, has been described as "having moved the art and science of coaching to a new level" and offers an integrated coaching approach that leverages multiple perspectives for greater creativity, impact, and meaning.

Patricia Rachel Schwartz, MA, provides coaching and leadership training for executives and teams. She is a Professional Certified Coach (ICF) and a Board Certified Coach (CCE) with expertise in strengths-based approaches that ignite innovation, infuse the organizational culture with positive energy, and drive bottom-line results. She has over thirty years of experience in leadership and management, and has trained and coached thousands of leaders. She is also an expert in major gifts coaching for large nongovernmental organizations. Schwartz serves on the faculty of the College of Executive Coaching, an international postgraduate institute. In prior training work, she designed and implemented mid-career leadership programs for domestic and international leaders, including an international Management Certificate Program at the University of Massachusetts. Ms. Schwartz is a strong advocate for our ability to boldly create extraordinary futures for ourselves and our companies.

Randall P. White, PhD, is a founding partner of Executive Development Group LLC in Greensboro, NC, and an international thought leader in the field of executive coaching and leadership development, an executive coach, and facilitator. He teaches with Duke Corporate Education (Durham and London), is an HEC affiliate professor (Paris, Doha, and Beijing), co-head of leadership in the EMBA program at HEC, and teaches leadership in the TRIUM Global EMBA program. Dr. White co-authored the best-selling business book, *Breaking The Glass Ceiling: Can Women Reach the Top of America's Largest Corporations?* and in 1996, co-authored *The Future of Leadership: Riding the Corporate Rapids into the 21st Century.* He has also co-authored *Four Essential Ways That Coaching Can Help Executives* (1997) and *Relax, It's Only Uncertainty* (2001). He serves on the Division 13 Coaching Psychology Credentialing Committee, is a reviewer for the Consulting Psychology Journal, and was recently elected a member-at-large of APA's Council Leadership Team. Dr. White is the former director of specialized client applications at the Center for Creative Leadership. He received his doctorate in social psychology from Cornell University.

ABOUT THE AUTHORS

Sandra L. Foster, PhD, PCC, is a business coach and peak performance psychology expert now based in Charleston, South Carolina, after living and working in Europe for eight years. She is a licensed psychologist, a Chartered British Psychologist, and holds the International Coach Federation Professional Certified Coach Credential. She has been a College of Executive Coaching senior faculty member since 2001. She was a principal in Korn/Ferry International's Leadership & Talent Consulting group, based in London and then in Los Angeles, before returning to independent coaching and consulting practice. Her clients are executives, emerging leaders, and entrepreneurs, as well as musicians, actors, and writers. Dr. Foster received her doctorate from Stanford University and served on the faculty as acting assistant professor and consulting associate professor. She speaks internationally on performance enhancement for leaders and positive psychology in coaching. Dr. Foster is the co-author of two sport psychology books and numerous scholarly articles and book chapters.

Jeffrey E. Auerbach, PhD, MCC, a licensed psychologist, is the founder of the College of Executive Coaching. He designs and delivers executive coaching programs globally.

Dr. Auerbach is a specialist in positive psychology–based and emotional intelligence–enhancing coaching approaches. He designs and delivers custom leadership programs to develop peak-performing leaders. Dr. Auerbach speaks internationally on executive well-being, emotional intelligence, and executive peak performance.

Dr. Auerbach is past vice president of the global board of directors of the International Coach Federation. Auerbach is the author of the classic coaching book, *Personal and Executive Coaching: The Complete*

Guide for Mental Health Professionals, now in its twentieth printing, and the widely used *Well-Being Coaching Workbook: Everything Needed for the Coaching Participant.* He holds a PhD in psychology and is a graduate of the University of California, Santa Barbara, the Chicago School, and Antioch University.

Dr. Auerbach holds the Master Certified Coach Credential, the highest level of credential in the coaching industry, from the International Coach Federation.

■ ■ ■

THE COLLEGE OF EXECUTIVE COACHING

The College of Executive Coaching was founded in 1999 by Jeffrey E. Auerbach, Ph.D. The college provides International Coach Federation accredited training to coaches and delivers executive coaching and leadership programs globally. In addition, we provide internal coach training certification programs for organizations and our faculty are available for training and keynote presentations. Certification in coaching involves in-person and/or distance learning curriculum to develop knowledge, skill and experience. Our certification programs are open to professionals with graduate degrees. Our faculty consists of twelve Ph.D. level professional coaches.

Most of the applicants to the training program are experienced, successful professionals who are motivated by a desire to create positive, meaningful change for their clients and our world. As highly trained professionals they know they can help people achieve their highest goals and they seek to be compensated well for their services.

Our diverse faculty provides you with a variety of role models and coaching styles to help you develop a coaching approach that matches your strengths.

The training program consists of a post-graduate level curriculum to provide you with the coaching and business skills you need to have a highly marketable coaching practice.

CONTACT INFORMATION:

College of Executive Coaching
897 Oak Park Blvd. #271 • Pismo Beach, CA 93449
(805) 474-4124
www.executivecoachcollege.com
training@executivecoachcollege.com